Knowledge, Power, and the Congress

William H. Robinson
& Clay H. Wellborn

Library of Congress

Knowledge, Power,
and the Congress

Knowledge, Power, and the Congress

William H. Robinson
and Clay H. Wellborn, Editors

Congressional Research Service
Library of Congress

Congressional Quarterly Inc.

Washington, D. C.

Book and cover design by Kachergis Book Design, Pittsboro, N.C.

Printed in the United States of America

LIBRARY OF CONGRESS CATALOGING-IN-PUBLICATION DATA

Knowledge, power, and the Congress / edited by William H. Robinson and
  Clay H. Wellborn.
      p.   cm.
    Papers presented at a symposium sponsored by the Council of
  Scholars of the Library of Congress.
    Includes bibliographical references and index.
    ISBN 0-87187-632-9.—ISBN 0-87187-631-0 (pbk.)
    1. United States. Congress—Congresses. 2. Policy sciences—
  Congresses. 3. Knowledge, Sociology of—Congresses. 4. Power
  (Social sciences)—Congresses. 5. Legislative bodies—Congresses.
  6. Legislative power—Congresses. I. Robinson, William H. (William
  Herbert), 1938-   . II. Wellborn, Clay H. III. Council of Scholars
  (U.S.)
  JK1067.K64   1991
  328.73—dc20   91-28262
                                                      CIP

Contents

Foreword

I t is a great pleasure to present this collection of papers delivered at a symposium entitled "Knowledge, Power, and the Congress: A Bicentennial Perspective," held at the Library of Congress, March 8–9, 1989. This symposium was one of several bicentennial celebrations of Congress scheduled by the Library of Congress over a period of several years. In its more than two hundred years, Congress has not only distinguished itself as the world's longest lasting and most important legislature, but it has also become extraordinarily well informed, independent, and knowledge-based.

The creation of the Library of Congress under Thomas Jefferson provided a unique place of intersection between knowledge and power in our fledgling republic in its early days. We honor Congress in our own time by exploring areas of potential improvement and by comparing our experiences with those of the growing number of other legislative republics. It is with a view toward the future that we undertook this inventory of past and present experience.

The symposium, made possible by the support of the Arcana Foundation, was sponsored by the Council of Scholars of the Library of Congress. The council is a distinguished group of scholars who offer advice on keeping the library's collections and services attuned to the needs of Congress and the nation's scholars. The Library of Congress fulfills its unique role as a link between the vast research community of this country and its legislature by gathering and sifting the best of what is known and conveying it to Congress on a timely basis. The Congressional Research Service in particular has a key role in this process. We hope to help Congress meet the needs of the nation and better understand and cope with the complex world in which we live.

James H. Billington
Librarian of Congress

Preface

The links between knowledge and power in a political setting are both practical and normative. Politicians and philosophers, from Bacon to Nietzsche, have grasped the notion that knowledge is power. The Chinese have exploited this nexus for thousands of years.

America's own Founders personified the union of knowledge and power. The Republic was built on the solid foundation of concepts and ideas imported from the best thinkers abroad. Our first statesmen studied and learned from their own experience the principles of democratic pluralism and the appropriate limits on power that they incorporated in the Constitution and in the institutions of American government.

Once established, the practice of government remained anchored in this tradition of joining knowledge and power. As Laurence E. Lynn, Jr., one of the contributors to this volume, has observed in another setting, the Lewis and Clark expedition represented Jefferson's search for relevant, documented knowledge to guide public policy in the development of the West. His insistence on detailed documentation, astronomical observations, and attention to history and culture set a high standard for scientific, interdisciplinary analysis for public policy.

The complex problems of modern governance and the unique pressures on Congress are testing this rational model. The modern phenomenon of "information overload" is trying the ability of even the best and the brightest to apply what they know to solving the problems at hand. The confusion of an overabundance of isolated "factoids" threatens to drown the decision-making process in minutiae. T. S. Eliot's phrase from *The Rock* comes to mind: "Where is the wisdom we have lost in knowledge? Where is the knowledge we have lost in information?"

On the occasion of the bicentennial of the U.S. Congress, the Library of Congress undertook an assessment of the present state of knowledge, power, and the Congress. At the invitation of the Librarian of Congress and the library's Council of Scholars, distinguished contributors from government and academia met with a small group of scholars, policy analysts, and members of Congress at a symposium to discuss the role of knowledge, information, and scholarship in the legislative arena.

The papers presented at the symposium fell into three broad categories: the historical and philosophical dimensions of the relationship between knowledge and power in Congress; the role of knowledge in congressional consideration of specific economic, defense, and social issues; and the relationship between knowledge and power in foreign legislatures.

Several recurring themes run through the essays. One theme is the distinction between two kinds of knowledge in the political arena. There is ordinary, or common sense, knowledge, as distinguished from professional, or expert, knowledge. The two kinds of knowledge can conflict with each other or can even lead to different kinds of lawmaking. A second theme is the relationship between congressional organization and the way knowledge is used by Congress. A third is the effect of the limitations of knowledge and understanding on congressional deliberations.

The symposium opened with remarks by James C. Wright, Jr., then Speaker of the House. Wright affirms that "knowledge, power, and free government are inextricably intertwined." With today's information explosion and communication networks, Congress has an urgent need to assimilate knowledge and to put it to practical use. To maintain an informed national legislature, Wright says, members of Congress have increased their staffs and created research organizations. The most important of these is the Congressional Research Service. Yet despite these developments, most members find that the sheer lack of time diminishes their ability to read, study, and assimilate information. Nevertheless, Wright concludes that there is no substitute for members of Congress reading books and journals.

In the first paper Theodore J. Lowi distinguishes between amateur and professional knowledge. He suggests that the professionalization of knowledge has created the illusion that our society is more complex than nineteenth-century society seemed to nineteenth-century legislators. He concludes that the professionalization of knowledge, reinforced by large staffs and low member turnover, has diverted Congress from the concrete to the abstract. Congress's change from enacting laws that govern behavior to creating laws that govern systems amounts to "legiscide." Lowi urges Congress to return to amateur knowledge, to reject systems, and to embrace the limited but more effective piecemeal approach.

House Speaker Thomas S. Foley (then majority leader) spiritedly rejects Lowi's assertion that our society is no more complex than that of the nineteenth century. Foley questions Lowi's interpretation of congressional turnover and disputes his suggestion that Congress has declined because of its present lawmaking approach.

Gordon S. Wood, reviewing the state of knowledge in the First Congress, observes that far less information was available to Congress then than now. Politics was a "small and intimate business," whose leaders relied on private conversations and personal correspondence for information. Nevertheless, argues Wood, the distinctions between professional and amateur knowledge and between policy research and ordinary knowledge were as important then as they are now.

Wood identifies the difficulties that faced the first Congress in acquiring information and discusses the value of congressional debates as a "source of information and shared wisdom." He argues that tensions between the executive and the legislative branches are not new, having been present at the outset.

Joseph Cooper disagrees with Wood's conclusion that the Federalist vision triumphed and expands on Federalist versus Anti-Federalist differences on the role of values and interests in politics. James Sterling Young directs his remarks to the nature and sources of political knowledge that informed the exercise of political power by those who governed the young nation. Noting that most of them had previously served in representative bodies, he distills two of the lessons they learned: how to control the exercise of executive authority and how to make policy through a process of consensus finding.

In the next paper Nelson W. Polsby discusses the structure of the modern Congress and the implications of that structure for the use of knowledge and power. Congress has modernized its own capabilities for policy analysis not because of the increasing sophistication of the executive branch, as reflected in its complex proposals, but because of its mistrust of the modernizing presidency, with its evolving institutional changes—increased politicization, professionalization, and management expertise.

Polsby contrasts today's Congress, which he calls a transformative legislature, with parliamentary and rubber stamp legislatures. To understand the legislative outcomes of what Congress does, one must understand the complex internal structure and workings of this institution, which is sui generis among legislatures.

During the past four decades, Polsby says, the Senate has moved from being a closed and "states-regarding" inner club to the current "nation-regarding" period in which "cultivation of general perspectives on public policy are common." The House of Representatives has developed a vast accumulation of knowledge through continuity and division of labor in committee service, which has brought "the sizable dividend of influence over public policy" to the House as an institution.

Elaborating on Polsby's paper, Frank Freidel comments on the cycling of relative power between Congress and the executive branch and on the effect of presidential roles on the development of the modern Congress. David Brady notes that technology and demographic change act as both constraints and as incentives to make institutional modifications to accommodate changing circumstances within the legislature.

Allen Schick enlarges this characterization of the modern Congress in the next paper. He develops the theme of two different kinds of knowledge, much as Lowi does in drawing a distinction between amateur and expert knowledge. Schick, however, distinguishes between ordinary knowledge and policy analysis. Ordinary knowledge is unsystematic and biased—the kind of knowledge that recognizes when there is a problem. Ideally, policy analysis is systematic, objective inquiry into public policies and programs. Its goal is to understand the extent to which a problem has been ameliorated or eliminated.

Schick contends that during the 1980s, when policy analysis matured and ordinary knowledge flourished, Congress became "awash in advice and information." He cautions, however, that policy research may lose out in the competition with ordinary knowledge. He urges policy researchers to improve their understanding of the ways ordinary knowledge accumulates, "not because conventional wisdom is right—it often is not—but because an understanding of this kind would enrich the value that research adds to society."

Carol H. Weiss argues that Schick's dichotomy of ordinary versus policy knowledge tells only part of the story. The main competition, she believes, is between policy research and political interests. David E. Price agrees with Schick's basic points but expands his dichotomy by adding "particularistic knowledge," which comprises the needs and interests of particular groups and communities, to the categories of knowledge used by policymakers.

Taking a different approach, Mancur Olson speaks not to knowledge but to its limitations—and especially to its opposite, ignorance. Olson asserts that in examining the relationship of knowledge to political power we must acknowledge what he calls rational ignorance, an individual citizen's recognition "that the benefits of individual enlightenment about public goods are usually dispersed throughout a group or a nation rather than concentrated upon the individual who bears the costs of becoming enlightened." Olson, who argues that this fact explains a variety of phenomena, discusses the implications of rational ignorance for collective action, for society's susceptibility to such ideologies as supply-side economics and industrial policy, for special-interest lobbies, for fads in public policy, and for the reelection strategies of politicians.

In his comment on Olson's paper, Newt Gingrich, arguing that economics is not a good basis for understanding how humans function, presents his views on rationality and its limitations. Jodie T. Allen suggests that Congress can improve on rational ignorance and gain from analysis by asking the right questions.

Three papers in this volume examine the link between knowledge and power in selected policy areas of concern to Congress: national security, economic policy, and social policy.

Ernest R. May argues that just as knowledge, power, and national security are interrelated, so are ignorance, weakness, and national insecurity. Knowledge and power are reciprocals. "The less raw power a nation has, the greater its need for knowledge, and vice versa." Because the United States has relatively less power in today's world than in earlier years, it has a correspondingly greater need for knowledge.

May cautions that we should avoid confusing knowledge with information and assuming that only organization and money are needed to create knowledge. He recommends that the United States be more open with the intelligence it collects, sharing that information with scholars. Most of the information government gathers through its intelligence community needs protection for only a short time, and more thought should be given to how that knowledge is used.

Stephen J. Solarz concurs with May's recommendations and elaborates on some of the points made in the paper, particularly the importance of anticipating surprises and the need for challenging assumptions underlying the policymaking process. He suggests that each government agency establish an Office of the Historian so that institutional memory might be brought to bear on every policy decision.

Lawrence H. Summers examines the nation's economic policy and the need for policymakers to cope with a world that is becoming increasingly integrated. This integration is driven by transportation and communication technologies and by the reduction of political and military conflict among nations. Summers believes that it is important for policymakers to recognize several points. First, because economic integration is mutually beneficial, international coordination will become increasingly important. Second, the divergence between American corporations and American interests will grow, with implications for tax and antitrust policy. Third, it will be necessary to encourage international coordination to the extent that nation-states want to tax, regulate, and affect economic activity. Fourth, it is wise to invest in American skills and education to improve those skills. Fifth, to maintain economic balance, it is essential to follow prudent macroeconomic policies.

Commenting on Summers's presentation, Isabel Sawhill argues that the United States has no "well-considered and well-coordinated economic policy" to deal with the goals of reducing inflation, lowering unemployment, promoting growth, and ensuring a fairer distribution of income—goals that should be subject to explicit public debate. William A. Niskanen questions Summers's conclusions about the extent of integration of the world economy, particularly Summers's recommendations for increased international coordination of economic policy and his conditional endorsement of free trade only when other nations also practice free trade.

Turning to social policy, Nathan Glazer contrasts today's sobriety about what government can do to resolve social problems with the optimism of twenty-five years ago. He sketches the high expectations of the 1960s, when it was thought that energy, commitment, intelligence, and ingenuity in government could transform society. The predominant theme of that era was that knowledge guides power. From such thinking came the War on Poverty and other sweeping approaches to solving societal problems. Those efforts provided few successes says Glazer. Knowledge did not prove to be up to the task of leading power, because social scientists believed they knew more than they really did. Glazer argues that although the strategy of identifying problems and designing governmental programs to solve or ameliorate those problems has its attractions it excludes or reduces the importance of traditional values.

Laurence E. Lynn, Jr., and Richard P. Nathan disagree with Glazer's pessimism about applying knowledge to solving social problems. Lynn concludes that policy intellectuals have a legitimate and essential role in, and a contribution to make to, the effective governance of society. Nathan argues that social science can help policymakers by analyzing conditions and trends, by designing demonstration studies, and by evaluating programs already adopted.

Views of knowledge and power in parliaments of other countries are offered by Denis Healey, who represents the British view, and by Gordon A. Craig, who comments on examples from European history.

Denis Healey notes some basic differences between British and American approaches to acquiring and using knowledge in a legislative setting. British legislators do their own work without the help of the relatively large staffs of their American counterparts. Arguing that "active and intelligent members of Parliament" can get the knowledge they need without the extensive support available to our members of Congress, Healey stresses the importance of newspaper reading, of written questions to the government, and of the opportunity for members of Parliament to serve in ministerial positions, where decisions and action are required despite inadequate information. He is skeptical of experts, saying they often do not understand their subjects.

Asserting that the tendency of European legislators to be "less men of knowledge than knowledgeable men" was not necessarily a disability, Gordon Craig points to lessons in European legislatures of the nineteenth and early twentieth centuries. Generalist legislators could usually manage the ordinary business of a nation, and they found specialists to help with complicated matters. In Zurich, for example, the legislature mobilized expert knowledge through cantonal councils and commissions and transformed the canton into a progressive industrial and intellectual center. On the other hand, notes Craig, the German Reichstag and the French Assembly, through a lack of common sense and a failure to draw upon available expert knowledge, did not take steps to alleviate the crisis brought on by the world depression. The result was the dissolution of legitimate parliamentary government.

The essays in this collection demonstrate that basic questions about knowledge, power, and the Congress—whether Congress should rely on the executive branch for information, what kind of information senators and representatives need to fulfill their legislative and representational responsibilities, and what they should know about the world beyond the boundaries of the states and districts they represent—are as important now as they were two hundred years ago. Over the years Congress has responded to these perennial questions in a variety of ways. Among its responses have been the establishment of the Library of Congress, the development of the library's vast collections, and the creation of the Congressional Research Service.

The questions about the role of knowledge in the practice of governance are relevant not only for the U.S. Congress but also for the legislatures of new and emerging democracies. Like our own Congress, new and reestablished legislatures are understanding the limitations of mere information and the effects of knowledge and understanding on legislative deliberations. Recognizing the importance of the links between knowledge and power, the Library of Congress is pleased to offer these essays to the U.S. Congress and to the growing world community of democratic legislatures.

William H. Robinson
Clay H. Wellborn
Congressional Research Service

Introduction: The View from Capitol Hill

James C. Wright, Jr.

There is a direct link between knowledge, power, and the Congress. My earliest recollections from higher education are the words engraved upon the tower at the University of Texas: "The cultivated mind is the guardian genius of democracy." These words are by Mirabeau B. Lamar, brother of Lucius Quintus Cincinnatus Lamar and second president of the Republic of Texas. At the base of that same building are the words from Scripture: "Ye shall know the truth, and the truth shall make you free." Knowledge, power, and free government—they are inextricably intertwined.

Surely, events are happening in the country and in the world today that make it ever more imperative that Congress act from a base of knowledge. The earth, seemingly, has shrunk. For purposes of transportation or communication, we are much closer in Washington today to London or Paris or Moscow than were our predecessors in the capital a century ago to Richmond, Virginia. Such an explosion of knowledge has occurred that it is difficult for us to assimilate it and put it to practical use. It is not that there is a lack of information, but we have an ever-increasing need for knowledge if we are to be effective legislators and if we are to lead our nation, caught up as it is in a rapid change of events in which yesterday's dream becomes today's reality and tomorrow's history.

Congress has many institutions dedicated to providing legislative committees and members of Congress with timely information. The Library of Congress is the most prominent of these institutions. It was created by Congress at the insistence of Thomas Jefferson after Congress's books were destroyed in the War of 1812. Jefferson sold Congress his extensive

I

library as a replacement. Some people commented that it was a waste of the federal government's money to buy a library with such esoteric books. But Jefferson responded, "There is no subject to which a Member of Congress may not have occasion to refer."

We get information from various sources. Our knowledge comes in bits and pieces and is assimilated by an imperfect instrument—the human brain. One of the principal problems confronting us today is that we are so caught up in the daily trivia of life that we have no time for reflection. There is little time for reading, certainly among the leadership. When I was in Congress I was constantly being given learned treatises that I would have liked to read unhurriedly. Yet I was constantly frustrated because I could not take the time to do so. I would set those materials aside for an unhurried moment, when I might read and reflect upon them without interruption. The moment never came.

All members of Congress come to work with their days preordained, bound to a list of activities to which their staffs have committed them. There is no time to sit and read and think and study. Weekends are equally busy. A few years ago Betty and I decided that we would try to budget our weekends. One in three I would spend with a colleague or colleagues in their districts, as those in the leadership are called upon to do. A second weekend in the three I would spend in my own district. I would go to Fort Worth, my constituency, and maintain the necessary contact with people at home. The third weekend, Betty and I would have for ourselves, for recharging batteries, for doing something recreative just for us. That was in January. In October of that year, Betty reminded me that in those ten months there had been only three "third weekends."

I think that is symptomatic of the problems that most of us have in being, if not scholarly, at least capable of reading, studying, and assimilating information, upon which we can act. It is a bit like providing the fuel for a fire. We all begin to burn out if we do not find new logs to throw on our fires.

Our government derives its just powers from the consent of the governed. That is not a mere slogan. Citizens frequently write their representatives in Congress. While I was in Congress, in an average day I received approximately 230 letters from my district, in addition to letters that came to me from around the country because I was the Speaker.

In the winter of 1989 members of Congress received a virtual snowstorm of communications stimulated by radio talk show hosts. The letters informed us that the Commission on Executive, Legislative, and Judicial

Pay, which recommended that representatives receive a raise, had not convinced the public that a raise was in order. Since congressional powers derive from the consent of the governed, we rejected the pay raise. But the mail we received was information, if distasteful. Although we may have felt that the analyses given by the talk show hosts were incomplete, we could do nothing but resign ourselves because that was how people felt. Yet that knowledge was indispensable.

About thirty years ago Walter Lippmann wrote a gloomy volume called *Public Philosophy*.[1] Lippmann said that Western leaders were for the most part insecure and intimidated individuals, driven by the necessity to be popular at home to make the wrong decisions. They usually did not what was right but what would be popularly received as right. I think that observation is somewhat harsh.

The explosion of knowledge ought to facilitate the dissemination of information that would make wise public policies acceptable. But the knowledge available to Congress is of limited comfort if that knowledge is not broadly available to the public.

Although information is more immediately available to the public through television than ever before, television's marvelous capacity to enlighten is often not realized. Unfortunately, it shrinks viewers' concentration, offering quick blips of information rather than thoughtful commentary. Television has brought the level of public debate from the thoughtful level of public discourse delivered by Daniel Webster and Henry Clay and John C. Calhoun to the sixty-second sound bite or even the fifteen-second news bite. Office seekers have been reduced to sloganeering rather than presenting voters with thoughtful concepts.

Still, Congress is responsible for informing itself. And members have created institutions to assist them. The most important is the Congressional Research Service. Sen. Robert LaFollette brought this idea from Wisconsin in 1914, suggesting the Legislative Reference Service, which was created at that time.

In 1945 the Joint Committee on the Organization of Congress recommended that the legislative branch "modernize its machinery, coordinate its various parts, and establish the research facilities that can provide it with the knowledge that is power." Although Congress did reorganize itself in the late 1940s, the news and editorial commentaries were scornful of the legislative branch for not being equipped to cope with the explosion of knowledge and for not having matched the executive branch in its access to resource material. Reacting to this criticism, Congress busied itself with developing new sources of information and expertise to confront the executive branch's overpowering range of knowledge.

Under the Legislative Reorganization Act of 1970, Congress attained what we then called "analytical parity" with the executive branch. Since the early 1970s the staff of the Congressional Research Service has increased from 258 to about 800. We did what the editorialists, the political scientists, and the critics said we should do. And now Congress is attacked for spending too much on itself and for creating an empire of staff members.

Another important resource is the House Information System, which has burgeoned since 1971. It is a computer-driven operation connected with the offices of the members. In one month while I was in the House, members and staff sent out some 600,000 computer commands to request information from the House Information Service (HIS). This service provides members with economic statistics, current news, federal grants, and information on the status of legislation. Every month more than 1,500 computer requests would arrive between the hours of midnight and 7:00 A.M., which shows either that a member's work is never done, or that the hors d'oeuvres at those after-hours receptions induce insomnia.

The Congressional Budget Office is a reliable source of information about economic forecasting. Its record is superior to that of the Office of Management and Budget in predicting inflation, growth rates, and other economic data. It can determine, in all likelihood, how much a given program will require in spending in a given fiscal year as opposed to the amount authorized for it.

So legislators can get statistical knowledge, but I am convinced that there is no substitute for members of Congress availing themselves of books and journals, even if they must fight to find the time to do so. This vast treasure house of knowledge that is readily available must be available in a truer sense to their minds.

Congress is criticized for everything it does. There is nothing new about that. Nicholas Longworth, Speaker of the House from 1925 to 1931, said in 1925 that during his twenty years in Congress he had been vilified, excoriated, criticized, calumniated, and abused in vocal and written form and that every free-born American considered it a duty to look down upon Congress and every native-born humorist to make jokes at Congress's expense.

Today members of Congress are criticized when they travel abroad. It seems clear to me, however, that if they are to acquire the knowledge necessary for wielding power, they must learn about what they are dealing with. Legislators cannot shrink in isolation, and consider themselves effective, if they have no base of information about the world. Members have a responsibility to travel, to become informed about other countries, when they are so frequently required to make judgments about our relations with those countries.

Surely Congress must try to learn what is happening in the Soviet Union. It must comprehend what is happening in the Pacific Rim, where development is burgeoning. It needs to disengage from the Cold War mythology that said no country once crushed under communism can become a capitalist society, that it is never possible to retrieve a country from the clutches of leftist dictatorship.

We know now that those myths are not true. The countries of Eastern Europe are emulating the West. We must release ourselves from the foolish thralldom of ideas of a generation ago. This requires a willingness to open our minds to new sources of knowledge.

Today, when our ecosystem is threatened by pollution, when the nations of the world are spending some $2 billion every day on implements of destruction, when 42,000 children die each day from malnutrition or disease, and when nuclear armageddon could be minutes away, wisdom based upon knowledge is surely what we must seek.

NOTE

1. Walter Lippmann, *Public Philosophy* (New York: New American Library, 1955).

I

Historical and Philosophical Considerations

1. Toward a Legislature of the First Kind

Theodore J. Lowi

Two hundred years ago, as Congress was trying to establish its new Constitution, France was revving up for its revolution. The two beginnings were equally inauspicious. Between opening day, March 4, 1789, and April 6, Congress was not even able to convene, for lack of a quorum in the Senate. On July 14, Bastille Day, Louis XVI was in Versailles. Historians tend to agree that Louis spent the day hunting, but they disagree on what he did and said that evening. Someone, the king or a forger, wrote three words in his journal: "Mardi, quatorze, rien." Tuesday, the fourteenth, nothing. Whether the king wrote that passage or not, if he went hunting on the fourteenth, it was because he knew of no compelling reason not to. Congress's inability to meet and Louis's ability to join the chase are together a fitting introduction to the problem of knowledge and power.

These are not the best of times for Congress, and it could become the worst of times. In the 1980s Congress bashing became a popular sport. An obscure lieutenant colonel could emerge from the White House basement to become a national hero by bashing Congress. Conservatives led the offense where once they were among Congress's most ardent defenders. Congress was blamed for imposing strict requirements on the executive, such as the Delaney clauses and the Boland amendments. Congress was faulted for delegating too broadly, then faulted later for interfering and also for not interfering through the budget process. President Ronald Reagan got good press for blaming Congress for the nation's historic deficits, and he got good press for disregarding Congress altogether—not only for conducting his own foreign policy but for regulating or not as he saw fit.

In 1989–1990, when President Bush's approval rating was soaring above 80 percent, Congress's was less than half that. These are not the best of times for Congress. Why?

At some point in the mid-1960s, according to my calculations, Congress began what can only be understood as institutional suicide. I call it "legiscide," a bleeding away of Congress's constitutional authority through a succession of laws that delegated essential legislative power to the executive branch when emergencies did not require it. Apologists say this devolution of legislative power was inevitable and also good, because Congress is unable to legislate clear rules of conduct for a society that has become so complex and fast moving.

If this is true, the displacement of Congress by presidential government comes down to a question of knowledge and, like the French monarchy's, its decline is probably irreversible. A legislature, composed as it is, mainly of amateurs, cannot survive as a legislature in a complex society and is doomed to the role of budgeter of authority, its function merely to say which agency shall have jurisdiction over what area and perhaps to make marginal adjustments in appropriations. Two hundred years of legislative experience at national and state levels can, however, support an opposite argument, one that may appear to be more critical of Congress than that of the apologists but is nevertheless more optimistic about the future of Congress.

The Golden Age of the Legislature

During the nation's formative years, Congress was dependent on the executive, as it is now. For example, Congress required the secretary of the treasury, Alexander Hamilton, to report on several important policy issues. Hamilton responded in 1790 and 1791 with formal reports, two of which stand among the greatest state papers ever written: the *Report on the Public Credit* and the *Report on Manufactures*. Yet, Congress did not delegate to the president or the secretary of the treasury the power to make policy. Congress itself produced the legislation assuming the war debts, establishing a national bank, formulating the first national excises and tariffs, and drafting the amendments that were to become the Bill of Rights.

After the first decade or so, with the founding a success, Congress was spared most of the heavy burdens of government because the Constitution had assigned these duties to the states. More to the point, the laws adopted by the state legislatures in the nineteenth century were far superior to Congress's laws today. They were superior in legal integrity, embodying clear rules of conduct, for government agencies and for citizens. The nineteenth century was truly the golden age of the legislature.

This statement appears to be paradoxical. On the one side is the nineteenth century's record of superior legislation. On the other side are three contradictory facts: First, state legislatures were relatively unstable, with far more turnover than in today's Congress. Second, state legislatures had virtually no staff, and they had no budget to hold frequent hearings, hire consultants, or commission research. Third, and most important, society to nineteenth-century legislators must have been more complex than today's society is to today's members of Congress.

Since this seeming paradox goes directly to the question of legislative knowledge, let me offer two illustrations. In the 1840s little was known about capitalism—about joint stock companies, fractional reserve banking, insurance, mechanization. According to the *Oxford English Dictionary*, the concept of capitalism did not even appear in common usage until the late 1840s. Yet state legislation on such matters was quite specific as to the obligations the law sought to impose on the conduct of the participants.

As a second illustration, little was known in the 1840s, indeed even in the 1870s, about the cause and spread of disease. Yet the states had appropriate and timely public health laws, with legal integrity. In other words, legislatures more than one hundred years ago did not enact such nonlaws as Congress enacts today—statutes that merely note the problem and name the goal (in an eloquent title and preamble) and then turn over to an agency the authority to make the actual rules. Even in the 1970s, when Congress occasionally tried to be specific in its legislation, the best it could do was to specify the deadlines and demand that the agencies impose the appropriate technology. It delineated no rules of conduct. And without rules of conduct there is no true law.

Why the success of the legislature of the golden age and Congress's relative failure today? Why the success of the nineteenth-century state legislatures if their society was as complex to them as ours is to us? The difference lies not in the superior knowledge held by the early legislators but in two different ways legislators can deal with ignorance. Legislators always lack knowledge of how their world works. In all matters of law, there is an equality of ignorance. The difference between legislative attainments in the two eras can be found in the use of two different approaches to knowledge, or better, the embrace of two different kinds of knowledge.

Amateur Knowledge and Professional Knowledge

Knowledge inthe There may be more than two kinds of knowledge, but my intention here is not to develop a fully articulated theory of knowledge. I can identify two kinds of knowledge, and they are sufficient to pursue my argument. The first kind is amateur knowledge, knowledge arising from sensory experience. The second is professional knowledge, based on formal agreements about experience.

Amateur Knowledge

Amateur knowledge is accessible to everyone; it is layman's knowledge, drawn from living. It was the knowledge used by nineteenth-century legislators. Politically, it could be called constituency knowledge because it was drawn from a representative's living a lifetime in the district and being of as well as from the district. Legislatively, amateur knowledge is knowledge of more than people and of their opinions and demands. It is also knowledge of the fundamental conflicts in the district that result from differing expressions of fundamental needs, of injuries, of sources of injury, and of widespread inconveniences. The legislation arising from such knowledge is direct and reactive, as in the old expression, "There ought to be a law."

Because amateur knowledge is limited, professionals are skeptical of it: "Common sense will tell you the world is flat." Experienced-based knowledge is a poor resource for making generalizations, and, in legislation, it is limited primarily to describing symptoms. To search for causes requires an ability to theorize that goes beyond the world of amateur thinking. Scientists with any humility will admit that in all but simple cases (which perhaps even amateurs can handle) determining causation is difficult even for those possessed of professional knowledge. This is why most modern professional knowledge deals in systems and probabilities—that is, it ignores the behavior of specific components and virtually replaces concrete connections with statistical association.

For example, in the nineteenth century amateur knowledge could cope with environmental issues, not because legislators understood their environment but because they dealt piecemeal with specific inconveniences and injuries, usually treating them as nuisances. Laws could be concrete and appropriate and expressed in straightforward legal rules, relative to the specific environmental experiences people were having. These same nuisances were later grouped together into an abstract category, and, for purposes of public policy, given a name: conservation. Later the category was given another, more abstract, name: the environment. Then it was given a goal orientation: environmental protection. Often the matter was expressed even more abstractly—ecology—and made into a system: the ecosystem.

Generally, categories of law and policy have advanced over the years from concrete to abstract, from amateur to professional, from particles to systems, and from specification of particular conduct to an exalted rhetoric of desired outcome. Some examples include the following: from nuisance to conservation to environment and ecosystem; from dole to charity to public assistance to social insurance to social security to welfare to human resources; from disease control to treatment to cure to health to health delivery system; from war to defense to national security. The tendency in formulating these labels seems always to be toward abstraction, theory, and system; toward inclusive definitions of the situation; and at the same time toward goal orientation or wish fulfillment and away from specific conduct and its immediate consequences. Today's society seems complex to policymakers because of the way they define it.

Formal Knowledge and the Bureaucracy

These observations lead to the second kind of knowledge, professional knowledge. By examining the concept of professional knowledge, I will show why this approach to knowledge has spread, yet has had such a devastating effect on the twentieth-century legislature. Professional knowledge is formal knowledge organized around concepts and definitions of reality agreed upon in advance. Although it is ultimately tied to the senses, every effort is made to transcend the senses. Professional knowledge is contrived knowledge.

Professional knowledge is far more powerful than amateur knowledge. Professional knowledge is formal knowledge in that it is self-consciously designed for a purpose, and that purpose is to get things done. Formalization makes knowledge particularly powerful in analyzing complex problems. Because of its analytical utility, professional knowledge is favored by the academic disciplines. It is highly compatible with the bureaucratic/

administrative process. There are four reasons for the special compatibility of formal knowledge with bureaucracy.

First, formalization reduces experience and accumulation of experience into routines. This is good for science. It is also good for bureaucracy. Philosopher Arnold Brecht once defined bureaucracy as "voluminous routine business." Formalization converts knowledge into information. Formalization made the information revolution possible. Bureaucracy made the information revolution successful. Formalization permits the conversion of knowledge into information. For science and bureaucracy it is vitally important to measure things. Information can be measured; knowledge cannot be.

Second, although information is costly, bureaucracy can handle the high capital outlay and can drastically cut unit costs through repeated use. Unlike the resources that produce energy, information resources, once collected, do not require replenishing. Adding information to the resource base entails only a marginal cost.

Third, information enhances management within a bureaucracy. Since information is an agreement about what knowledge is relevant, all members of an organization become dependent on it and on each other. Management can be defined as control and manipulation of organizational information.

Fourth, bureaucratic investment in information is justifiable. Administrative agencies are organized to deal with a special problem or area or process that requires continued attention and analysis of general patterns within their areas of responsibility or bearing upon them. These agencies require constant input of data concerning all persons and phenomena defined as related to their mission. Defining an agency's jurisdiction as a system and delegating to it the difficult task of pinpointing specific causes produces an explosion of possibilities. This demand for data, not totalitarianism, explains why, according to the National Institute of Standards and Technology and the Office of Technology Assessment, the federal government in the late 1970s invested $6 billion in information technology and subsequently spent another $10 billion in 1983 and an estimated $15 billion in 1985. This demand, not totalitarianism, also explains why, according to estimates in the early 1980s, there were fifteen computerized dossiers on every individual in the United States, amounting to more than three billion dossiers on computer, not counting the millions of paper dossiers in government file drawers. In 1986 OTA concluded that computerized exchanges of personal information were creating a de facto national data base covering nearly all Americans.

Limitations of Knowledge

With all the power of professional knowledge, it has at least one serious limitation. There is no truth in it. Professional knowledge is an approximation. Because it is derived knowledge, the units of reference, whether bits of information or complex concepts, are artificial conventions; that is, they are agreed-upon definitions or measurements, in which one thing stands for another. That is what an index (or indicator) is: an indirect measurement of a phenomenon that cannot be measured directly. Examples of indicators in policy discourse include the gross national product (GNP), consumer price index (CPI), unemployment figures, and the monetary measures M_1, M_2. Everyone uses indicators and indexes without realizing there is no truth in any of them. A thermometer is a direct measure of body temperature, but it is also used, by agreement, as a means of providing an index to infection in the body. The Dow Jones average is an index, a useful convention but a very partial reading of the day's stock market results. Ratings of the president's job performance and other opinions are clearly partial. Dozens of other indexes are used in public discourse and in academic and public policy analysis. Few of them are appreciated as indexes, and most are eventually accepted as direct measures and treated as truths about the phenomena to which they refer. This practice is a profound weakness in formal knowledge.

Former senator Barry Goldwater once referred to GNP as the gross national lie, and he was not exaggerating all that much. GNP is a useful if flimsy measurement of the phenomenon to which it refers. But when an index or any other formalization of reality is off by even a fraction, consequences in action can be greatly magnified. In the academic sciences slight misrepresentations may not be so serious, perhaps resulting only in a failed experiment. When indicators are taken as truths and become guides to programmatic action, however, a small distortion at the outset can become a grievous error. Bill Mauldin was prescient in his World War II cartoon depicting a general as he stood on an alpine peak poring over a map. His aide has a finger on the map and, as he points with the other hand, says, "General, sir, according to our calculations, we are on that peak right over there."

Serious-minded scientists and technologists, aware of the limitations of indirect measures, regularly seek "reality checks." This is why real bomb tests must sometimes be made. And this reality checking may now be the most important function of our embassies. In the age of satellites and sophisticated telecommunications, the importance of embassies is diminished, but they can still offer a sight-and-sound supplement to the information gathered technologically. Furthermore, no sane financial adviser would rely solely on the Dow Jones average without directly examining some real companies.

When policymakers trust formal information as reality, however, the distortions can be dangerous. Former secretary of defense Robert McNamara offers a case in point. He and his "whiz kids" gave us our first Pentagon driven entirely by formal knowledge. McNamara frankly admits in his 1968 autobiography that the Pentagon grievously overestimated Soviet strength in 1961–1962 and that estimates significantly distorted President Kennedy's Cold War policy.[1] Analysts based their estimates largely upon such things as interpretations of U-2 overflight photographs and expenditures in rubles that could be over or under reality by billions of dollars, depending on the value assigned to the ruble. In another area the Pentagon used body counts as an index to the effectiveness of our conduct of the Vietnam War.

Finally, one must not overlook the element of politics in formal knowledge. Wherever there is room for interpretation, partisans will conscientiously and sincerely push the reading of an index in their favor and call it science. But that is not a superficial subterfuge of politics. Indexes do in fact leave room for self-interested interpretation, and that must be seen as an inherent limitation of formal knowledge, all the more dangerous when its users treat it as truth rather than approximation. Formal, professional knowledge is still powerful, however, and is a boon to effective government. As long as its limits are recognized, its compatibility with bureaucracy is a good thing.

Knowledge in the Legislature

Professional knowledge, however, has not been good for the legislative branch. It has eroded the separation of powers to the extent that Congress insists on speaking in the essentially foreign language of bureaucracy. When Congress adopts professional knowledge, it does not necessarily gain more knowledge. It simply exchanges one form of knowledge for another, to its disadvantage.

As Louis XVI learned too late, a government can be knowledgeable about many things and still be ignorant of the genuine needs of the people.

This was not so important before the "rise of the common man" in the eighteenth century, but since then constituency knowledge has become as important as market knowledge, knowledge of natural resources, or any other formally defined area of knowledge. Constituency knowledge is a special category of amateur knowledge. It is the basis of representative government in general and of Anglo-Saxon representative government in particular. The Anglo-Saxon system is built upon several assumptions.

The first and most important principle of representation is geography, and the district is the unit of representation. The unit of representation is not the individual. It is not the majority, nor special interests, nor groups or classes. Anglo-Saxon representation is geographic representation. Equality of numbers—as in the expression, "one person, one vote"—did not become an important principle in the United States until the 1960s, when Congress's conception of itself and of relevant knowledge had changed.

Second, districts should be meaningful social units. There should be some historical reason for their boundaries, as defined by preexisting town and county lines.

Third, elections should be frequent. Given the inefficiency of travel and communications in 1787, the constitutional provision for two-year and six-year terms must be considered a strong commitment by the Framers to the criterion of frequency.

Fourth, and a logical extension of the third assumption, legislative turnover should be brisk, with members holding relatively brief tenure. Otherwise, what is the use of frequent elections? The rate of incumbent reelection in the 1790s, incidentally, was about 40 percent, compared to an average of more than 90 percent in the House and Senate today.

Fifth, representatives should be amateurs, neither professional legislators nor government functionaries. The constitutional prohibition of an individual's holding office simultaneously in both branches attests to this. Elected representatives should be of the district as well as from the district. The Constitution requires only that a House or Senate member be "an inhabitant of the State in which he shall be chosen," but it has been extremely rare for House members not to reside legally within their district. Sen. Robert Kennedy, D-N.Y., is the only person in recent memory who became an inhabitant of a state just prior to and for the purpose of running for Congress.

When these simple, human-scale criteria are met, the problem of knowledge in the legislature is to a large extent solved. Elected representatives can bring meaningful, practical knowledge to the legislature if a geographically defined unit of representation, of whatever size, is a meaningful living unit; if the representatives have lived a substantial part of their lives in their districts; and if some electoral competition exposes real local conflicts, needs, and sources of injury and inconvenience.

The classic conflict posed by Edmund Burke between loyalty to the district and responsibility for the nation was solved in American republican theory. Life in the district gives the elected representative the requisite knowledge. The institution of representative government takes care of the nation. As James Madison put it in *Federalist* no. 10, when the government is delegated

to a small number of citizens elected by the rest ... [the effect is] to refine and enlarge the public views by passing them through the medium of a chosen body of citizens, whose wisdom may best discern the true interest of their country and whose patriotism and love of justice will be least likely to sacrifice it to temporary or partial considerations. Under such a regulation it may well happen that the public voice, pronounced by the representatives of the people, will be more consonant to the public good than if pronounced by the people themselves, convened for the purpose.... In the extent and proper structure of the Union, therefore, we behold a republican remedy for the diseases most incident to republican government.

Congressional Adjustment to Change

Major changes in Congress began only after the Great Depression forced new governing roles on Washington. Thanks to the ability of state governments to meet the demands placed on them by the Constitution, Congress did not confront the collapse of the strict federal structure until the depression, when it found itself constitutionally dominant but institutionally weak. A few spurts of policy activity in the late 1880s and again after 1910 had given Congress little preparation for dealing with a fully interstate economy. The Senate was still intoxicated with its ninety-six wordaholics deliberating under permissive debate rules. Earlier reforms had weakened party and parliamentary leadership. From 1900 onward all measures of party support and party discipline showed steady decline. Committees had proliferated. Congress had given away its budget powers in 1921, and the presidency had not yet learned how to use them. Three adjustments to the crisis presented by the depression were inevitably fast and poorly thought through.

First, Franklin D. Roosevelt sought and Congress approved programs that were not merely larger than ever but were constitutionally novel for the federal government. To the traditional domestic function of promoting commerce through public works and protective tariffs, Congress added two entirely new kinds of government functions: regulation of the economy and redistribution of wealth and status among broad income classes and sectors through policies of progressive taxation, credit and monetary manipulation, and social security. Both new functions had to be constitutionally tested, and both were approved by the Supreme Court in a separate line of cases.[2]

Second, because of the urgency of the situation, Congress did not bother to enact legislative rules to guide implementation but rather delegated that authority to the agencies. These broad delegations of legislative authority were also tested in the Supreme Court and were declared unconstitutional.[3] In the ensuing years, however, Congress disregarded the nondelegation doctrine, and the Supreme Court in effect let the issue stand.

These first two adjustments—two new kinds of government functions and broad agency delegation—were immediate and involved Congress as an institution acting upon other institutions and upon society at large. The third adjustment was internal. Having beefed up the presidency, Congress then moved to reinforce its own powers. The culmination was the La-Follette-Monroney Act of 1946, which revamped the committee system and significantly expanded the professional staff of individual members of Congress and the permanent staff of the committees.

Delegation of Power and Similarities with the Executive Branch

Two of the three adjustments—delegation and professionalization—were the beginning of congressional "legiscide." I view 1961–1962 as the beginning of legiscide because Congress, in the 1960s, continued to write laws with broad and undefined delegation, although there was no longer an emergency and Congress was in a position of strength rather than weakness and crisis. But the legislative branch had begun to set the stage for legiscide as early as 1946, as it modeled itself after the executive branch. Congress had begun to change its nature, not merely its structure.

Congress's professional capacity expanded from nearly 1,300 personal aides in 1935 (870 in the House, 424 in the Senate) to more than 11,000 professional staff in 1986 (7,920 House, 3,774 Senate). In addition, by 1986 there were 20,000 other professional staffers working for Congress in the congressional support agencies—including the Congressional Research Service, Congressional Budget Office, Office of Technology Assessment, and the 30 percent of the General Accounting Office that works directly for Congress. Since at least the 1970s the number of congressional staff members has been larger than those in the departments of State, Labor, or Housing and Urban Development.[4] Individual members can call on committee or support agency staff for policy research as well as for help with constituency issues. Members avail themselves of staff to such an extent that they no longer feel confined to specialize on the policy issues under the jurisdictions of the committees on which they serve. Members instead approach each policy issue through the assistance of committee and personal staff and through the research provided by the service agencies. A ranking member of a committee and one or more subcommittees can have a working staff exceeding one hundred professional people.

In 1942 a distinguished political scientist, Arthur W. Macmahon of Columbia University, described the already noticeable expansion of congressional staff in the appropriations process. Among other considerations, Macmahon was concerned that as Congress became increasingly involved with administrative oversight, especially through the power of the purse, staff additions to accomplish this could rob the institution of its distinctiveness. Macmahon concluded that

closer cooperation in the routine handling of appropriations . . . must be developed cautiously. . . . Even [a practical minimum] would require enlarged permanent staff for the committees. . . . The most valuable contribution of legislative oversight is to galvanize the disciplines of administration itself. . . . The [congressional] staff necessary for continuous inquiry could be maintained only at the risk of a harmful division of responsibility, while such staff would still lack a first-hand sense of operations. *The hazard is that a body like Congress, when it gets into detail, ceases to be itself.* . . . (Emphasis added.)[5]

Let me extend Macmahon's argument further with an interpretation based on nearly fifty years of history since he first recognized the problem. Everyone studying congressional staffers has noted their professionalism, career commitment, and tendency to resemble the agency career people with whom they deal. According to Harold Seidman, a career Budget Bureau staffer, "growth of a congressional bureaucracy accentuated the innate disposition of the Congress to concentrate on administrative details rather than basic issues of public policy." [6] Ultimately, according to Brookings scholar James Sundquist, congressional staffers force members of Congress into becoming "managers of professional staffs" rather than legislators engaging in deliberation and true collective decision making.[7]

Although I am sympathetic with their arguments and have written about some of them, I think we have all missed one important point: the tendency of professional staffers to think alike even when they disagree on recommendations or conclusions. Professors and politicians know that whoever establishes the terms of discourse usually wins the argument. Since congressional staffers, like agency staffers, are professionals, they prefer the same kind of knowledge, a knowledge that comes from analysis. This is what the bureaucratization of Congress has accomplished.

It is now almost universally agreed that professional knowledge takes precedence over amateur knowledge, which may be why the very notion of amateur knowledge sounds rather quaint. The consensus can be seen in the curricula and faculty of law schools, business schools, and schools of public policy and public affairs, where most career officials in all branches of government are trained. Case studies and other impressionistic methods are being overshadowed, often displaced, by systems analytic methods. Courses in decision making focus on formula decision making. Economics is replacing law as the language of the state.

The proliferation of schools of business and more recently of schools of public affairs has been a response to the victory of professional knowledge in its fullest technological meaning. But perhaps even more telling is that law schools are undergoing similar mutations. In recent years law professors with the brightest reputations are those who have made their names in the relatively new field called law and economics. According to Yale law professor Bruce Ackerman, law and law schools will lose their traditional power position in American society unless they learn to take into account all the facts and not merely those comprehended by testimony in the case at hand.[8] Yet, taking into account the whole system of causes and effects surrounding a particular case and all possible cases like it is alien to the language and thoughtways of law, both in courts and in legislatures. As Oliver Wendell Holmes observed, "the life of the law has not been logic: it has been experience" [9]—that is to say, amateur knowledge.

Legislatures are able to deal with amateur knowledge by general rules of conduct, while courts are constitutionally obliged to dispose of particular cases. Both institutions deal with actual conflicts, and some of the best products of legislation are laws codifying court-developed precedents. Both institutions work from the particular to the general through cumulation of concrete experiences. Econometric modeling and economic indicators represent a distinctly different approach to knowledge, one with which most legislators are poorly equipped to deal because it moves from the general toward the particular (but rarely reaching the particular). If society through these lenses looks more complex, the distortion is largely a product of the lenses themselves.

There are many other signs that Congress is becoming more like the executive branch as it delegates its legislative powers. One indication is that incumbents, particularly in the House, can virtually claim automatic reelection. The reelection rate for incumbent House members was 79 percent in 1948 and 98 percent in 1988. (The rate in the Senate went from 60 percent in 1948 to 93 percent in 1982, then to 90 percent in 1984 and 75 percent in 1986. The lower rate in the Senate and the variation is attributable mainly to the fact that only 33 senators must run in each election, and small numbers distort results.) Reelection produces professionals, and this also insulates the institution from society, as Harvard professor Samuel Huntington noted as early as the mid-1960s.[10] There is, of course, turnover in Congress. Of the 435 representatives elected in 1972, only 122 would still have been in Congress in 1988, even if no election had been held, because 313 members retired during those sixteen years. This kind of turnover, however, does not deeply counteract the insulation and professionalism that come from virtually assured reelection. Rather, turnover by retirement could be considered an element that encourages insulation and professionalism: Retirement is a career trait of an established institution.

A related sign is the change in the relation of members to their districts. With the decline of local political parties, members have become individual entrepreneurs, devoting more of their resources than ever to their constituencies. The resources spent have changed significantly, however. Improved transportation enables members to return home more frequently than in the past. Even more significant is the expansion of staff for district offices, services, and research. As Norman Ornstein and his associates observed, "more than two-fifths of the personal staff of representatives and one-third of those of senators now work in district or state offices—a dramatic increase since the early 1970s."[11] With the additional staff, the functions have changed, "to develop a personal presence before their constituencies . . . to orchestrate electioneering, polling, voter mobilization and campaign finance activities themselves."[12] This puts a different light on the raw observation that members are spending more time at home than formerly.

In Washington, although the number of days Congress is in session has not gone up appreciably since 1960, the number of hours per day in session has risen, from about 4.0 hours in 1960 to 6.4 in the 1980s. In addition, states and congressional districts are becoming increasingly heterogeneous. Since 1962 the stress on numerical equality of districts has pushed state legislatures in their redistricting to the point at which they are violating the original constitutional assumption of geographic representation that districts be formed around recognizable social units. The artificiality of most numerically equalized districts, coupled with the increasing heterogeneity of all residential areas, including the states, has compounded the insulation of the professionalized member, producing what an anthropologist would call social distance. When analyzing culture from a distance, one must rely on substitutes for direct observation and experience.

Applying this to Congress, we find the use of computer-generated mailing lists, a practice now universal among staffers who work for House and Senate members in the districts. These lists are not assembled from door-to-door canvassing by local party workers or by the members. They are produced by systematic analysis of the voting rolls, by the aggregated voting backgrounds and socioeconomic character of the neighborhoods, and, above all, by sample surveys. A poll can reveal a lot about people and their preferences. Yet the knowledge it produces is artificial. It is a professionally designed instrument and can be produced better by professional staff members or consultants than by the members. The voter preference questions are particularly artificial, often reported in the form of scale scores or index rankings. What is salient to the district can get lost in standardized questionnaires. Open-ended surveys designed to elicit spontaneous responses and genuine local concerns are expensive, hard to analyze, and usually created by teams of academics without pressing political goals.

As Macmahon feared, the rise in the number of staff would also affect the internal life of Congress, making it more like the executive branch. Kenneth Shepsle has captured this feature of the change very well:

Growth [in staff] transformed legislative life and work. In the 1940s the House had its norms and the Senate its folkways ... members who were neighbors ... or who traveled back and forth to Washington [together] came to know each other exceedingly well. But even more distant relationships were based on familiarity and frequent formal and informal meeting. By the mid-1960s this had all changed. The rubbing of elbows was replaced by liaisons between legislative corporate enterprises, typically at the staff level. Surrounded or protected by a bevy of clerks and assistants, Members met other Members only occasionally and briefly on the chamber floor or in committee meetings.[13]

Legislators become still more like bureaucrats when the influences come from outside their districts. The House leadership and other members can rhapsodize about the renewed attentiveness of representatives to their districts. Beyond the fact that much of that attention comes through staff and polling, the additional reality is that representatives learn the details of their districts by artificial means, but they pick up policy ideas, issues, and commitments from interest groups that go beyond their districts. Although legislators have always been the prime target of interest groups, these groups took on new and problematic meaning as parties and committees devolved more and more power on the individual legislators. The emergence of political action committees has simply exacerbated the existing problem: More and more financing comes from outside the districts, and most of it is tied to policy discourse. These interest group/PAC constituencies are more similar to agencies than to traditional geographic districts because their interests are specialized and their communications to Congress tend to be formal statements produced by professional staff. I see this as a negative trend because the high status of professional knowledge (which abounds in the staffs of well-financed corporate groups) is being reinforced by political incentives for members of Congress to participate in the professionalized policy discourse.

Finally, Congress has been drawn into the ambit of professional knowledge and bureaucratese by the replacement of congressional policymaking (that is, significant legislation) by the budgetary process. In its valiant effort to retrieve some of the power it had delegated to the executive through hundreds of broad and ill-defined statutes, Congress adopted the Congressional Budget and Impoundment Control Act of 1974. This act created the Congressional Budget Office (CBO), two new standing committees, and a new congressional budget process. The CBO became a new source of professional knowledge for Congress. But more important, a much larger proportion of Congress's collective workload was dedicated to the budget resolutions, the reconciliation acts, the proposals for deferrals and rescissions, the supplementals, and, all the while, the coordination of budget ceilings with authorization and revenue provisions. In 1970, for example, 45 percent of all House roll calls were budget related (121 of 266). In 1975, 52 percent (320 of 612) were budget related, and the number has remained well above 50 percent since 1975. In the Senate the percentages run a few points higher, reaching an all-time high of 71 percent in 1981, with 62 percent in 1983 and 60 percent in 1985, the nonelection years.[14]

Meanwhile, as many students of the budget process have observed, the

Office of Management and Budget (OMB) has become less a budget bureau and more an instrument of presidential policymaking, implementation, and control. This is a perfect reversal of roles, with Congress preoccupied with the most administrative and least policy-oriented aspect of government. We are too often instructed that policy and administration are impossible to separate. Here is a clear case of separation and reversal, with Congress becoming increasingly professional in order to cope with the professionalization of policy in the function of budget. In an earlier formulation I called this policy-without-law.

A New Kind of Lawmaking

By delegating its legislative powers to the executive branch, Congress has been drawn into a basically alien form of discourse, a more complex form of discourse that makes modern life appear more complex. It has become hazardous for a member to stand up on the floor of Congress and say, "There ought to be a law," unless this declaration is backed by extensive hearings, cost-benefit analyses, impact analyses, and so forth. In addition to the Library of Congress and Congressional Research Service, the agencies, and the think tanks and consultants, Congress has had to create—and take note of the name—an Office of Technology Assessment, whose professionals not only evaluate technology but also are asked how to use technology to make policy.

Having been cast adrift in a sea of artificial forms of data, Congress tends to make law in terms of what it is provided. Congress is given a pattern determined by professional analysis, and it passes a statute ordaining an outcome or a goal in terms of the pattern. This is a new kind of lawmaking.

Just as there are at least two kinds of knowledge, there are two kinds of law. One is law that governs people. This is law composed of rules, rules backed by sanctions, that impose obligations on conduct. This is law as it is traditionally understood, in a juridical and a legislative sense. This is law that governs people.

Law of the second kind is law that governs nature or the universe; it is concerned with physical laws. This kind of law is a hypothesis about the way nature works; it is a guess about the regularities and behavioral patterns of particles in a defined system, whether the particles are atoms, individuals, or historical events. If a pattern is so regular that it is lawlike, it is a law of the second kind.

Law of the first kind is very different from law of the second kind, and the result is devastating when law of the second kind is adopted as if it were the same as law of the first. An example, slightly exaggerated, will help to illustrate the point.

Specialists from agencies, congressional committees, interest groups, and elsewhere bring to Congress a proposal for legislation based upon lawlike patterns, drawn from professional knowledge derived artificially and confirmed by statistics and by causal theories with good scientific standing. Members of the relevant committee see the pattern as irrefutable and undebatable. Although some members oppose taking action, they all recognize that no amount of additional knowledge can refute the pattern with certainty. Meanwhile, defining the problem in broad, systemic terms strengthens Congress's conviction that a society comprised of systems is too complex for amateurs to understand. Rather than rejecting the whole-system, whole-pattern approach and reverting to piecemeal legislation on a few known aspects of the problem (laws of the first kind using knowledge), Congress enacts the pattern as law. In effect, it ordains the goal; it states what the outcome shall be. The following is an only slightly exaggerated example of law of the second kind treated as law of the first kind:

Whereas the best estimates show dirty air [defined in parts per billion], and whereas such air is harmful [defined by a biomedical theory estimating increased lung cancers], now therefore let there come to pass clean air [defined very precisely in parts per billion]. In pursuance of this goal, the agency will make whatever rules and whatever precise standards, using the best available technology, that will give us clean air by [whatever precise date is provided].

Another more recent example suggests that Congress continues to be unaware of the existence of two kinds of law. Professional staff develop an economic model to estimate the size of the drug market and to calculate the dollar value (another index) of the loss of life and property attributable to it. These drug data—rather flimsy estimates—are translated directly to budget data, and out pops a policy, composed of a preamble vowing to end drug abuse, an appropriation, and an authorization for a legal drug czar to fight the illegal drug czars. This is a different kind of law.

How Laws of the Second Kind Affect Agencies

Two direct consequences flow from Congress's adoption of laws of the second kind. The first effect is on the agencies. The second is on the scope of rights and the role of the federal courts, taken up in the next section.

When Congress responds to a flood of professional knowledge by enacting a law of the second kind, ordaining as a goal the pattern defined in the research, it is in effect turning back the entire information base as delegated legislative power. But that information base is inadequate, even when the agency itself produced the original knowledge, because it does not tell the agency what the priorities are, what parts of the system ought to be addressed first in order to attain the system goal. This inadequacy generates contradictory activity. First, the agency feels an urgency to turn out rules, because without priorities, everything is compelling. This tendency helps to explain the explosion in the number of rules and rules proposals generated in the 1960s and 1970s. At the same time, the agency is pressed to engage in new research, to determine the priorities, and to translate the systems study of professional knowledge into concrete rules and benefits for real people. Undertaking research delays agency action even as it increases agency activity. People grow impatient, seeing as dilatory all the new research, while also seeing as trivial the rules that seem to bring the agency no closer to attaining the grandiose system goal ordained in the statute.

This appearance of dilatoriness by the agency leads directly to the second consequence: the effect of laws of the second kind on Congress and the courts. As people grow impatient with the agency's lack of progress, they claim the goal as a matter of right and sue for a remedy.

Obligations and Rights: Rules Statutes Versus Goals Statutes

The difference between law of the first kind and law of the second kind is related to the distinction made by New York law professor David Schoenbrod between "rules statutes" and "goals statutes": a rules statute identifies a particular conduct and either restricts it or encourages it; a goals statute ordains the outcome and leaves the rules to the agency.[15] I take the distinction a step further: rules statutes convey obligations and goals statutes convey rights.

When Congress enacts a goals statute—a law of the second kind—ordaining a desired outcome, such as clean air, safe consumer products, or better working conditions, it is conveying a right to that outcome, whether intended or not. The responsible agency may later make rules restricting or encouraging the relevant conduct, but the emphasis on goals in a goals statute remains as a cause of action. Since no agency rule can attain more than a fraction of the legislated goal, each new rule or action by the agency is an inadequate remedy for the right denied by continued lack of fulfilment of the legislated goal. The right conveyed by a legislated goal is not a right in a constitutional sense; it is a legislated right that can be terminated by subsequent legislation. As long as it stands, however, the goals statute conveys rights. Brandeis professor Shep Melnick reports that since 1975 handicapped youths have had a legally enforceable right to a "free appropriate public education." [16] The legislation ordains free public education as a goal, saying nothing about whether it is a right. The interpretation of it as a right comes from litigation, and, as Melnick puts it, "over the past decade the courts have developed an elaborate federal common law on the placement and treatment of handicapped children." He is critical of "the amount of power [the Education for All Handicapped Children Act] gives to the judiciary." [17] On this last point I think he errs. The power to provide remedies for rights was already in the judiciary. The right was conveyed by the act, and the right was a claim on the judiciary that was difficult if not impossible for the judiciary to ignore.

The litigation explosion that earned for the federal courts the title "imperial judiciary" arose largely from Congress's enactment of laws of the second kind. Conservative critics have argued that big government programs, particularly those enacted in the 1960s and 1970s and designated "social policy," were all part of a left-wing program of class legislation aimed at changing the capitalist system. The conservative argument strengthened in intensity as well as cogency as the federal courts began to liberalize their rules of standing, class action, and third-party suits, making it possible for a group or individual to sue the U.S. government— that is, the agency—even when the plaintiff did not satisfy the Article III requirement that there be a real "case or controversy" in which the plaintiff had a substantial personal stake in the outcome of the case. Suits have been successfully brought to force an agency to go farther than it has been able or willing to go (as in a mandamus suit) or to stop an agency action (as in New York's vast Westway redevelopment plan), even when the person or group had no direct "nexus" with the injury or benefit being claimed, or had only an aesthetic connection. Since many litigants in the 1970s were members of or sponsored by liberal public interest groups, critics were convinced of a left-wing plot. But since most of the participants were upper middle class, were zealously committed to the stated public interest goals, and seemed unmindful of whether protection of the snail darter or education for handicapped children would transform capitalism, another explanation for the explosion of rights litigation is called for. It is readily at hand: Congress.

When Congress adopted laws of the second kind, it created rights. Sometimes the legislation explicitly created the right—usually called an entitlement. But beyond that, legislatures create statutory rights every time they ordain a goal as if it were a rule. Harvard law professor Laurence Tribe has tried to synthesize this complex situation:

An appropriately defined statutory right may confer standing upon virtually anyone who can allege any kind of injury going beyond the purely ideological. The Court has explicitly distinguished the constitutional requirement of "injury in fact" from its preference for cases that may vindicate "individual rights," for cases brought by the "best suitable" litigant, or for cases involving injuries "peculiar to the [litigant]" or to a distinct group of which [the litigant] is a part.[18]

I differ with Tribe on only one point. He uses the term "an appropriately defined statutory right"; I believe that goals statutes confer such statutory rights whether stated or not, indeed whether intended or not.

It is not necessary, nor would it be possible, to demonstrate that the federal courts have been under a left-wing spell or have been eager to seize the kind of power implied by the accusation of imperialism. A simpler explanation is that federal judges are responding to their natural calling. Wherever a right has been denied, there must be a remedy. This response differs from the traditional understanding of rights and standing to sue for rights, but the difference is not because the courts are now more permissive than ever—although indeed they are. The difference is for two other reasons: First, these suits are brought to win substantive group rights to an outcome or benefit rather than for individual, procedural rights to a process. Second, the suits are brought mainly against agencies to force them to take action or otherwise to do their duty. If members of Congress do not realize they are conveying rights when they ordain goals, that is evidence not that courts are imperial or that plaintiffs are socialists but that members of Congress are lacking in appropriate knowledge.

Cornell professor Jeremy Rabkin hits hardest on the revolution in standing to sue. As he puts it, "the question in a conventional lawsuit is never whether the would-be plaintiff has 'standing' . . . but whether he actually has a personal right to what he seeks from the court. There is no separate law of standing—because the whole argument is about what the plaintiff, himself, is entitled to receive." [19]

Although Rabkin's point is excellent, he overlooks the fact that we are not dealing with conventional lawsuits because we are not involved with law of the first kind. Rabkin makes another unassailable point. In areas of law in which citizens have the greatest and most substantial personal stake, such as crime, the courts

have remained adamant that no private citizen may force the government to commence criminal proceedings against another. . . . It is well-known that not every criminal prosecution is enforced to the fullest extent. . . . [Yet] there is no judicial check on the discretion of the Justice Department to refuse to prosecute. . . . With all the potential for bias and mischief in such unfettered discretion, few judges imagine that prosecution policy would be improved by allowing private advocates to challenge the exercise of this discretion.[20]

These comments apply to the realm of what Rabkin calls the "old administrative law," which is to be distinguished from the "new administrative law," where suits to force agencies to act are being brought successfully by lawyers "overwhelmingly leftist in their political outlook" and among whom "well over half expressed support for the proposition that 'the U.S. should move toward socialism.'"[21]

We do not need the mention of socialism to perceive that the areas in which courts have permitted tremendous citizen and public interest group intervention involve what I have called laws of the second kind, which underlie what Rabkin refers to as the "new administrative law." Criminal law is an example of law of the first kind. There the courts tend to respect administrative discretion on whether and how agencies might take action as a way of introducing flexibility into the obligations imposed by the laws and as a way of permitting professionals in the agencies to use their professional judgment. Since criminal laws impose obligations and sanctions on individual conduct, the courts must there be concerned with the constitutionally defined rights of persons accused of violating the rules. Courts, even in the age of open access, are not likely to grant standing to persons who merely perceive a benefit from more vigorous prosecutions and an increase in guilty verdicts.

But suppose Congress adopted a "safe streets act," based on statistical studies of crime waves, that ordained safe streets and authorized the Criminal Division of the Justice Department and the nation's drug czar to make the rules and regulations necessary to eliminate the crime wave by the year 2000.[22] My hypothesis is that the courts would find it difficult to maintain a strict standard for standing in these criminal prosecutions. Laws of the second kind cannot be precise about conduct, but they can be quite precise about goals. Statutes of recent years have been precise, down to the level of carcinogens or percentage of pollutants. When agencies use their discretion regarding the goal, people consider themselves deprived of benefits to which they are by statute entitled, and courts have to see it that way also.

What It Means for Congress

In 1969 I published a book arguing that liberalism was undoing itself. Liberalism failed to appreciate the constitutional limits on what democratic governments can do, and it replaced constitutional criteria with abstract, goal-oriented, interest group definitions of the public good. As a liberal I am not unqualifiedly happy to have my predictions confirmed. Liberalism is indeed down for the count, with almost no public figure willing to take on the mantle and with George Bush winning the 1988 election on a liberal-baiting campaign. What I had not fully anticipated is the extent to which conservative intellectuals also embrace legislative delegation and broad administrative discretion. This shift goes beyond partisanship and the fact that Republicans have held the White House for twenty of the past twenty-four years. Their position is based largely on contempt for Congress and pessimism about the capacity of democratic government to govern by rule-of-law.[23] Writing the book today, I might very well have entitled it *The End of Congress* rather than *The End of Liberalism*.[24]

Congress's delegation of legislative power to administrative agencies is inevitable. And under proper circumstances, where rules of conduct accompany the delegation, delegation can save a legislature. But delegation of the second kind is a curse. Goals statutes do not just undermine liberalism; they derange the administrative and the judicial processes.[25] Goals statutes also reach back into Congress.

Laws of the second kind arise mainly from professional knowledge. Once they become statutes, they draw members of Congress further into a discourse of data bases and systems theories, into the web of professional analysts who are more at home in the language of economics than in the language of law. More seriously, laws of the second kind undermine Congress by taking policy decisions outside the realm of Congress and distancing them from the ordinary politics of representative government. We can call this the "shrinking of Congress." Two dimensions of it will be addressed.

First, we can readily see Congress's shrinkage in the displacement of substantive policymaking by budget making and reconciliation. We can understand this same development—mentioned earlier to document the extent of professionalized discourse, particularly the language of economics—in the context of the declining scope of congressional power. Budgetary discourse not only confines Congress to "numbers work," as Allen Schick has observed. For example, as Schick notes, "the annual debate on defense policy was conducted in terms of percentages of real growth or decline, not in terms of force levels, defense objectives, or the role of the United States on the world scene." (See Chapter 4.)

This confinement to budgeting was not merely a temporary reflection of Ronald Reagan's policy of no new policy, although that probably explains the downturn in the number of bills Congress acted on in the 1980s. In fact, budgetary discourse is only part of a long-term shrinkage of congressional authority that affects, at a minimum, the increase in the deficit and the rise of uncontrollable expenditures. President Reagan was at least half right in observing that the deficits are Congress's responsibility. Sustained deficits unrelated to revenue and economic conditions indicate an inability of representative government (which includes the presidency) to establish substantive priorities.

On top of that is the phenomenon of the uncontrollables, a very interesting term. Uncontrollables are "off-budget" legislative commitments that are put above regular budgetary or appropriations actions; the level of expenditure for these items can be altered only by later substantive legislative action. Uncontrollables include such expenses as housing programs, in which the government guarantees FHA and VA mortgages in case of default. This category also includes deposit insurance, which mandated the savings-and-loan bailout, and the so-called entitlements, particularly health and welfare programs, many of which are indexed to the cost of living. In brief, in the years between 1967 and the late 1980s, "relatively uncontrollable" expenditure rose from 59 percent of the total federal outlay to well over 75 percent.[26] This is not merely shrinkage of congressional responsibility. It is downright legiscide.

Finally, we can see Congress's shrinkage most dramatically in the rise of court-made rights and the politics of rights. Congress could probably reverse much of the first kind of shrinkage. Except for interest on the federal debt, uncontrollables, after all, can be controlled by statute. But in this second kind of shrinkage, the genie may be permanently out of the bottle.

Rights, as Ronald Dworkin says, are trumps.[27] To establish a claim as a right is to set it above normal plurality and majoritarian politics. Politically, a right is a claim that cannot be denied except by an extraordinary decision process specified in advance. A constitutional right in this context is a higher order of right simply because the process of denial is the most difficult. Other rights exist, as on a continuum, depending upon the difficulty in denying the claims based on them. One point, however, is clear about all claims called rights: such claims are beyond the reach of ordinary politics. An important strategy in American politics is to convert a claim into a right, thus making the claim much more secure. The more rights conveyed, the cheaper each right becomes. But that is another part of the story. My concern here is that laws of the second kind make it easier for special interests to convert claims into rights and that immoderate success produces further institutional derangement.

To the extent that claims became rights, politics became less parliamentary. Lobbies have proliferated in Washington, but their focus has shifted outward from Congress to the agencies and downward from Congress to the election of members. What used to be called the "new lobby"—the media, mass mailings, public relations—is more conspicuous than ever. Direct action politics, in fact, ideological politics, is more noticeable. Just as Mancur Olson was explaining why groups do not succeed unless they can provide their members with personal services,[28] we witnessed, on the left and on the right, the birth of a host of public interest groups whose members are sustained by ideology. It is no accident that nearly all the public interest law firms serving public interest groups were founded in the late 1960s and afterward.[29] They were founded during the golden age of laws of the second kind, and their prime motivation was to realize the rights inherent in such legislation.

Congress is no longer at the center but at the periphery of representative government. The Constitution makes the legislative branch a major participant, but Congress's own actions have diminished the value of that participation. Consequently, the national government has a new two-party system. The liberal party holds sway in Congress, where the main action is retreat, in an attempt to defend the accomplishments of the New Deal. The conservative party controls the presidency and executive agencies. The conservatives are winning. Because they can restrict and reverse liberal programs through management, by exercising some of the discretionary powers Congress delegated to the agencies, they do not need to control Congress to win.

The courts have loosened the executive-legislative relationship, and the conservatives revile Congress because it is susceptible to claims of rights by public interest litigants in suits against agencies. As long as Congress enacts or fails to repeal legislation of the second kind, however, judicial review in effect will be proexecutive and antilegislative because courts generally accept the constitutionality of agency statutes and because many public interest suits seek not to restrict agencies but to prod them to further action. All this is at the expense of Congress and should be cause for concern. When Congress loses, the nation loses. There will be a new and drastically diminished American republic if right-wing intellectuals succeed in arguing that the true American republic is comprised of "good people" controlling the presidency, the presidency controlling the agencies, and the agencies making right decisions in the public interest. In this vision Congress is spectator; when it tries to be more, its actions are taken as intrusive, obstructive, and extravagant. When national security is the issue, Congress's role as opposition party is decried as obstructive and downright treasonous.

In the not too distant past some highly advanced, highly cultured countries, such as Italy, France, and Germany, tried to reject legislative institutions as anachronistic, inefficient, and unworthy of the politics of a great power. We know what these countries got in place of representative government. Congress bashing is indicative of the impatience Americans already have with the legislative branch.

If the decline of Congress is historically determined, it is irreversible, and the continuity with 1789 will be broken. If, however, the decline of Congress is of its own making, it can be reversed. Two difficult but simple steps are required.

First, Congress must return to the pursuit of amateur knowledge and, rejecting the systems approach, embrace the piecemeal. The objective and obligation of representative government is to cope with problems, not to solve them. The method should be one of successive approximations, learning from the experience of previous steps. To pretend that society's problems are solvable by ordaining a solution is worse than no action at all. The proposed solution can be dressed up in the ceremonial rhetoric of goals, but it is as primitive as witch doctors doing rain dances. And it is more harmful because it undermines representative government. No more grandiose goals. Just let Congress soberly establish some standards of conduct for particular problems as they are experienced.

Second, members of Congress should retreat to the Constitution and reflect on Article I, Section 1, clause 1: "All legislative powers herein granted shall be vested in a Congress of the United States." If these legislative powers are understood to mean laws of the first kind, the future of Congress is assured.

NOTES

1. Robert McNamara, *The Essence of Security: Reflections in Office* (New York: Harper and Row, 1968), 57–58.
2. *N.L.R.B. v. Jones & Laughin Steel Corp.* (1937) approved Congress's exercise of regulatory power; *Helvering v. Davis* (1937) approved redistribution power.
3. *Panama Refining Co. v. Ryan* (1935); *Schechter Poultry Corp. v. United States* (1935).
4. Norman J. Ornstein, Thomas E. Mann, and Michael J. Malbin, *Vital Statistics on Congress, 1987–1988* (Washington, D.C.: Congressional Quarterly, 1987), 135–140.
5. Arthur W. Macmahon, "Congressional Oversight of Administration: The Power of the Purse-II," *Political Science Quarterly* (September 1943): 413–414.
6. Harold Seidman and Robert Gilmour, *Politics, Position, and Power,* 2d ed. (New York: Oxford University Press, 1986), 40.
7. Quoted in ibid., 41.
8. Bruce Ackerman, *Reconstructing American Law* (Cambridge: Harvard University Press, 1984), 106.
9. Oliver Wendell Holmes, *The Common Law* (Boston: Little, Brown, 1963), 7.
10. Samuel P. Huntington, "Congressional Responses to the Twentieth Century," in *The Congress and America's Future,* ed. David B. Truman (Englewood Cliffs, N. J.: Prentice Hall, 1965), 5–31.
11. Ornstein, Mann, and Malbin, *Vital Statistics,* 136.
12. Kenneth A. Shepsle, "The Changing Textbook Congress," in *Can the Government Govern?* ed. John E. Chubb and Paul E. Peterson (Washington, D.C.: Brookings Institution, 1989), 242.
13. Ibid., 241–242.
14. Ornstein, Mann, and Malbin, *Vital Statistics,* 192–193.
15. David Schoenbrod, "Goals Statutes or Rules Statutes: The Case of the Clean Air Act," *UCLA Law Review* 30 (April 1983): 740–828.
16. R. Shep Melnick, "Judicial Activism Meets the New Congress" (Paper prepared for the Conference on the American Constitutional Experiment, Gordon Public Policy Center, Brandeis University, Waltham, Mass., March 1987), 6.
17. Ibid., 7.
18. Laurence Tribe, *Constitutional Choices* (Cambridge: Harvard University Press, 1985), 109.
19. Jeremy Rabkin, *Judicial Compulsions* (New York: Basic Books, 1989), 63–64.
20. Ibid., 76–77.
21. Ibid., 11–12.
22. This hypothetical example sounds extreme until it is compared to such ordinary cases as the 1972 Water Pollution Control Act amendments which, among other things, ordained that discharge of pollutants in navigable waters shall "be eliminated by 1985."
23. In addition to Rabkin, *Judicial Compulsions,* see Donald Brand, *Corporatism and the Rule of Law* (Ithaca: Cornell University Press, 1988), 290–319.

24. Theodore J. Lowi, *The End of Liberalism: Ideology, Policy, and the Crisis of Public Authority* (New York: Norton, 1969; 2d ed., 1979).

25. Ibid., esp. 2d ed., chaps. 5 and 11.

26. Ornstein, Mann, and Malbin, *Vital Statistics*, 179, 187.

27. Ronald Dworkin, *Taking Rights Seriously* (Cambridge: Harvard University Press, 1977), 269. That is, counterarguments based on utility or public policy cannot defeat claims of legal rights.

28. Mancur Olson, *The Logic of Collective Action* (Cambridge: Harvard University Press, 1965).

29. Study cited in Rabkin, *Judicial Compulsions*, 290, fn9.

Comment

Thomas S. Foley

There is some truth in Theodore Lowi's interesting thesis, but I believe it to be oversystematized and extrapolated. The first part of his thesis seems to be an outcry against professional knowledge at all levels. Any systematized, organized, secondary, or reductive knowledge seems somehow to offend his sense of the basic verities of human character. My impression is that he believes the typical member of Congress to be like Rousseau's primitive natural man. Back in his district or state he sits in the local café, a straw in the corner of his mouth, susceptible only to the empirical knowledge that can be gathered over a cup of coffee. He hears no statistical information, reads no compilations, does no systems analysis. He comes to Washington, this Babylon on the Potomac, surrounded by the experts, the systematizers, the systems analysts, the professors, and (worst of all) the economists—all of whom try to infuse his basic goodness with the taint of professional knowledge.

I cannot accept Lowi's notion that our society is for its own time no more complex than that of our predecessors. In the 1880s somebody proposed closing the Patent Office on the ground that all useful knowledge had already been achieved. We would not be guilty of that kind of hubris today. I think we recognize the explosion of information and knowledge. That explosion is not always a satisfactory reality in our lives, but it is a reality. Moreover, I do not agree that the environmental problems faced by Congress in the nineteenth century—such as nuisances created by pig sties—are the same as the environmental problems facing Congress today— such as the destruction of the ozone layer. The problems we face now— in the environment, in the relations between individuals, and in the areas of energy and nuclear power and the threats to the global climatic systems—are more complex than those of the nineteenth century. Ours is a different world entirely, and I reject the thesis that the golden age of Congress dealt with as many complexities in its time as we do in ours.

There is no question that political systems are having trouble dealing with the complexities of modern life. Not everything those in government do is commendable. It is true that there are instances of congressional clumsiness, overregulation, complication, and indecision. But what is the solution?

Lowi suggests that the solution, at least at the congressional level, is frequent elections and brisk turnover—that is, defeat, particularly in contested elections, of as many incumbents as possible. He is not alone in suggesting that there is insufficient turnover in Congress. This conclusion has been drawn by some who point to recent congressional elections, when more than 90 percent of incumbents facing reelection for the House were returned to office. In fact, President Reagan once said that more turnover has taken place in the Supreme Soviet than in the House of Representatives.

If it is true that turnover in Congress is desirable, we already have a fair measure of it. Of the members of the House serving in the 101st Congress in 1989, only 45 percent were serving in 1980, 19 percent in 1974, and 10 percent while Lyndon Johnson was president. I think turnover in the House is fairly reasonable; it certainly does not indicate the twenty-to-thirty-year bureaucratic career pattern that some people imagine representatives follow. The U.S. Congress is not a House of Lords with life tenure. Although 92.4 percent of the House was reelected in 1988 and 89.7 percent in 1990, a very healthy turnover of between 15 and 20 percent has occurred in every election cycle throughout the postwar period, not only because of contested elections but also because candidates died, retired, or pursued other offices.[1]

Contrary to what some critics assert, Congress did not engorge itself with staff in the early 1960s and create the impossibility of defeat. With only a couple of exceptions, the retention rates since the end of World War II until recently have been fairly constant. That is the statistical, professional, derived knowledge on this issue.

Common sense would tell us that everybody stays in Washington forever and becomes a committee chairman. Common sense and observation tell us that Congress has acquired bigger staffs that have become more professional (in a good and bad sense) and that are knowledgeable in a wider range of subjects—including economics, law, statistics, and natural sciences—than ever before. That is not a bad thing. If Congress is going to communicate with the executive branch agencies, made up of bureaucratic specialists in derived, organized, and professional knowledge, Congress needs its own professionals. And it is just as well that it has its own communicators rather than somebody else's.

I plead not guilty to the charge that members of Congress are personally acquiring highly developed, systematized knowledge. We all know from sensory experience and from what Lowi calls amateur knowledge that not all members of Congress are well prepared, well educated, or scholarly. In fact, a typical image is that of the patient staff member with a Ph.D. in nuclear engineering trying to explain to a senator or representative what reactor cores do when they overheat and what meltdown means. I would, in other words, plead guilty to Lowi's charge: we members of Congress are not now nor have we ever been all that smart.

Has Congress Declined?

Lowi's suggestion that Congress has declined is another questionable assumption. In whose opinion has it declined and with regard to which of the other branches? Presidents do not seem to think Congress has declined. Every president I have known in recent years has bitterly complained about the micromanagement of Congress, the overwhelming presence of Congress, the brooding domination of Congress, and the unrelenting intrusions of Congress into the prerogatives of the executive branch.

I agree with Lowi about the judiciary, however. Perhaps because I am the son of a judge, I agree that the judiciary has occasionally exceeded its role in providing individuals with entitlements and rights. Although this subject deserves considerable discussion, I would suggest here only that my concern arises not so much, or at least not solely, from the courts' handling of enabling entitlements of legislative enactment as it does from their widened judgment about constitutional rights. The courts have ruled that individuals enjoy privacy rights that are constitutional, antidiscrimination rights that are constitutional, and economic rights that are constitutional. All of these areas are thus beyond even the reach of Congress, if it wished to impose restrictions. The judicially broadened interpretation of equal protection under the Fourteenth Amendment has led to much of the complaint about judicial excess. As Charles Evans Hughes said, the Constitution is what the judges say it is. And the judges have been writing the Constitution with a much larger hand in recent decades.

In our divided government of separate powers it is interesting to observe how various groups have viewed the three branches. In the late 1920s and early 1930s, for example, the conservative community, the business community, and those who sought the protection of capital and property looked to the Supreme Court as a natural ally; the liberals—those who wanted some changes in what they regarded as the fixed controls of society by economic power—looked to the legislature. In the 1930s Louis Boudin ranted against the powers of judicial protection of property.[2] (And again the property elements we are talking about are the foundation and protection of capitalism.) In the 1950s, however, one had merely to look at billboards calling for the impeachment of Earl Warren to see the reaction of conservatives—or at least ultraconservatives—to the activist, liberal Court of Earl Warren. The Court had become the target rather than the savior. By the early 1960s James McGregor Byrnes was complaining about the deadlock of democracy, claiming that the executive was fettered by a Congress that was unwilling to move.[3] On the other hand, during the Vietnam War the "imperial presidency" was at fault, and Congress had to liberate the country from the evils of that war. Under Ronald Reagan's presidency the conservatives, rallying around the executive branch, talked about congressional micromanagement. They pointed to the necessity of preserving the president's power to control foreign policy even beyond constitutional restrictions, proclaiming the president's fundamental right to maintain security of the state.

These discussions go back and forth. To some degree they indicate how proponents of political viewpoints in our society latch on to one of the three branches of government as they determine which might suit their philosophy or advance their interests.

Some observers have said that Congress, particularly the Senate, has become overstaffed. It is argued that members' staffs have expanded outrageously and gained power. Sometimes staffers are arrogant, taking on the characteristics of their principals. Senators have so divided their time that they sometimes empower individual staff members to be the "senator for international monetary payments" or the "senator for clean air attainment" or the "senator for defense procurement." These specialized clones can be formidable indeed.

Some areas of the House may be overstaffed—perhaps not. It is true that some chairmen and some committees have greater success in acquiring staff and exercising power than others, although I would not say that power in Congress is always directly attributable to staff size and therefore directly attributable to knowledge. John Dingell of Michigan has perhaps one of the best professional staffs in the House; he is extremely powerful. So is Dan Rostenkowski of Illinois, who has relatively fewer staff members. Nevertheless, most observers of Congress would agree that the skill, en ergy, and tenacity of these two chairmen are more responsible for their influence than the relative size of their staffs.

The problem is not that members are dominated by their staffs. It is rather that staff size is to some degree seen as a symbol of potency. How many are there in your clan? How large is your army? If you have a big staff, you must be important.

Unlike Lowi, I do not believe that Congress is under the control of staff members who constitute a professional, mandarin elite. Members of Congress still approach problems with a healthy provision of amateur knowledge, instinct, and intuitiveness. If a staff presentation conflicts with that intuition, the member might well avoid the staff advice.

Members of Congress are still primarily individuals, not scholars, who represent their geographic areas. When Congress is composed of more members holding doctorates than master's degrees, we may have a problem. But we have not reached that stage yet. Unlike their counterparts in countries with more elitist traditions, such as Great Britain, Americans are frequently skeptical of people of great ability and wide experience or superior education. They naturally want their representative to be someone like themselves.

Constituents and Elections

It is not true that members of Congress are locked up in Washington, D.C., never breaking out of the cocoon of professional knowledge and academic discourse. Representatives go home often. I sometimes suspect that if we allowed members to use their voting cards from their district offices, they would be so happy to cast their votes from Pocatello, Idaho, or Spokane, Washington, or Ypsilanti, Michigan, or Tallahassee, Florida, that they would seldom come to Washington. We might run the risk of never getting a quorum. It is in part because we do not permit voting from the districts that representatives and senators are willing to come to the capital. This is a healthy indicator that members still do reside near their constituents, that the geographical heart of representation still beats, and that members still observe the Tuesday-through-Thursday club. As a matter of fact, legislation is usually scheduled only on Tuesday, Wednesday, and Thursday so that members can spend the long weekend in their districts. They are not likely to be at home relaxing during those long weekends; they are much more likely to be hard at work with their constituents.

Returning to the question of elections, I agree that most contested incumbency races result in the election of the incumbent. At the same time, however, members probably today feel less secure in their position than they did twenty-five years ago, even with the advantages of PAC money, franking privileges, and other perquisites of incumbency. But that is another issue.

Let me just plead as one who has been in Congress for more than twenty-five years that I am not certain that the institution would be benefited, its role enhanced, or its power magnified if we had a rolling turnover of two-year or two-term members of Congress. And I do not think the purpose of frequent elections mandated by the Constitution was necessarily to remove the incumbents. Lowi asks why we have frequent elections if not to unseat incumbents. I would argue that we have frequent elections to have the *opportunity* to unseat incumbents. I am not suggesting that the way to make Congress powerful and efficient in a competitive, modern world is arbitrarily and regularly to change its members. I think, in fact, the opposite would happen. A quick turnover of a large number of representatives would inevitably enhance a relatively permanent feature of Congress, the professional staff. The influx of many new members would increase the power of the professional staff, and the staff would become Congress's institutional memory and continuing civil service. It would interact as it does today with the executive branch, the agencies, the Library of Congress, and the various interest groups, while members of Congress would be led around the track for a couple of years before retiring home to tell their grandchildren about their term in Congress.

Although Lowi's observations contain some truth, I do not think the situation is as bad as he says. Perhaps Congress has promised solutions to the country's problems that it cannot deliver. I do not think that is because we are trapped in professional knowledge. The promises reflect popular demand; they reflect popular instinct. People want a clean environment. If we were to ask average citizens whether the United States should be competitive in international affairs or clean up the environment, they would not think we had asked a sensible question. They would say we should do both. If we stated a good, they would support it.

I do not believe Congress is in decline. The problems besetting us are to some extent transitory. Our efficiency from time to time may be questionable, but Congress was not designed to be a highly efficient organization.

Finally, with all of its problems, with the lobbying of the interest groups and organized political efforts, Congress still reflects the attitudes of Americans, even though the institution has always been held in contempt. Mark Twain said, "It could probably be shown by facts and figures that there is no distinctly native criminal class, except for Congress." Cartoonists and political critics going back to the foundation of the Republic have found Congress to be a wonderful target. Their lampoons are nothing new, but in many cases the individual members do have the confidence of their constituents and reflect their needs, desires, and collective wisdom. The task of the modern representative, as Edmund Burke said, is to rise above the wisdom of the district. Theoretically, constituents elect their representatives for their judgment as well as their opinion. It is unfortunate that in the election after Burke made this statement he was defeated, a fact that is never mentioned.

NOTES

1. Norman J. Ornstein, Thomas E. Mann, and Michael J. Malbin, *Vital Statistics on Congress, 1991–1992* (Washington, D.C.: Congressional Quarterly, 1992), table 2–7; Library of Congress, Congressional Research Service, *Reelection Rates of House Incumbents: 1970–1988*, CRS Report No. 89–173 (Washington, D.C.: Congressional Research Service, 1989), 12, 13.
2. Louis Boudianoff Boudin, *Government by Judiciary* (New York: Godwin, 1932).
3. James McGregor Byrnes, *The Deadlock of Democracy: Four-Party Politics in America* (Englewood Cliffs, N. J.: Prentice Hall, 1963). See, for example, 2–7.

2. Knowledge, Power, and the First Congress

Gordon S. Wood

In many respects Congress today is better off than the First Congress of 1789. The present members of Congress undoubtedly know more about more things than did congressmen at any time in American history. Data and information of every conceivable sort about our society, our economy, and our government pour into Congress from every direction. We have more institutes, more academic centers, more specialized studies of ourselves and the world than we can comprehend. An array of media—radio, television, books, newspapers, journals, magazines, research reports—overwhelm Congress and the rest of us with an abundance of facts and figures that multiply daily. Not only are more Americans now going to college than ever before, but, despite our gloomy talk of cultural illiteracy, more Americans are also better informed than at any time in our history.

When we look back two hundred years to the beginning of our national history and the meeting of the First Congress, we find a very different situation. Although the quality of the political leadership of the Founders overawes us—they were, we tell ourselves, "a galaxy of leaders who were quite literally incomparable"—they certainly knew much less than we do today, and they lived in a society that had far less information available to it than we do.[1]

Life in the Late Eighteenth Century

In the late eighteenth century the United States still was an underdeveloped society, relegated three thousand miles from the centers of Western civilization to the very edges of Christendom. When, in 1790, Gouverneur Morris pressed the British foreign secretary, Lord Leeds, as to why His Majesty's government had not yet sent a minister to the United States, Lord Leeds replied that the government wanted to send a good man, but it was difficult to find one: "It is a great way off, and many object on that score." [2]

By today's standards Americans were ill-informed and severely lacking in knowledge. Perhaps half the society was illiterate, and even those people who were literate read little beyond their Bible and their almanac. There was not much else for them to read in any case. There were only thirty-six printers in the country in 1789.[3] Books were a rare luxury, and a young stranger with a trunk of books was regarded with curiosity and wonder. In 1789 the New York Society Library, a private organization, gained permission to occupy an upper room in Federal Hall to help persuade the national government to stay in New York City. The library had only 250 subscribers, who had access to its three thousand volumes from 12:00 noon to 2:00 in the afternoon on Monday, Wednesday, and Friday.[4] There were fewer than a hundred newspapers in the country, and most of these were ephemeral and contained fewer than a half-dozen pages. Periodicals were even more unstable, blossoming for a moment and dying like exotic plants. At the end of 1788 there were only three American magazines, each struggling to survive. Although a half-dozen more would be created in 1789, by 1795 only five remained.[5]

A college education was not at all as common as it is today, and only about half of the members of the First Congress had gone to college. The dozen or so colleges in existence in the 1780s awarded fewer than two hundred B.A.s a year, which is why Benjamin Rush called them the "true nurseries of power and influence." [6] Columbia College's commencement was held in May 1789, with the U.S. president, vice president, and Senate in attendance (the president of the college was also senator from Connecticut). Only ten students received B. A. degrees.[7]

By our standards people and information moved at a snail's pace. Letters or newspapers carried by ships, stagecoaches, or riders on horseback were the only means of communication over any distance. Many still relied on private carriers, since the postal system was just getting established. In 1789 there were only seventy-five post offices and fewer than 2,400 miles of post roads to service four million people over half a continent. Few areas of the western United States and none of the new territories—Vermont, Kentucky, or Tennessee—had any postal service. Albany, for example, was the only interior town in the state of New York served by the post office. The mail moved slowly: a letter sent from Virginia by Governor Randolph on December 27, 1787, to New York did not arrive until March 7, 1788. Few people sent letters: many people could not write, and the post was expensive. The cost of delivering a single letter a few hundred miles could equal a good part of an ordinary person's daily wages (which is why the congressional franking privilege was so highly valued).[8]

People moved no faster than did information, for travel was not easy. It took weeks for some members of the First Congress to travel from their home states to the national capital at New York City. Even a stagecoach from Boston traveling eighteen hours a day took six days to get to New York. Philadelphia was three days away.[9] Consequently, the First Congress had difficulty getting itself together. Fifty-nine representatives and twenty-two senators were supposed to convene on March 4, 1789, in New York. But on that date only a handful had arrived. During the next few weeks the members dribbled in, several each day. Not until April 1 did the House of Representatives have the quorum it needed to organize for business; the Senate got its quorum a week later on April 6.

In that distant, different world of the Founders, politics was still a small and intimate business, and political leaders relied mainly on private conversations and personal correspondence among "particular gentlemen" for their social connections and information.[10] Knowledge of Congress's activities was not widely available. Members communicated with their constituents back home by sending letters to prominent friends who would show them to a few other influential persons.[11] The practice of circular letters to constituents summarizing congressional business had not yet become common. There was no *Congressional Record* yet. Senate debates were closed to the public until 1795, and although the debates of the House of Representatives were open from the beginning (an innovation in the Western world), they were recorded at the discretion of newspaper reporters, who took down only what they thought might be interesting to readers. It was not until 1834 that all these early reports and fragments of congressional debates were compiled and published as the *Annals of Congress*.[12]

Knowledge Then and Now: Congress and Society

These differences between life in the late eighteenth century and today are important, for they give us historical perspective on our own situation.

But if pushed too far, comparisons and contrasts become anachronistic and not very helpful; they work only to accentuate our sense of diminution in relation to the Founders. The question we implicitly seem to ask is, if they had so much less knowledge and information than we do and yet accomplished so much, what is wrong with us?

That is not the question we ought to be asking. Nor should we be simply comparing the knowledge available to us with the knowledge available to Americans of the late eighteenth century. Although by today's standards the United States of 1789 was ill-informed, by eighteenth-century standards it was not. In fact, some Americans quite justly thought that the United States was the "most enlightened" nation in the world. Literacy rates, at least in the North, were higher than almost any other place in the world, and Americans were well on their way to becoming by 1810 the greatest newspaper-reading public in the world.[13]

Rather than contrasting knowledge then and now, we might better make comparisons between knowledge available to members of the First Congress and that available to late-eighteenth-century society as a whole. In these terms the difference between the situation today and that of two hundred years ago does not seem all that remarkable. Indeed, many of the problems growing out of distinctions that we draw between "professional" and "amateur" knowledge and between "policy research" and "ordinary knowledge" were present at the time of the First Congress. What kind of representatives should the members of Congress be? How much should they rely on the executive branch for information? How much should they know of the world beyond their districts? And what kind of knowledge—professional or amateur, expert or ordinary—should members of Congress use to fulfill their responsibilities? These were questions just as important two hundred years ago as they are today.

The First Congress, as the initial governing body, faced a unique challenge, and those representatives and senators who gathered in New York two centuries ago were awed by what lay ahead of them. Not only would the members of Congress have to pass some promised amendments to the new Constitution, but they would have to fill out the bare framework of a government that the Philadelphia Convention had created, including the organization of the executive and judicial departments. Some therefore considered the First Congress a second constitutional convention. Congress was the first of the institutions created by the Constitution to be organized; indeed, during its first session, in 1789, it was virtually the entire national government. The subordinate executive offices were not filled until late in the summer, and the judiciary was not established until just before adjournment in the early fall of 1789. The challenges and responsibilities were daunting, and many members of the First Congress felt overwhelmed by them.

Difficulties of Acquiring Information

At the time of the American Revolution, observed Fisher Ames of Massachusetts, the first of America's national bodies—the Continental Congress—had needed "heroic qualities" above all. But the objects of this Congress of 1789, he said, required less heroism and "more information." [14] Information, however, was not easily obtained. Members of the First Congress had no staffs and no think tanks to help them, nor were there any academic studies nor a Library of Congress nor a Congressional Research Service to draw on. Not surprisingly, members of both houses of Congress complained of a "want of information" in their efforts to launch the new government. James Madison, the dominant figure in the first House of Representatives, urged his fellow congressmen at the outset "to exert themselves in giving and procuring information" on the matter of tariffs so that revenue gathering for the new government could begin "as speedily as possible." [15]

William Maclay, the fifty-year-old senator from rural Pennsylvania, had fifteen years of legislative experience and, although he had not gone to college, was reasonably well educated. But as a gentleman-farmer he was scarcely prepared to deal with commercial issues. Looking back, we can readily sympathize with his painful efforts to acquire some smattering of commercial knowledge quickly to help him legislate intelligently on matters of tariffs and trade. There were few statistics available and no studies of American trade, and Maclay groped for assistance. He hoped that some useful information might be found in the New York newspapers but concluded that "the bulk of the Papers consist of advertisements." [16]

Maclay knew that most members relied on private conversations for up-to-date knowledge about the world, including matters of commerce. But coming from the back country, he did not know any merchants well. He realized that some of his Pennsylvania colleagues, including his fellow senator, the one-time merchant Robert Morris, and representatives Thomas Fitzsimons and George Clymer, were receiving "private communications" concerning trade matters from knowledgeable citizens in

Philadelphia, although he was not. He consoled himself by saying "I am much less known." Then, however, he was dismayed to discover that others, including even Sen. Charles Carroll of Maryland, had received help and documents from Fitzsimons, and he had not, even though he had "taken as much pains to collect information as any of them." He badgered people for information and asked Morris more than once for assistance— for the article on salt in a customhouse paper he knew Morris had and for a copy of the current London prices of imported goods with the duties marked for comparative purposes that Morris had long promised him.[17]

Maclay finally spoke in the Senate on the tariff issue, but only after he had studied an abstract of the imports into Philadelphia given to him by the collector of the port. To show his audience that he "spoke not at random or without book," he displayed the abstract in the handwriting of the collector. Once he gained confidence on these trade matters, the talkative Maclay was often on his feet in the debates, on one occasion even enlightening his senatorial colleagues with "a Short History of the British Navigation Act." [18]

Everywhere in the First Congress there was a scramble for information, for authorities to cite, for knowledge to display. Everything seemed new, unfamiliar, unprecedented, and the members struggled to agree on what to do, on what examples to follow, not only in matters of tariff and trade policies but also in what seems to us to be elementary matters of rules and ritual. How to receive the president in the Senate chamber? How to communicate between the two houses? How to address the president and each other? Should the Senate have a sergeant-at-arms and, if so, what should he be called? They ransacked ancient and modern history for examples and precedents, wondering whether "the framers of the Constitution had in View the Two Kings of Sparta or the Two Consuls of Rome," when they created a president and vice president, or whether a fourteenth-century Italian reformer obsessed with titles was not an object lesson for them.[19]

Often they turned to English history and the English Parliament for precedents. In discussing the manner in which Congress ought to hear the president's address, for example, Sen. Richard Henry Lee of Virginia recalled from his stay in England as a young man that the king addressed Parliament with the Lords seated and the Commons standing. But then Sen. Ralph Izard of South Carolina reminded his colleagues how often he too had visited the English Parliament and told them that "the Commons stood because they had no seats to sit on." Vice President John Adams compounded the confusion by saying that every time he had visited the Parliament on such occasions "there was always such a Crowd, and ladies along, that for his part he could not say how it was." [20] Many believed, not wrongly, that these precedents smacked of monarchy and quickly came to resent having "the measures of the Parliament of Great Britain hung about our necks in all our public proceedings, and observations from their practice perpetually sounding in our ears." [21] They wanted Congress's precedents drawn from the practices of the American state legislatures, and of course they were often the source.

There were virtually no lobbyists to help the members of the First Congress in their search for information; even their constituents back home were often too far away to give guidance. In the spring of 1789 Congress postponed consideration of the duty on molasses to give the Massachusetts representatives time to obtain more knowledge from their constituents "so they might meet the discussion with greater ability." But, as Rep. Benjamin Goodhue confessed, the Massachusetts members were unsuccessful in receiving any communications from their home state, and therefore they had to "proceed to consider and judge the question by those lights which [their] own minds afford." [22]

The Value of Congressional Debates

Consequently, a premium was put on debates in Congress as a source of information and shared wisdom. The House of Representatives encouraged open and free deliberations by its common practice of going into the Committee of the Whole, where the restrictions on discussion were looser and the rules governing debate more informal than in the full House.[23] The House thereby became, as Fisher Ames complained, "a kind of Robin Hood society, where everything is debated." [24] Many northern congressmen thought the House was following the pattern of the Virginia House of Delegates in conducting much of its business as a Committee of the Whole, and thus they blamed the Virginians for the endless talk and the slowness of business.[25] "Our great committee is too unwieldy," complained Ames. Fifty members or more trying to amend or clean up the language of a bill was "a great, clumsy machine ... applied to the slightest and most delicate operations—the hoof of an elephant to the strokes of mezzotinto." [26]

The debates, however, were not only lengthy but sometimes remarkably

thoughtful. Of course members of Congress had much more time to pre-
pare their speeches then than they do today. Because there were few select
committee meetings and other distractions, nearly all members attended
the daily five-hour sessions punctually, at least at first, and many were often
more attentive to what their colleagues had to say on the floor of the
House than they are today.[27] Ames "listened," as he said, "with the most
unwearied attention to the arguments urged on both sides" so that "his
own mind might be fully enlightened." [28]

Ames himself was an elegant and compelling speaker. Almost overnight
his oratory established his reputation as one of the most able members
of the House; indeed, he became what we would call a celebrity. People
congratulated themselves on having visited the gallery of the House to
hear Ames speak. He was self-conscious about his speaking and frequently
wrote his friend George Minot about the techniques and mistakes of his
performances in the House along with commentary on those of others.
He thought Madison, for example, an impressive reasoner but concluded
that speaking was "not his forte." [29]

Rhetoric, still a central subject of a liberal education, was highly prized,
and members were anxious about how they appeared, how they sounded
in public, and they fretted over the accuracy of transcriptions of their
speeches in the press. They were eager to bolster their arguments with the
ideas of celebrated thinkers, sometimes for substance, as in the case of
Madison's using Adam Smith in the debate over commercial regulation,
and other times for appearance, as in the case of Senator Izard of South
Carolina, who, in a debate over secret balloting in the Senate, as Maclay
caustically reported, "quoted Harrington to show his reading." [30]

Then, as now, some members of Congress knew more than others, and
expertise was highly valued. There is no doubt that Madison's extraordinary dominance over the proceedings of the First Congress came not
merely from his reputation but from his broad knowledge and careful
preparation for what had to be done. He prepared for the opening debate
on revenue in the House of Representatives by comparing the state laws
on the subject and by collecting whatever statistical information he could
on the commerce of the various states.[31] His colleagues reported that he
was "a thorough master of almost every public question that can arise, or
he will spare no pains to become so, if he happens to be in want of
information." Although Madison was not a strong speaker, he made 150
speeches in the first session of the First Congress alone. Others likewise
gained reputations for knowledge. Because Congressman Thomas Fitzsi-

mons of Philadelphia was "supposed to understand trade," it was natural that he assume "some weight in such matters." [32] Ames quickly saw what expertise could do and thus "resolved to apply closely to the necessary means of knowledge, as I know it is the only means of acquiring reputation." [33]

One of the reasons the House of Representatives in the early Congresses dispensed with standing committees was because it soon came to rely on the heads of the executive departments to draft most of its bills. At the end of July 1789 the House of Representatives set up a Committee of Ways and Means to advise it on financial matters, but on September 2 the Treasury Department was created. On September 11 Alexander Hamilton was appointed secretary of the treasury, and six days later the House discharged its Committee of Ways and Means, stating that it would rely on Hamilton for its financial knowledge. Not until 1795, after Hamilton's resignation, did the House reestablish its Ways and Means Committee.

Executive-Legislature Tension

The current problems of executive-legislative relations and the disparity of information and knowledge between the executive and Congress were present at the outset. Indeed, some congressmen wanted the United States to develop a British style parliamentary government with more ministerial direction over Congress than the Constitution presumably provided. But many others were horrified at that prospect. If we establish "the doctrine of having prime and great ministers of State," warned Elbridge Gerry of Massachusetts, we would "soon see them distinguished by a green or red ribbon, or other insignia of Court favor and patronage." He and other representatives objected to the deference shown by Congress to experts such as Hamilton in the executive branch; their objections continued well into the Second Congress and beyond. It was one thing for the executive departments to give information to the legislature, declared Abraham Baldwin of Georgia in 1792, but it was quite another for the executive departments to draft laws for the legislature. The "information" the executive gave to Congress "should relate merely . . . to statements of fact and details of business, but the laws should be framed by the Legislature, after they have acquired this information." The role of Congress, said Baldwin, was more than revising and rejecting what the executive proposed. If separation of powers were to be properly maintained, "it is dangerous to intrust those who have a prospect of deriving some advantage in the execution of a law, to have any hand in framing it." Baldwin felt so keenly on this point of separation that he was opposed "even to the introduction of the two Secretaries [of the treasury and war departments], the other day, to answer interrogatories in the House," fearing that "such a precedent . . . might prove a dangerous one, and lean to an interference in more important points." Rep. John Mercer of Maryland likewise objected to opinions coming to Congress from the executive. "If they are to influence me, they are wrong; if not to influence, they are useless." Some had suggested that the treasury secretary's reports resembled Adam Smith's *Wealth of Nations* and that congressmen could learn from them. Mercer was contemptuous of this view: "We do not come here to go to school, or to hear lectures from the Secretaries on finance or any other subject." [34]

Others argued, as James Madison did, at least at the outset, that the public good often dictated congressional dependence on the executive for knowledge and information. Although he would change his tune in the next Congress, in 1789, during the First Congress, Madison thought that "well-digested plans of a well informed officer" were far less dangerous than the "inconsistent" and "unproductive" schemes that had burdened the state legislatures in the 1780s because of their "want of information." Even after Madison shifted his position and began to resist Hamilton's influence in the House, others continued to argue that Congress necessarily had to pay attention to the superior wisdom of executive officials. To pay off the public debt, said Fisher Ames, everyone agreed that a plan was essential and that "it must be framed with wisdom and digested with care." The only question is what branch could do it better. "Neither this House nor a select committee," Ames declared, "are pretended to be already possessed of the knowledge which is requisite to the framing [of] a system for a Sinking Fund. The very materials from which this knowledge is to be gleaned are not in the possession of this House—they are in the Treasury Department." Common sense, said Ames, therefore determined that "knowledge of our financial affairs, and of the means of improving them" was "most accurately" obtained from the officer in the executive branch "who is appointed and commissioned" for the very purpose of understanding such financial affairs "and to whom every day's practice in his office must afford some additional information of official details, as well as of the operation of the laws." [35]

But others asked how one man in the executive could possess more information than the collective members of the House drawn from every district of the country. In the process they opened up the question of what popular representation and popular knowledge in Congress really meant. It may be that Congress lacked expertise and particular information in some matters, said William Findley of Pennsylvania, but that was no reason to allow others to usurp its responsibilities. He had no doubt that Secretary of the Treasury Hamilton was "very capable," but the minister's "eminent abilities, or his want of them" were irrelevant. Congressmen may feel themselves unfit for the business of the debt, but nevertheless the House had to fix its own principles on fiscal matters and explore and make its own financial plans. "And capacity and information will grow out of the investigation." Different members would propose different approaches and "by comparison and discussion, they will become the better acquainted with the subject." The general interests of the community, said Findley, were not matters known only by a few department heads and experts who had gone to college and had read Adam Smith. "Knowledge" of the general interest "must grow out of a representation of all the local interests," and "this can only be found among the members of this House. . . . Certainly this House contains in itself more extensive knowledge of the people's wants and pressures, of their situation and prepossessions, and of their resources, than the most enlightened Minister can possibly do." [36]

At the very beginning Elias Boudinot of New Jersey directly confronted this conception of representation and categorically denied that congressmen "coming from different parts of the Union are the most proper persons to give information." In fact, he said, there were "no persons in the Government to whom we could look with less propriety for information on this subject [of finance] than to the members of this House." They all came from different occupations and from different parts of the country filled with local prejudices and "without the least preparation to bring forward a subject that requires a great degree of assiduous application to understand." [37]

Few were willing to be as bold or as explicit as Boudinot, for his argument seemed to suggest, as one congressman put it, "that one person could be a better judge of the means to improve and manage the revenue, and support the national credit, than the whole body of Congress." It stuck "at the root of all legislation founded upon the great Democratic principle of representation." [38] But with men in the cabinet such as Hamilton, who had far more knowledge of commerce, banking, and other technical matters than did the members of Congress, many believed it only sensible to rely on the executive departments not merely for information but for drafting bills. When Princeton graduate and newly elected senator from New York Aaron Burr early in 1791 vaguely recalled that philosopher David Hume had some "ingenious thoughts" about banking, but that he had "not leisure to turn to them" or even to read "with proper attention" Hamilton's proposal for a national bank, then we can more easily understand why many congressmen readily deferred to Hamilton's expertise.[39] Ames complained of "the yawning listlessness" of many of his colleagues "in regard to the great objects of the government." But he concluded that it was perhaps better for Congress that only a few members understand what was going on as long as that few had the confidence of the rest; if all in Congress were "such knowing ones," they would continually "contend for supremacy," and there would be no cohesion or stability at all.[40]

These debates over the nature of representation and the kind of knowledge the representatives were supposed to bring to their legislative tasks were not new. In fact, such debates had been at the heart of the controversy over the formation of the Constitution in 1787–1788. Most of the Federalists, as the creators and supporters of the Constitution were called, had voiced an understanding of the representative's role that was much more similar to that expressed by Elias Boudinot than to that of William Findley, who had originally opposed the Constitution. The Federalists of 1787 had hoped that members of Congress would be not only gentlemen— still a meaningful distinction in that eighteenth-century world—but, more important, the most liberally educated and enlightened gentlemen in the society, those free from the parochial concerns and narrow local interests of the ordinary people they represented.

It is not too much to say that the Federalists or the Founders were anxious to avoid in the new national Congress what we today take for granted as democratic politics. They were not modern men; they did not believe in pluralism, interest group politics, logrolling, or pork barreling, and some of them did not even care if they were paid salaries or not. Many of them believed that public service was a sacrifice required of certain gentlemen because of their talents, independent wealth, and social rank; they saw office holding as a burden, undertaken, said Jefferson, in accord with Roman principles. It "contributes neither to advantage nor happiness. It is but honorable exile from one's family and affairs."[41]

Today we smile knowingly when we hear politicians talking about the burdens of office and their dedication to public service, but for many of the Founders these classical ideals still had great power. People in the eighteenth century did not yet clearly conceive of politics as a profession or as an occupation. Men were to be called to office; they were not to seek it. The Founders did not like electioneering or political parties, and they regarded running for office or campaigning in one's own behalf as dishonorable. They therefore conceived of Congress as a very different body from what it soon became.

Congressmen were not to represent the particular interests of their local constituencies as much as to stand above them and make wise and impartial judgments. In the Massachusetts ratifying convention Theodore Sedgwick defended the two-year term for congressmen, arguing that it would take at least a year for a man to "divest himself of local concerns" and gain a "general knowledge of such extensive and weighty matters" as the new Congress would address.[42] This general knowledge was perhaps not the scientific information based on analytical research that representatives to-day seek to acquire, but it was certainly something other than the ordinary amateur knowledge that a member picked up from his neighbors and constituents. Ideally, members were to transcend the local interests and knowledge of their districts or even of their states. When Congressman Boudinot expressed displeasure in the first session at hearing "any thing that sounds like attachment to particular States" and declared that he was "as much the representative of Massachusetts as of New Jersey, and nothing shall prevail on me to injure the interest of the one more than the other," he was voicing the highest aspirations of many of the Federalists.[43]

The Founders hoped that the new Congress, because of its distance from local interests and its small size (smaller in fact than nearly all of the state assemblies), would filter talent in such a way as to avoid the factionalism and the localist and special-interest legislation of the state assemblies, which had caused so much trouble during the 1780s. Many Federalists considered the state legislatures to be too large and their electoral districts too small and therefore thought them to be composed of the wrong kinds of men—men such as ex-weaver William Findley who was narrow-minded, uneducated, and parochial. The more numerous the body, wrote Madison in the *Federalist* no. 58, "the greater is known to be the ascendancy of passion over reason" and "the greater will be the proportion of members of limited information and of weak capacities." By reducing the number of representatives and enlarging the electoral districts in the new national Congress, the Founders hoped to make it more difficult for ordinary obscure men with parochial interests and illiberal outlooks to get elected. If the people of North Carolina, for example, could elect only five men to the federal Congress in contrast to the 232 they elected to their state assembly, they were more likely in the case of the few national representatives to ignore ordinary men with "factious tempers" and "local prejudices" and "limited information" and "weak capacities" and elect those men with "the most attractive merit and the most diffusive and established characters." (*Federalist* no. 10, no. 58.)

When Madison in the *Federalist* no. 10 spoke of getting men into the national government "whose enlightened views and virtuous sentiments render them superior to local prejudices," he meant men like himself, gentlemen who had been to college and had a liberal education and who were capable of being "disinterested and dispassionate" umpires among the society's many selfish interests and partisan passions.[44] When, in his first inaugural address, President Washington paid tribute to the qualifications of the members of Congress, beholding in them "the surest pledges" that "no local prejudices or attachments, no separate views, nor party animosities, will misdirect the comprehensive and equal eye which ought to watch over this great assemblage of communities and interests," he expressed the deepest hopes of the Founders.[45]

These were classical republican hopes and dreams that could not be fulfilled. They ran too much against the democratic realities of American politics, as some members of the First Congress soon came to understand. "I came here expecting every man to act the part of a God," Maclay confided to his diary at the end of August 1789: "That the most delicate Honor the most exalted Wisdom, the refined Generosity was to govern every Act and be seen in every deed." Instead, he found only too often "rough and rude manners Glaring folly, and the barest selfishness, apparent in almost every public Transaction." The expectations of the Founders that the members of the new Congress would be impartial and disinterested gentry, standing above state and local interests, were not being realized. Those who "expected a Roman senate" said Fisher Ames, when he saw the new Congress, "will be disappointed." And the opponents of the Constitution in 1787–1788, "the *antis*," he added, "will laugh at their own fears. They will see that the aristocracy may be kept down some years longer." [46]

The Anti-Federalist View of Leadership

In the 1787–1788 debate over ratification, the Anti-Federalists, as the opponents of the Constitution were called, had expressed fears, not without justification, that the new federal government would become an aristocracy. They rejected the need for any liberally educated elite to act as umpires among the contending interests of the society and challenged the classical conception of disinterested leadership that underlay the Federalist plan for the new government. They did not believe that a virtuous, gentlemanly elite, such as the Federalists talked about, existed. To be sure, there were gentlemen who had gone to Princeton or Harvard and who therefore, said William Findley, thought they were "born of a different race from the rest of the sons of men [and] able to conceive and perform great things." But congressmen, the Anti-Federalists declared, did not have to divest themselves of their local interests and acquire some special cosmopolitan knowledge in order to legislate on weighty and extensive matters. This was "a novel idea," said William Heath in the Massachusetts ratifying convention in answer to Theodore Sedgwick. Congressmen, Heath said, did not have to go away to some far-removed District of Columbia and read research reports to learn their duty. Their duty, their representativeness, ought to be instinctive, based on ordinary knowledge acquired by living among their neighbors. "The representative is one who appears in behalf of, and acts for, others; he ought, therefore, to be fully acquainted with the feelings, circumstances, and interests of the persons whom he represents; and this is learnt among them, not at some distant court." The Anti-Federalist position was that educated patricians, such as the Federalists wanted in Congress, could never feel "sympathetically the wants of the people." Such cosmopolitan gentry were not as disinterested as they claimed but were as self-serving as anyone else in the society. No one, the opponents of the Constitution argued, however elevated or however liberally educated, was free of the lures and interests of the marketplace.[47]

There is no exaggerating the historic importance of this challenge by the Anti-Federalists: they took on an enlightened tradition of public leadership that went back to Aristotle and Cicero, laying bare the democratic realities of American society and politics with a boldness and originality that we today can scarcely appreciate. They offered Americans an understanding of themselves that was far more accurate, hardheaded, and modern than anything the Federalists put forward. The majority of the Anti-

Federalists went beyond Madison's *Federalist* no. 10 to argue that American society was so fragmented and diverse—composed of so "many different classes or orders of people. Merchants, Farmers, Planters, Mechanics, and Gentry or wealthy Men," all equal to one another—that the Federalists' classical conception of political leadership by an educated and enlightened elite had lost all relevance. In such a pluralistic, egalitarian society, they said, men from one class or interest could never be acquainted with the "Situation and Wants" of those from another class or interest. "Lawyers and planters," whatever their genteel pretensions, could never be "adequate judges of tradesmen's concerns." The interests of the society were so varied and discrete that only individuals sharing a particular interest could speak for that interest.[48]

The Federalists were foolish to tell people that they should overlook their local interests. Local interests, the Anti-Federalists said in a remarkable anticipation of former House Speaker Tip O'Neill's maxim about American politics, were all there really were. "No man when he enters into society, does it from a view to promote the good of others, but he does it for his own good." Since all individuals and groups in the society were equally self-interested, the only "fair representation" in government, concluded the "Federal Farmer," the most highly regarded of the Anti-Federalist polemicists, ought to be one where "every order of men in the community . . . can have a share in it." Consequently any American government ought "to allow professional men, merchants, traders, farmers, mechanics, etc. to bring a just proportion of their best informed men respectively into the legislature." Only an explicit form of representation that allowed Germans, Baptists, artisans, farmers, and so on, each to send delegates of its own kind into the political arena could embody the democratic particularism of the emerging society of the early Republic. The Anti-Federalists offered the first comprehensible defense of pluralism and interest group politics in American history.[49]

The Anti-Federalists lost the battle over the Constitution, but they did not lose the war over the kind of national government the United States would have for a good part of the next century. Their understanding of American society and politics in the early Republic was too accurate and too powerful to be put down, as the Federalists themselves soon came to appreciate. Even the elections for the First Congress in 1788 revealed the practical realities of American democratic life that contradicted the Federalists' classical republican dreams of establishing a government led by disinterested, educated gentlemen.

The Democratization of Representation

Thomas Hartley of Pennsylvania, a stout Federalist, realized that the new congressmen from his state should be "men of knowledge and information, well attached to the new plan and should have characters unexceptionable as to their integrity." If we had such men, he told a Federalist friend, it would not matter "to what profession or interest they belong." Unfortunately, however, outside Philadelphia "there are but few men who have abilities and leisure and are fit objects for choice." There were simply not enough educated and disinterested gentlemen spread about the state, which is why Federalists in Pennsylvania, like those in several other states, urged that members of Congress be elected at large instead of by districts: "you have a better chance of obtaining good men than obliging the electors to vote for separate Representatives in districts." [50]

Still, even many Pennsylvanian Federalists who wanted at-large elections were not willing to go so far as Hartley in ignoring what interest or profession the representatives belonged to. The senators and congressmen, it seemed, were to be spokesmen for their constituents rather than umpires after all. By 1788 it was clear even to the Federalists that one of the state's two senators had to be from the country and represent agricultural interests and that the other had to be from Philadelphia and represent trading interests.[51] One Federalist leaned so far toward pluralism as to urge that at least four of the state's eight congressmen must be attached "to the farming or landed interest"; two more ought to "understand foreign and domestic trade," and two ought to be "learned and judicious law characters." Northumberland County Federalists would also have preferred cosmopolitan and disinterested college-educated gentlemen as representatives, but, realizing that such men "cannot easily be found," the county instructed its delegates to the Federalist meeting at Lancaster "that different men adapted to the different interests" of the state be chosen: four involved in agriculture, two in commerce, "one person remarkably attached to the principles of manufactures, and an eminent law character." Almost as an afterthought, the county meeting, which was chaired by William Maclay, already elected as one of the two senators from the state, brought up the problem of German representation. "Although as Pennsylvanians we declare ourselves actuated by one common interest, and abhor every idea of national distinction," the county could not ignore the fact that one-third of the population spoke German; thus it urged that "a part of the representation should be qualified to do business in that language." [52]

This proposal touched off a furor in Pennsylvania politics. The Federalist meeting at Lancaster on November 3, 1788, to draw up a Federalist ticket of congressmen and presidential electors felt some of the pressure for German representation; consequently, it placed two Germans on the ticket, one for Congress and another for the electors. But others thought that this was not enough. A broadside published on November 13 (perhaps written by Benjamin Rush) addressed "To the German Inhabitants of the State of Pennsylvania" blasted the ticket for its inadequate representation of Germans. The state, the writer declared, had elected or will elect two senators, eight congressmen, and ten presidential electors—in all twenty persons. According to the proportion of Germans in the population, there should have been six or eight Germans among the twenty candidates. But instead, "for political reasons . . . very condescendingly," the Federalist ticket placed only two Germans on the ticket, one for Congress and one for the electors: "Two whole Germans, therefore, among eighteen Englishmen. . . . Is this not degrading the character of the Germans to the lowest degree? And who of our countrymen, that deserves the name of a German can bear such treatment with cold blood?" Germans needed to have in government men of their own kind who spoke their own language; they could not count on the English to know and to look after their interests.[53]

This broadside turned German representation into a major issue in the Pennsylvania elections for the First Congress. Some alarmed Federalists tried to cool passions, conceding that the Germans were "most useful members of society" whose opinions "ought to be attended to," but not to the extent of endangering support for the new federal government. Once aroused, however, the Germans' dissatisfaction "at having so small a representation in the Federal ticket" could not be appeased. Some tried. Why should the Germans be singled out for attention? "If any national distinctions can possibly be made in the future laws of the empire, why are not these anxious writers equally concerned for the Scotch and the Irish? Why are they not desirous that they also should have their due proportion of federal representation?" Such "invidious distinctions" among the citizenry were ridiculous. But it soon became clear that these distinctions of ethnicity, as well as those of occupation and religion, were here to stay. The Germans, voting as a bloc, went on to elect three German congressmen from Pennsylvania—every German candidate they could find on the Federalist and Anti-Federalist tickets.[54]

The situation in Pennsylvania was exaggerated because of the particular heterogeneity of the state. But it was only an exaggeration of what was present elsewhere in America, particularly in the North.[55] America's democratic future of local politics, special interests, ethnic voting, and popular electioneering was already visible in 1788–1789. Nearly everywhere the Founders and other Americans groped to understand what was happening, and many of them sought to resist the spread of democracy. But the movement was relentless, and within a few years it transformed the political landscape of the country, changing the way people thought about political leadership, representation, localism, electioneering, political parties, and the nature of Congress.

By the first decade of the nineteenth century it seemed to many gentlemen, like Benjamin Latrobe, the noted architect and engineer, that the Anti-Federalists had not really lost the struggle over the Constitution after all. To be sure, the new federal government was now well established, but it was not dominated by the kind of enlightened and educated gentry that the Founders had expected. "After the adoption of the federal constitution," Latrobe explained to the Italian patriot Philip Mazzei in 1806, "the extension of the right of Suffrage in all the states to the majority of all the adult male citizens, planted a germ which has gradually evolved, and has spread actual and practical democracy and political equality over the whole union. There is no doubt whatsoever but that this state of things in our country produces the greatest sum of happiness that perhaps any nation ever enjoyed." But the cost has been high, said Latrobe, in a remarkable anticipation of what Tocqueville would observe three decades later.

The want of learning and of science in the majority is one of those things which strikes foreigners who visit us very forcibly. Our representatives to all our Legislative bodies, National, as well of the States, are elected by the majority *sui similes*, that is, unlearned. For instance from Philadelphia and its environs we send to Congress not one man of letters. One of them indeed is a lawyer but of no eminence, another a good Mathematician, but when elected he was a Clerk in a bank. The others are plain farmers. From the county is sent a Blacksmith, and from just over the river a Butcher. Our state legislature does not contain one individual of superior talents. The fact is, that superior talents actually excite distrust, and the experience of the world perhaps does not encourage the people to trust men of genius. . . . This government of what may be called, an unlettered majority, has put down even that ideal rank which manners had established, excepting in our great cities depending on commerce and crowded with foreigners, where the distinction between what is called the Gentlemen, and others still subsists.[56]

Governing this popular egalitarian society would not be easy. If the age-old distinction between gentlemen and ordinary people was now blurred, if political leaders were no longer to be men of special talents with special knowledge and expertise, and if no one in the society was really disinterested, who would assume the roles of neutral umpires? Who was to judge among the different clashing interests, occupations, religions, and ethnic groups in the society and promote the good of the whole? All the Anti-Federalists and their Republican successors had as an answer was the view, attributed to Jefferson by Latrobe, "that the public good is best promoted by the exertion of each individual seeking his own good in his own way." [57] Allowing ordinary persons to define and pursue their own happiness in this individualist manner was no doubt democracy—indeed, a democracy more popular and prosperous than any in history—but it was not quite the society or government that the Founders had envisaged.

NOTES

1. Henry Steele Commager, "Leadership in Eighteenth-Century America and Today," *Daedalus* 90 (1961): 652.

2. Gouverneur Morris to George Washington, April 7, 1790, in *Senate Executive Journal and Related Documents*, vol. 2, Documentary History of the First Federal Congress of the United States of America, ed. Linda Grant DePauw et al. (Baltimore: Johns Hopkins University Press, 1988), 454.

3. Peter Parker, "The Philadelphia Printer: A Study of an Eighteenth-Century Businessman," *Business History Review* 40 (1966): 38.

4. Thomas E. V. Smith, *The City of New York in the Year of Washington's Inauguration, 1789* (Trow's Printing Co.: New York, 1889; repr., Riverside, Conn.: Chatham Press, 1972), 206.

5. Frank Luther Mott, *A History of American Magazines, 1741–1850* (New York: Appleton, 1930), 28–38.

6. Quoted in Lawrence A. Cremin, *American Education: The National Experience, 1783–1876* (New York: Harper and Row, 1980), 119.

7. Smith, *City of New York*, 194.

8. Wesley Everett Rich, *The History of the United States Post Office to the Year 1829* (Cambridge: Harvard University Press, 1924), 69, 182; Merrill Jensen et al., eds., *The Documentary History of the First Federal Elections, 1788–1790* (Madison: University of Wisconsin Press, 1976), I:14.

9. Smith, *City of New York*, 102, 194.

10. Gordon S. Wood, "The Democratization of Mind in the American Revolution," in *Leadership in the American Revolution: Library of Congress Symposia on the American Revolution* (Washington, D.C.: Library of Congress, 1974), 78.

11. Winifred E. A. Bernhard, *Fisher Ames: Federalist and Statesman, 1758–1808* (Chapel Hill: University of North Carolina Press, 1965), 75, 104.

12. Joseph Gales, comp., *Annals of the Congress of the United States* (Washington, D.C.: Gales and Seaton, 1834).

13. Charles E. Hyneman and George W. Carey, eds., *A Second Federalist: Congress Creates a Government* (Columbia: University of South Carolina Press, 1967), 24.

14. Fisher Ames to George Richards Minot, May 27, 1789, in *Works of Fisher Ames as Published by Seth Ames*, ed. W. B. Allen (Indianapolis: Liberty Press, 1983), I:633.

15. *Annals of Congress*, I:117, 120, 124.

16. Kenneth R. Bowling and Helen E. Veit, eds., *The Diary of William Maclay and Other Notes on Senate Debates*, vol. 9, Documentary History of the First Federal Congress of the United States of America (Baltimore: Johns Hopkins University Press, 1988), 65. (Hereafter cited as Maclay, *Diary.)*

17. Ibid., 56, 59–60.

18. Ibid., 67–68, 77.

19. Ibid., 5–6, 27, 28, 37.

20. Ibid., 11.

21. *Annals of Congress*, I:363.

22. Ibid., 209.

23. Ralph V. Harlow, *The History of Legislative Methods in the Period Before 1825* (New Haven: Yale University Press, 1917), 127.

24. Ames to Thomas Dwight, June 11, 1789, in Allen, ed., *Works of Ames*, I:642.

25. Actually, Madison said, it was not the Committee of the Whole that accounted for the delays; it was the newness of everything. There were "difficulties arising from novelty." "Scarcely a day passes," he told a friend, "without some striking evidence of the delays and perplexities springing merely from the want of precedents." But "time will be a full remedy for this evil," and Congress and the country would be better for going slowly. (Madison to Edmund Randolph, May 31, 1789, in *The Papers of James Madison*, ed. Charles F. Hobson [Charlottesville: University Press of Virginia, 1979], XII:190.)

26. Ames to Minot, July 8, 1789, in Allen, ed., *Works of Ames*, I:683.

27. During a single two-year Congress today, the House may hold as many as 4,500 committee meetings.

28. *Annals of Congress*, I:352.

29. Ames to Minot, May 29, 1789, in Allen, ed., *Works of Ames*, I:638.

30. Maclay, *Diary*, 82.

31. Hobson, ed., *Madison Papers*, XII:54.

32. Ames to Minot, May 29, 1789; May 18, 1789, in Allen, ed., *Works of Ames*, I:637–639, 627.

33. Ames to Minot, May 18, 1789, in ibid., 627.

34. *Annals of Congress*, I:601; III:703–705, 706–707.

35. Ibid., I:604–605; III:715–716.

36. Ibid., III:447–452.

37. Ibid., I:599–600.

38. Ibid., I:600.

39. Burr to Theodore Sedgwick, February 3, 1791, in *Political Correspondence and Public Papers of Aaron Burr*, ed. Mary-Jo Kline et al. (Princeton: Princeton University Press, 1983), I:68.

40. Ames to Minot, May 27, 1789, in Allen, ed., *Works of Ames,* I:633.

41. Jefferson to Francis Willis, Jr., April 18, 1790, in *The Papers of Thomas Jefferson,* ed. Julian P. Boyd (Princeton: Princeton University Press, 1950), XVI:353.

42. Jonathan Elliot, ed., *The Debates in the Several State Conventions on the Adoption of the Federal Constitution* (Philadelphia: Lippincott, 1896), II:4.

43. *Annals of Congress,* I:216. John Brown Cutting told Jefferson that New York's election to the U.S. Senate of Rufus King, who had just moved to the state from Massachusetts, was "the most signal instance of disregard to local attachments and prejudices that I have known any state in the Union manifest." (John Brown Cutting to Jefferson, September 15, 1789, in Boyd, *Jefferson Papers,* XV:427.)

44. Gordon S. Wood, "Interests and Disinterestedness in the Making of the Constitution," in *Beyond Confederation: Origins of the Constitution and American National Identity,* ed. Richard Beeman et al. (Chapel Hill: University of North Carolina Press, 1987), 92.

45. James D. Richardson, comp., *Messages and Papers of the Presidents, 1789–1897* (Washington, D.C.: U.S. Government Printing Office, 1900), I:52.

46. Maclay, *Diary,* 149, 141; Ames to Minot, April 4, 1789, in Allen, ed., *Works of Ames,* I:564.

47. Elliot, ed., *Debates in the State Conventions,* II:13, 260; Herbert J. Storing, ed., *The Complete Anti-Federalist* (Chicago: University of Chicago Press, 1981), III:95.

48. Wood, "Interests and Disinterestedness," 101–102.

49. Ibid.

50. Thomas Hartley to Tench Coxe, October 6, 1788, in Jensen, *First Federal Elections,* I:304.

51. Ibid., 296, 306.

52. *Pennsylvania Gazette,* July 30, 1788, in ibid., 247; "Instructions of the Northumberland County Delegates," October 16, 1788, in ibid., 314.

53. "To the German Inhabitants," November 13, 1788, in ibid., 339.

54. *Federal Gazette,* November 18, 1788, in ibid., 347; *Pennsylvania Packet,* November 215, 1788, in ibid., 362, 363. As if to confirm the Anti-Federalist view that all politics were local, one of the elected Federalist congressmen from Pennsylvania, Thomas Scott of Washington County, announced his resignation before he could take office. Scott did not want to give up his position as prothonotary of the county; apparently, being a federal congressman could not compare with the power of the clerk of the county court. The Federalists, however, feared that if Scott did resign, Anti-Federalist demagogue William Findley might replace him. Consequently, they worked out an agreement whereby Scott's son was appointed prothonotary, and Scott stayed on as congressman. (Ibid., I:234, 426.)

55. In Massachusetts, for example, those who wanted only "the best and most competent characters" chosen as congressmen in the election of 1788 were opposed by those who wanted an "equal and real representation" in the government of all the diverse interests of the society. (Ibid., I:468–472.)

56. Latrobe to Mazzei, December 19, 1806, in *Philip Mazzei: Selected Writings and Correspondence,* ed. Margherita Marchione et al. (Prato, Italy: Edizioni del Palazzo, 1983), III:439.

57. Ibid.

Comment

Joseph Cooper

Gordon Wood's analysis of Federalist and Anti-Federalist thought on the relationship between knowledge and power raises the most critical issues of democratic politics: the validity of the concept of the public interest and its relationship to the role of political institutions. Unlike many political scientists who approach Madison primarily as a pluralist theorist, Wood quite correctly concludes that the Federalist vision of the American republic is a public interest view. In contrast, the Anti-Federalist vision is an interest group view, quite close to modern pluralist thinking in the United States. He suggests that it is the interest group vision of the Anti-Federalists, not the public interest vision of the Federalists, that has prevailed over the course of American history. Whatever their views of Madison, many political scientists would agree. I do not, and I propose to explain why I see the Founders as the ultimate winners as well as the immediate winners of the historic debate in the late 1780s over the future of the American republic.

The Conflict in Visions

To begin, let me briefly summarize the two visions. The Federalists believed that the ends of government were to promote justice and the public interest, that the institutions of government should contribute to the achievement of those ends, and that in the United States mechanisms such as representative government, federalism, and a separation of powers would provide effective means for achieving both justice and the public interest.

The Anti-Federalist position, as identified by Wood, shares the major presumptions of modern pluralist thought. Both positions deny reality to any overarching notion of justice or of the public interest. Such conceptions are seen at best as delusions and at worst as rationalizations of the interests of those in power. Democratic political institutions thus do not serve as mechanisms for identifying the public interest through rational deliberation; rather, they serve as mechanisms for articulating, aggregating, and accommodating individual preferences or desires, based largely on self-interest. As a result the well-being of the community has no meaning beyond the summation of such preferences, and it is achieved by self-interested behavior and the trading of advantage rather than by some quixotic search for the public interest. Given these brief sketches, the following points should be noted regarding the key assumptions and salient differences of the two visions.

First, the Federalist and Anti-Federalist positions disagree fundamentally on the role of reason and values as opposed to power and interests in politics. The Federalist position assumes the existence of rational order in the world, both physical and moral. All desires or preferences are not equal. What is desirable is not simply what is desired, but what reason identifies when applied in a disinterested manner to the problems of social choice. Policy choices thus differ inherently in their relationship to the protection of the natural rights of the individual (that is, justice) and the promotion of the permanent well-being of the community (that is, the public interest).[1] Moreover, one can assess the status of policy choices in these regards objectively through rational deliberation, and such deliberation can and should provide the basis for reconciling conflicts in policy views.

In contrast, the Anti-Federalist and pluralist positions are positivist on the question of moral order and see reason as a reliable guide only on questions of means, not ends. Reason, as a result, cannot discriminate among desires or preferences. There is, in short, no objective way of determining what is desirable as opposed to what is desired. All desires or preferences thus become of equal worth. Similarly, no moral premium exists for disinterested as opposed to interested behavior. Finally, aside from the trading of advantage, no means of resolving conflict exists other than power—that is, allowing some preferences to dominate others.

Second, the two visions differ substantially on the basis and character of representative government. For the Federalists the need for representative government proceeds directly from the strength of human passions. Madison and his colleagues assumed that passion was a far stronger motive than reason, that individuals were far more likely to follow their self-interests than to act unselfishly. Hence, representative government is essential to protect against minority tyranny. Given human passions, however, representative government itself involves the strong possibility of majority tyranny. It thus has to be carefully designed institutionally to frustrate majorities based simply on self-interest and to promote the triumph of policies and actions that truly serve justice and the public interest.

In contrast, the basis of representative government in the Anti-Federalist or pluralist position stems directly from the absolute equality of preferences. If all desires or preferences have equal worth, all should have an equal influence in determining political decisions. This, in turn, means political institutions that give all preferences a fair and equal voice—in other words, the institutions of representative government. Similarly, the character of representative democracy is quite different. The pluralist view shares Madisonian presumptions about the power of self-interest but without Madisonian discrimination. The political system works best if individuals assert their self-interests and bargain on the basis of them. Political actors are not merely impractical but unwise and presumptuous if they engage in some disinterested search for the public interest. Rather, collective well-being results from the aggregation of preferences, and this is best left to the political system as a whole and the bargaining process it involves.

Third, the two visions present very different views of political leadership. For the Federalists political leadership is crucial. Given the strength of human passions, political leaders must be relied upon to supply the disinterested and rational deliberation necessary to attain justice and the public interest. In this regard the Federalists counted on two factors to make such a result likely. One was that representative institutions and indirect elections would free public officials to act rationally and deliberately. The other was that the people would rely on a leisured and educated aristocratic elite who were capable of providing the leadership required.

The role of political leadership in pluralist or Anti-Federalist thinking is quite different. The role of leaders is to represent faithfully the coalitions of interests that elect them and to bargain skillfully on their behalf. Neither of these functions is easy to ensure, however, since public officials too are self-interested. Hence, elections assume a far more critical significance than in the Federalist vision.

Assessing the Visions

Wood suggests that the Anti-Federalist vision rather than the Federalist vision has triumphed. He argues that American politics became just the kind of interest group politics the Anti-Federalists predicted and that the Framers' hope for reliance on the disinterested leadership of a leisured and educated elite was never realized. In short, he argues that a kind of democratic politics the Framers did not foresee or intend has largely frustrated the relevance and success of the Federalist vision.

I disagree on theoretical, historical, and normative grounds. First, in theoretical terms, it is clear that individuals do make judgments on moral or value grounds in politics and that these judgments affect outcomes. Thus, whatever their basis in objective reality, the facts are that such judgments are made and that they are influential. It is for this reason that societal consensuses on political values are critical in resolving conflict.

Even preeminent pluralist theorists, such as David Truman and Charles Lindblom, concede that American politics involve more than merely the conflict of interests.[2] They both acknowledge that shared values constrain the definition and assertion of interests. What can also be claimed, however, is that shared values provide a basis for reconciling interests, a basis for agreement in terms of shared purposes as opposed simply to the trading of advantage. For example, the politics of health care reflect not only the trading of advantage but the implications of past agreements on common purpose. We have only to look at a policy area in which there is deep value disagreement, such as abortion, to realize how dependent pluralist thought is on the happy circumstances of American society. In sum, then, it is not true that American politics operate simply on the basis of self-interest and bargaining. There is just not that much to trade, given the character of the agreements that must be forged, and what is available for exchange quickly loses its allure when value disagreements arise.

All this, however, is not to deny that the pattern of interests is also crucial. Even a public interest politics involve the satisfaction of some preferences rather than others and must rely on bargaining as well as on rational deliberation. If values constrain interests, it is also true that interests constrain values. Thus, value consensuses are unlikely or subject to breakdown where interest divisions are deep and difficult to accommodate. Still, we can conclude that there is reality or meaning to the concept of the public interest, although it is of a contingent nature. It exists to the degree that claims on government are disciplined and decided in terms of their rational relation to shared or common purposes. As such, no "invisible hand" guides the process. There can be "bad" as well as "good" outcomes, depending on the patterns of values and interests and the ability of political leaders to forge agreement on the basis of rational argument as well as bargaining.

Second, the Federalist vision can be defended on historical as well as theoretical grounds. Many of the institutions the Framers designed have worked, as the Framers intended, to check coalitions based simply on self-interest and to promote coalitions that express shared purposes and concerns. Even when American institutions have not worked as the Framers intended, however, the effect has often been to foster their goals. Undoubtedly, the Framers did not intend the kind of democratic party politics that arose. Still, electoral parties are not the factious force they understood parties to be on the basis of the eighteenth-century model. When a broad national party succeeds in uniting a variety of interests across a multitude of constituencies, it is because it provides a public philosophy that tempers and unites these interests on the basis of shared conceptions of common purpose. The New Deal was not mere logrolling, not mere interest group liberalism, and neither were any of the broad party coalitions that have altered the course of public policy in the United States from Jefferson to Jackson to Lincoln to Wilson to Reagan. Similarly, if rule by the kind of aristocratic elite the Framers envisioned did not come to pass, this does not mean that their view of the role of political leaders was incorrect, that the institutions they designed have not given leaders the leeway they intended, or that democratic politicians do not have as much ability to rise above parochial self-interest as a landed aristocracy. In short, what is true in theory is true in practice. American politics has not been and remains far more than mere interest group politics.

Finally, the Federalist position can be defended on normative, or ideal, grounds. It is true that the Founders' vision appears naïve to those who pride themselves on their realism. Realists, however, underestimate the role of reason and values in American politics. Whatever the weaknesses of the Federalist vision, the normative presumptions and implications of the Anti-Federalist or pluralist position are even more fragile empirically. To escape being reduced to the proposition that might makes right, the pluralist vision must be able to implement the single standard it possesses— it must be able to design institutional arrangements that give all preferences fair and equal access to and influence over political outcomes. Yet its ability to accomplish this end is subject to even greater skepticism than the ability of the Federalist vision to induce disinterested deliberation.

It is ironic that social choice theory, which shares the underlying positivist assumptions of pluralism, has nonetheless provided a set of findings that vitiate it. But this is the case. On the one hand, social choice findings on the paradox of voting demonstrate that arbitrariness cannot be avoided in systems for summing and aggregating preferences. In short, given positivist assumptions, no system of institutional arrangements exists for summing preferences that confers power without bias.[3] On the other hand, social choice findings on principal-agent relationships strongly indicate that the problem of ensuring the faithful representation of interests in democratic governments may well be beyond the ability of elections to solve in any manner that meets the needs of pluralist theory.[4] If we combine pluralist assumptions regarding the sovereignty of self-interest with the general character of elections, it is difficult to see how serious problems of moral hazard and adverse selection can be avoided or why representative government is not just another form of government in which rulers manipulate the ruled. Interestingly enough, the emphasis modern students of Congress place on the manipulative stratagems members of Congress employ to ensure reelection has more serious implications for pluralist thought than for Madisonian thought.[5] In sum, then, given its own assumptions, the Anti-Federalist or pluralist vision has problems of institutional design and political leadership that undercut both its supposed realism and its ability to provide a standard for assessing and legitimizing American democracy.

In conclusion, this long discussion of the conflict in visions highlights a critical point about the interaction of values, beliefs, and facts in public affairs. Politics is not physics. Our ideals and beliefs influence results. If we proclaim that politics is self-interest and that self-interest is beneficial, we will induce political actors to act even more selfishly than they otherwise might. Conversely, if we proclaim the importance of reason and civic virtue, we will induce more disinterested action in the pursuit of shared purposes than we might otherwise secure. Disputes over visions, therefore, are not empty exercises in scholasticism. Ultimately, the relevance and worth of the Founders' views are dependent, to a significant degree, on how we regard them.

NOTES

1. The distinction between justice and the public interest is preserved in the text because Madison distinguished between the protection of natural rights and the promotion of the public good. See Morton White, *Philosophy, the Federalist, and the Constitution* (New York: Oxford University Press, 1987), 208–227.

2. See David B.Truman, *The Governmental Process* (New York: Knopf, 1951); and Charles E. Lindblom, *The Intelligence of Democracy* (New York: Free Press, 1965).

3. See, for example, Kenneth J. Arrow, *Social Choice and Individual Values* (New York: Wiley, 1963); and William H. Riker, *Liberty Against Populism* (San Francisco: Freeman, 1982).

4. See, for example, Terry Moe, "The New Economics of Organizations," *American Journal of Political Science* 28 (November 1984): 739–777.

5. See David R. Mayhew, *Congress: The Electoral Connection* (New Haven: Yale University Press, 1974); and Morris P. Fiorina, *Congress: Keystone of the Washington Establishment* (New Haven: Yale University Press, 1977).

Comment

James Sterling Young

Gordon Wood's paper delineates a First Congress of the United States that hit the ground running, as Washingtonians today would say. It reveals the founding two centuries ago of an institution that instantly became and still remains the most powerful national legislature in the world. The first generation of senators and representatives—the Founders of Congress—seem to have been extraordinarily adept at governing. They and their infant institution proved equal not only to the challenge of a policy agenda that was daunting even by today's standards but also to the need for statecraft to nurture a new, still fragile Union.

Wood's vivid portrayal of the First Congress in action invites one to ponder what it was that made their remarkable performance possible. What could the Founders have known about the governing of a nation that made them so successful at it? What was the nature and source of the political knowledge that informed their exercise of political power?

Necessarily, they were novices at nation governing, for the nation itself was new. They were unused to making laws for all Americans, because they were the first generation of Americans to be allowed this authority. They did have knowledge of nation governing such as it was under the Articles of Confederation—government by the member states assembled in a single institution that had no coercive authority. But this way of governing had failed. They had knowledge also of the way the British had governed America. But this way was unacceptable. Government by hierarchy, with a king on top, lords next below, and commoners at the bottom—this was what Americans had united and revolted against. What Americans chose by adopting the Constitution was government by a set of separate institutions with no one on top. But the Constitution, like the nation, was new and untried.

Not only did the Founders have no tradition of nation governing on which to draw, but they had few of the sources of political knowledge that are available to those who govern the nation today. There was then no Library of Congress to enlighten them, and no Congressional Research Service, Congressional Budget Office, Office of Technology Assessment, or General Accounting Office. There were no schools of public affairs or think tanks to train them. There were no professional consultants to serve as coaches, no staff to serve as sherpas, and no Machiavellis to serve as strategists, so far as I know. Pollsters to tell the governors what the governed were thinking, journalists to tell them how they were doing, PACs to tell them which policies were rewarding, and academicians to tell them which were good and bad—all these were lacking. There were no transition teams to impart knowledge to incoming executives. There were no orientation programs to do the same for incoming legislators—and the turnover rates were very high in the early Congresses. Lacking, too, were left-behind cadres of colonial civil servants to provide administrative know-how, operational continuity, institutional memory, and links to the mother country while the governors of the first new nation got their bearings.

Yet these novices did not govern the nation like amateurs. They successfully completed the first transition in history from colonialism to independence. Head upon the heels of this accomplishment they effected the first nonviolent transformation of independent states into a nation-state. Quickly after the Constitution was ratified they moved to "extend the ground of confidence" in it by crafting a ratifiable Bill of Rights from a mass of conflicting and passionately advocated proposals for amendments. They legislated a solution to the new nation's near-bankruptcy and agreed upon a plan for the retirement of the national debt within their lifetimes. Without getting entangled in great-power politics, although inflaming anglophile-francophile domestic politics, the Founders foiled the mother country's schemes to lure the western states out of the Union and to evade its treaty obligations. They put Britain in its place and declined France's embrace.

Congress set up a national judicial system. Senate and House together created a new executive branch that permitted effective administration while ensuring the subordination of the civil and military establishments to the constitutional authority of both the president and Congress. Without tearing the nation apart, the Founders fought out a fundamental disagreement over national development philosophy and policy: Hamilton's plan to make America an industrial nation, administratively centralized, with a deficit-financed infrastructure and indebted to financiers; Jefferson's plan to make America a giant nation, debt-free and decentralized, with strong, self-financing member states. It took a few years, but the Founders decisively chose the Jeffersonian option and then, with the electorate's endorsement, moved with Hamiltonian energy and dispatch to implement their decision with a coherent package of domestic, fiscal, territorial, defense, and foreign policies.

All this was done without reinventing a king or recreating a Cromwell, without a junta or a coup, and without resort to Lockean prerogative. Everything was done by the initiative or the coparticipation or the approval of Congress.

So the Founders knew something about governing. One source of their knowledge is apparent from their public careers. The overwhelming majority of them had previously served in representative bodies—colonial assemblies, state legislatures, the Continental Congress. This was true of executives as well as senators and representatives. The pattern persisted, moreover, well into the nineteenth century. Except for Zachary Taylor every president from George Washington until Ulysses Grant came into office with legislative experience, as did a large majority of the cabinet members. Schooling in "the legislative way of life," as an admirer of yesteryear called it, was what the Founders had most in common with each other—and with at least four generations of presidents, cabinet members, senators, and representatives who followed them.[1]

It is hardly surprising that representative institutions were the main political training and recruiting ground for the governors of the young nation. Not until after independence was it possible for Americans to gain policy-level executive or judicial experience, since these sectors were the preserve of the British ruling hierarchy during the colonial period. The representative assemblies in each of the colonies were the only governmental institutions above the local level that Americans were allowed to control. During more than a century and a half of prenational political development, beginning in 1619 with the creation of the first representative assembly at Jamestown, the colonial assemblies evolved into policymaking bodies (though not to the same degree in all the colonies) and came to exercise powers far beyond the scope allowed in British instructions. Outlawed by royal edict on the eve of the Revolution, these representative institutions became the principal governing bodies of the former colonies as soon as the British were ousted. An all-colony representative body—"The United States in Congress Assembled"—was created as the governing body of the new confederation.

So the governors of the young nation received their practical political knowledge in institutions that were British in their provenance but most un-British in their purpose. They learned about governing by serving in institutions that the settlers had used to take over the government of their respective colonies from the British and to protect themselves from oppressive or careless governance by their rulers across the sea. It would seem, then, that the way of governing that the Founders knew best—and probably trusted most—was the way their forebears had learned to replace British colonial government with self-government long before they declared their independence.

Among the lessons learned in these legislative schools were two of enduring significance in American political life. One was how to exercise political power without possessing executive authority. The other, related to the first lesson, was how to make policy consensually rather than hierarchically.

As to the first lesson, note that in contrast with the American way old-world parliaments exercise political power by furnishing the membership and controlling the tenure of "the Government," the cabinet of high executives who make national policy. This way of exercising power was foreclosed to colonial Americans. Barred from the colonial governorships—barred indeed from all positions of authority in the British hierarchy including seats in Lords and Commons—and invested with advisory powers at most, colonial assemblymen had to invent a new way of controlling the exercise of executive authority. The particulars and the success of their strategy varied from colony to colony, but its elements seem to have been the same everywhere.

Capitalizing on their utility as channels to and spokesmen for the local communities whose delegates they were, assemblymen offered to the colony executives help they could not refuse and advice they could not ignore, save at the cost of making their jobs more difficult or their tenure less secure.

Assemblies helped out administratively, lending a hand in fiscal matters here, helping out in personnel placement there, and taking over such chores as auditing the colony's books and licensing lawyers. In the process they came to play a substantial role in colony administration, ranging from oversight to micromanagement. They provided political help also, such as advising the governor how to interpret British instructions or how to disburse revenues in ways that the local communities would not object to and might even applaud. They put the needs of their constituencies on the governor's agenda and helped formulate his responses. They assisted in translating affirmative responses into authoritative policies by drafting and voicing approval of the governor's policy edicts. And they made trouble by withholding help and voicing disapproval of unwanted edicts.

Colonial assemblies were thus the schools where Americans learned to lobby. They learned how to obtain by the art of carrot-and-stick and by pressure and persuasion what they could not command from those in positions of political authority. In the process representative institutions became partakers of executive power. People who served as delegates learned to be administrative superintendents as well. Legislators learned to live with a separate and independent chief executive, even how to turn one into a chief clerk. Indeed, they learned how to get along in a crunch without a separate executive. During the Revolutionary crisis, representative bodies served as interim governments of states and of the Union. We need no reminding that representative bodies alone framed and ratified the Constitution. We sometimes forget, however, that the separate and independent executive created by the Constitution had been a familiar fixture on the American political landscape for more than 150 years, a presence that had already been assimilated into the American way of governing.

Learning to be policymakers as well as representatives was a second kind of political knowledge gained through service to legislative bodies. Note again the contrast with the old-world way of making policy by deference to persons possessed of executive authority. In the old world the high executive makes policy, and the representative body ratifies it after questions from the floor. In the event of failure to ratify, a new government with a different policy is installed, and the norm of parliamentary deference to the executive resumes. This way of policymaking was foreclosed to colonial Americans. The only way they could secure self-government within the empire was to turn their representative assemblies into legislative bodies and learn how to make as well as ratify policy on the floor.

To make a representative institution into a policymaking institution was no mean feat. The success of this effort required much tolerance for conflict and contention, not to mention parochialism and localism, logrolling and filibustering, and unruliness and obstinacy. These aspects of colonial legislative behavior cropped up in Congress often enough for visiting Britons to make devastating comparisons with the disciplined (they did not say deferential) behavior of their Commons. Policymaking in a representative body required acceptance of diversity: unlike individuals had to behave as equals. It required also persons with cultural antipathies, contrary convictions, conflicting interests, clashing ideas, and competing loyalties to act as a body. And it required them as a body to come up with policies that the public and the executive could be persuaded to accept.

This was a demanding set of requirements, but the incentives to succeed were high. A deadlocked assembly lost its value for constituents and lost its utility for the colony executive, who might prorogue it and govern unilaterally by edict. For the early Americans, the failure of the assembly to produce acceptable policy meant the failure of self-government.

American representative bodies, then, became institutions where policies were arrived at by a process of consensus finding among "opposite and rival interests" more than by exercises of authority over the rank and file. Here Americans learned to legislate by lobbying within the body, using much the same strategies of pressure and persuasion on each other that they used in dealing with the executive. They contended with each other to obtain by coalition, compromise, and consensus the policies that no one member—party leader or not—could command of the whole body. Here Americans learned to be political leaders by being consensus finders, whether or not they sat in seats of high authority. In the legislative schools those who governed learned, for better or worse, that acceptable policy was the best policy and that it was better to spend time trying to discover what was acceptable before a law was made than to spend treasure and possibly blood in order to make it acceptable afterwards.

Small wonder it was, then, that a new and untried Constitution worked so well for the first new nation. The way of governing the Constitution prescribed—government by a set of separate institutions with no one on top—was consistent with the way of governing that Americans invented long before they had a nation to govern.

Small wonder, too, that Congress started out two centuries ago as the most powerful national legislature in the world and remains so today. Americans learned how to make their parliaments part of their government more than three centuries ago.

Nor is it surprising that the Founders, novices though they were at nation governing, did not govern like amateurs. Behind them were long years of American experience in dealing with and controlling the exercise of coercive state authority. The Founders were not the first but the ninth generation of Americans to be schooled in the arts and sciences of self-government. The knowledge that informed their exercise of power came not only from books and from across the sea but also from their own political culture. It came in significant measure from the culture that was seated in the representative institutions where successive generations learned, practiced, and taught a distinctively American way of governing.

That this way of governing would not be serviceable for all purposes soon became apparent with the disarray that attended the War of 1812 and was demonstrated beyond doubt in the decade that ended in the Civil War. There are those who argue that it is inadequate to the exigencies of the world we live in today. The legislative way of governing, with its reliance on consensus and its tolerance of contention, indiscipline, uncertainty, and delay, ought to be discarded, some say, in favor of an executive way, with its reliance on prerogative and its promise of action, decisiveness, and discipline (they do not say deference). Perhaps this old-world way of governing works better in the world of today. But if my reading of political history is right, Americans keep coming back to the legislative way, modifying rather than abandoning it as the world changes. The lessons the Founders learned and passed on to their successors seem to have become indelible in our political culture. Though they are set aside occasionally, they are never forgot.

NOTE

1. T. V. Smith, *The Legislative Way of Life* (Chicago: University of Chicago Press, 1940). Smith was an academic and a congressman at large from Illinois; he dedicated his book to "all living legislators" as an "appreciation of the legislative way."

3. The Making of the Modern Congress

Nelson W. Polsby

The U.S. Congress is singular in its importance as a legislative institution within its political system. Nothing very much like it exists in any of the 160 or so nation-states that make up the modern world. Most of the world's famous legislatures are parliamentary in character and hence are organizations that exist primarily as electoral colleges for governments. Typically, they are controlled by leaders of a single political party, and sometimes by a coalition of political parties. These legislatures are at best what the British sometimes call "talking shops"—arenas in which issues may be raised, questions asked, and speeches made. When the time comes to make laws, however, legislation is enacted more or less pro forma, as received. In parliamentary governments, when the automatic processes of legislative enactment do not run reasonably smoothly, it is time to elect a new government so that the proper functioning of the legislature can be restored.[1]

This description covers most functioning legislatures, although it does not take into account the rather frequent incidence in the modern world of rubber stamp legislatures, which do not have even the power to elect and dismiss governments independently nor the power to originate or shape individual items of legislation. Rubber stamp legislatures may exist on firm constitutional footings, as in many so-called peoples' republics, or they may meet strictly at the pleasure of a military dictator or of some other elected, anointed, or hereditary leader. Although they may share with Congress the appellation *legislature,* they are mere shadows in comparison with Congress. Congress writes laws, exercises political judgment, and transforms proposals that it receives from agencies other than itself. If one wishes to predict the output of a legislative arena, one must consult the intentions of the body, usually a one-party cabinet, that possesses the authority to control the program of the legislature in question. What the cabinet wishes, more or less, the legislature does. This is not, to put it mildly, the way Congress works. To understand the outcomes of the legislative process in a transformative legislature, of which Congress is by far the most conspicuous example, it is necessary to understand the internal wiring diagram of the institution itself.

These observations provide a serviceable theoretical rationale for examining Congress. Congress is complex and interesting; Congress is sui generis; and Congress matters.

The most obvious aspect of the complexity of Congress is its bicameral structure. Although a fair number of bicameral legislatures exist, the probability of both halves of a legislature possessing substantial power, in something like equal measure, and of each having its own institutional history is about as likely as the existence of fraternal Siamese twins. In this respect it is the Senate that is the more remarkable of the two houses; throughout its two-hundred-year history it has been virtually unique among upper legislative bodies in its success at retaining vital functions, in certain ways even revitalizing itself as time has gone on.

In this paper I shall attempt briefly to describe the aspects of the modern Senate and the House of Representatives that enable these bodies to make their own peculiar contributions to the modern American political system. I shall indicate how Congress manages to inform itself in the exercise of its powers. And I shall speculate briefly on the social and political forces that seem to have been conspicuously influential in creating the modern House and Senate and that may contribute to further institutional change.

Congress is an evolving institution. A proper portrait of the institution today would show influences that trace back to its beginning in the wording of the Constitution and in the first acts that set the constitutional provisions in motion. It would also show elements that reflect the rise and fall of sectional conflict and its persisting influence, the professionalization of the great institution-building period at the turn of the twentieth century, and the organizational results of the pulling and hauling on the institutional fabric that have taken place more recently. My portrait will be a sketch, outlining only recent events that seem to me to have significance for the development of the institution and its most important activities. This reflects my definition of modernity, which refers to contemporary structures and practices in contrast with whatever different structures and practices prevailed at an earlier time.

The Modern Institutions

The Senate's special role in the contemporary American political system is to incubate policy ideas and political innovations.[2] This function stands in dramatic contrast to the Senate's role as late as the 1950s, when it had positioned itself as a critic of and a respondent—frequently an inhospitable one—to the political innovations hatched in the executive branch and by activist presidents, which were forwarded to it by the House of Representatives. During the past three decades the Senate has evolved from being a rather negative repository of states-rights thinking, dominated by a mostly southern-led "inner club," and hence an agent of the devolved aspect of the federal system, into a predominantly nationally oriented body.[3]

The principal agent of this transformation has been the remarkable change in the life chances, and therefore in the political ambitions, of a large number of U.S. senators. In earlier years not so many of them entertained presidential ambitions. Today the Senate is the main institutional source of presidential hopefuls, and for a number of senators such aspirations play a significant part in guiding their behavior in the Senate. Even senators who realistically have little hope of advancing to the presidency now frequently seek national recognition for their legislative work and are not satisfied merely with the approval of interest groups and citizens in their home states.

Senators arrange to receive national recognition in two ways: by occupying leadership positions or actually leading on significant matters of public policy within the Senate, or by running for president.[4] To do the latter, some but not all senators do the former. Several of those who have been notably successful in presidential election politics have in fact not been notably successful in leading the Senate. The availability of the modern Senate as a platform from which—and not only an arena within which—senators might fulfill their political ambitions has changed the character of the institution.

This change in the Senate has had an important implication for the flow of information through the institution. Whereas senators in the era of the inner club could ration their participation in public policymaking to subjects that interested them or that deeply concerned their mostly unconcerned constituents, contemporary senators must have opinions about everything. With the institution's heightened appeal to the national publics has come the need for senators to be generalists. The issues that become hot topics in Congress require senators who nurture larger ambitions to position themselves. One mechanism for meeting the formidable information needs thereby created has been the establishment of highly professional staff. These staff members, lodged in senators' offices, in Senate committees, and in congressional agencies, are dedicated exclusively to serving senators. They are separate and distinct from the staff of the executive branch.

During the past forty years or so the House of Representatives has traveled its own evolutionary route. As the Senate moved from the era of the closed, states-regarding inner club to a brief period of centralization under Lyndon Johnson's aegis to the nation-regarding contemporary period in which senatorial self-advertisement, policy incubation, and the cultivation of general perspectives on public policy are common, the House mostly stood still. Between 1890 and 1920 most of the machinery of the modern House was put in place—notably the practice of seniority as a means of constituting committees, the establishment of committee jurisdictions, and the delineations of the roles of the House Speaker, the majority and minority leaders, and the whips. Rational-legal criteria were substituted for the exercise of political or personal discretion in making many of the choices that governed the internal management of the institution. Meanwhile, being a member of Congress developed into a professional career, requiring of the member almost constant attendance in the capital and a sizable commitment of years as a prerequisite of success within the institution. Leadership became a matter of promotion from within.[5]

The great asset of the House of Representatives as an institution among all the institutions that seek to put a stamp on national policy was and still is its division of labor. A legislative branch of 435 full-time members— as the House has had at its disposal since the 1920s—can in principle deploy its members to produce, across the board, a cadre of experts who have two valuable advantages. They possess a high degree of legitimacy by virtue of having been elected directly by the people, and they can accumulate a vast store of knowledge through devoted and lengthy service on committees organized according to subject matter. The House has organized itself in precisely this fashion: Overall, continuity in committee service has been the norm for members, and this has brought to the House as an institution the sizable dividend of influence over public policy.

No institution—not even the House, which in the sweep of world history may be taken as very near to a limiting case—stands still. Many commentators have remarked upon the developments of the 1970s, when change came to the House, but it will do no harm to review the principal features of these developments. Briefly, the House enhanced the strength of the most significant arm of its division of labor—subcommittees—while weakening another aspect of it—seniority—in favor of greater integration around party responsibility. Power was taken from committee chairmen and given to subcommittees, subcommittee chairmen, party rank and file on committees, and—frequently overlooked—to the Speaker, who was particularly empowered when acting on behalf of the party caucus. These changes on the whole have liberalized the House by greatly increasing the power of the Democratic party caucus—a body that had been moribund since the time of Woodrow Wilson.[6]

Causes: Proximate and Remote

Why did the Senate become a more nationalized body between the 1950s and the present? And why did the House become more liberal? When scholars deal with historical causes, as compared with physical or even social causes, they are in the realm of speculation. The existence of a given set of historical outcomes may be plain enough, but proximate, prior social events adequate to cause them may be so thick on the ground as to defeat the efforts of even the most careful analyst to disentangle them. At best we can assemble stories of greater or lesser plausibility. What is required of these stories is that they not incorporate facts known to be false or be incompatible with the best currently certified knowledge about how things ordinarily work. My best current guesses about the causes of the making of the most modern versions of the House and the Senate rely upon the effect on Congress of large events that had considerable significance outside Congress.

I am inclined to attribute the largest share of the change in the Senate to the influence of television. Because television is today so much a part of the daily lives of Americans, it is easy to forget how recent a phenomenon it is. The 1952 national party conventions were the first given full coverage by television networks. Only a year earlier much of the North

American continent had been spliced together to allow simultaneous transmittal of programs to an almost nationwide audience. The first politicians to feel the power of national television coverage in their own lives were those on a Senate committee investigating organized crime headed by Estes Kefauver of Tennessee.

For some time Kefauver's committee had been holding hearings all over the country. During the week of March 12, 1951, committee members met in New York, where for the first time their hearings were televised. *Life* magazine commented:

> The U.S. and the world had never experienced anything like it. . . . All along the television cable . . . people sat as if charmed. For days on end and into the nights they watched with complete absorption . . . the first big television broadcast of an affair of their government, the broadcast from which all future uses of television in public affairs must date. Never before had the attention of the nation been riveted so completely on a single matter.[7]

As Kefauver's biographer said, "the televising of the New York hearings . . . transformed Kefauver into a genuine national hero and vastly heightened his availability for the Presidency." [8]

Kefauver's television-powered leap from middle-level senator to a lifelong factor in Democratic presidential election politics dramatically demonstrated to senators something very important about changes in the conditions of their lives. It may have been a fluke of fate that caused lightning to strike Kefauver first rather than some other senator, but the structural properties of the situation were plain enough: people and events in Washington were going to be a lot more visible in living rooms all over America. Public visibility and name recognition were already assets of great significance to members of an occupational group that depended on electorates to return them to office, and after 1968 the presidential nominating process came to be wholly dominated by appeals to mass electorates. In some respects national television made national audiences easier to cultivate than audiences confined to the boundaries of a single state.

The most recent important changes in the House of Representatives were precipitated by somewhat different means. The proximate cause of most of the changes in House rules and procedures was a set of enactments made by the House Democratic caucus, for the most part over the objections or at least the passive resistance of the Speaker and the House Democratic leadership. For most of the twentieth century, and certainly as late as the 1960s, the Democratic caucus was useless as an instrument of party policy, either for the purpose of developing policy or enforcing it. Yet by the 1970s party policy was being made, and enforced, by the caucus. What had happened?

During Sam Rayburn's time as Speaker (roughly 1940–1960), the uselessness of the caucus was a product of the diversity of the Democratic party in the House. To thrash out policy in caucus and then to require adherence to the party position was to court the destruction of the party. The nub of the problem was the Dixiecrats. As diverse as were northern ideological liberals, northern machine politicians, and western Democrats, the conservative Democrats from the South provided an indigestible measure of diversity. Not all southern Democrats were in fact conservative. But in 1960, of the hundred-odd Democrats who represented districts from the eleven former Confederate states, about two-thirds voted against the rest of the Democrats in Congress a substantial amount of the time. Only one-third had party support scores that exceeded their party opposition scores by 2–1 or better.

Sixty-six Dixiecrats were too many for the Democratic leadership to fool with. By defecting en masse from the Democratic party line and voting with a reasonably united Republican party, the Dixiecrats could tip the balance of power in Congress away from what to a casual observer might appear to be an overwhelming Democratic majority.[9] So Rayburn seldom convened the Democratic caucus. Ticklish or high-priority matters customarily proceeded by back room negotiation. On one conspicuous occasion when he had to fight openly (over the packing of the House Rules Committee after the 1960 election), Rayburn chose as his arena of preference the House floor, where he won narrowly, rather than the caucus. This experience was a vindication of his longstanding strategic judgment that the caucus was fundamentally unavailable as a vehicle for serious party business.[10]

What rejuvenated the Democratic caucus was the revival of the Republican party in the South. During the twenty-year period after Rayburn died in 1961, the number of southern Republican congressional seats quadrupled. Virtually all these seats were at the expense of Dixiecrats. Indeed, a few southern Democrats in the House departed from the Democratic caucus by becoming Republicans. The net effect by 1980 was markedly to reduce the risks of using the caucus to enforce mainstream national Democratic policy perspectives on Democratic committee chairmen.

The revival of the Republican party in the South is a large topic indeed. I do not propose to do more here than indicate my belief that it has its roots in demographic changes, mostly migrations, that were in some important measure driven by changes in technology. The depopulation of the rural South during the fifty years from 1930 to 1980 is in part a story about the push of agricultural mechanization and the pull of factory jobs in the North—especially during World War II—and in the small cities of the South. This shift subtracted nonvoters and Democratic voters from some places and in others made southern communities more like northern ones. During the forty years from 1940 to 1980 the creation of the Sun Belt—which includes the old Confederacy and Arizona, New Mexico, and California—is a story about northern retirees, many of them well-off, conservative, and Republican, moving south to avoid the harsh northern winters. Much of the timing of this phenomenon can be attributed to the expansion of air conditioning into the region. The creation of white-collar, technical, and managerial jobs through federal expenditures on space and on the military no doubt accounts for some of the growth of Republican voting in some suburban districts of the South. And there is the special case of the Cubans of southern Florida, who sent a Republican to Congress in a special election in August 1989. Finally, there is the enormous influence of the voting rights act, which, in the first place, created black Democratic voters in the South and, in the second place, inspired the movement of Dixiecrats into the Republican party. Ultimately, persuasive explanations accounting for the making of the modern Congress—and for each succeeding modern Congress—will turn on factors outside Congress such as these.

Implications of Modernization for Knowledge

In 1970 I wrote an essay advocating that Congress should increase its access to professionally certified knowledge. In such areas as defense procurement and economic planning, I argued, the executive branch had availed itself of professional modes of analysis. If Congress wished to follow the proposals the executive branch was making and understand the justifications and assumptions underlying those proposals, it would have to do likewise.[11]

In the end, however, it was mistrust of the modernizing presidency, not the increasing sophistication of the executive branch, that drove Congress to modernize its analytic capabilities. This topic exceeds the scope of this paper, but I will record my conjecture that Lyndon Johnson's credibility gap and the increased politicization of the Bureau of the Budget under Richard Nixon were milestones along the path that led to the creation of the Office of Technology Assessment, the Congressional Budget Office, a revitalized Congressional Research Service in the Library of Congress, and a beefed-up General Accounting Office, with a management orientation (as contrasted with a post-audit orientation).

Nor did professionalization stop there. Congressional committee staffs grew by leaps and bounds in the 1970s, the staffs of members grew, and as they grew in size their attentiveness to policy increased.[12] In the 1950s and 1960s it was unusual for congressional staff members to expect to cycle through the government agencies downtown or the think tanks or local law firms as natural stages in their careers. By the 1980s this expectation was commonplace. By then Capitol Hill needed much the same qualities in its staff as did the rest of the policy communities in which it was enmeshed. Professional training before working on the Hill, not merely political experience in service to the member, became a norm for staff members, as did shorter stays on congressional staffs.

The rise of the presidential branch of government shifted the values of the executive office and senior bureaucrats from an emphasis on neutral competence to an emphasis on responsiveness to the president's political needs.[13] The growth of congressional staff can be read as a response to this. But some of the growth was also a response to the institutional changes in the House and the Senate already discussed. The decentralization of policymaking, as occurred in the House of Representatives, increased the number of decision-making nodes in the House's division of labor and created a demand for professional staff assistance at each new decision point. The Senate did not change its division of labor, but for each senator who wished to become an all-purpose fountain of policy wisdom in the pursuit of higher office—or merely to keep in the game as it was increasingly being defined by those pursuing higher office—a demand was similarly created for adequate professional advice and better behind-the-scenes preparation.

In many respects there is continuity rather than change in the congressional pattern of information gathering and processing. "Witnesses" still report to "hearings" and are frequently put under oath so as to "make a record." This lawyer's model of information processing consumes a lot of time and resources, and it may or may not always be appropriate. It would probably be instructive if advocates of different points of view were occasionally invited to interact with one another seminar-style under congressional auspices.

Despite the rigidities that remain in the rather equivocal encounter between Congress and the world of knowledge, it seems to me fair to say that the most recent changes in the most consequential structures and procedures of the House and Senate have, on the whole, greatly increased the capacities of Congress to bring information to bear on the decisions they must make.

NOTES

1. For further discussion of Congress in comparative perspective, see Nelson W. Polsby, "Legislatures" in *Handbook of Political Science,* vol. 5, ed. Fred I. Greenstein and Nelson W. Polsby (Reading, Mass.: Addison-Wesley, 1975), 257–319.
2. Case studies of political innovation in which the emerging role of the Senate as a policy incubator can be observed are contained in Nelson W. Polsby, *Political Innovation in America* (New Haven: Yale University Press, 1984).
3. The most important work on the modern Senate has been done by Ralph K. Huitt. See Huitt, *Working Within the System* (Berkeley, Calif.: Institute of Governmental Studies Press, 1990). The inventor of the "inner club" was William S. White. See White's *Citadel* (New York: Harper and Row, 1957); and Joseph S. Clark, *Congress: The Sapless Branch* (New York: Harper and Row, 1964). For a critique of White, see Nelson W. Polsby, *Congress and the Presidency,* 4th ed. (Englewood Cliffs, N. J.: Prentice Hall, 1986), 86–113, 251–257. Another good account of recent changes in the Senate is Alan Ehrenhalt, "In the Senate of the 80s Team Spirit Has Given Way to the Rule of Individuals," *Congressional Quarterly Weekly Report,* September 4, 1982, 2175–2182.
4. See Stephen Hess, *The Ultimate Insiders* (Washington, D.C.: Brookings Institution, 1986).
5. See Nelson W. Polsby, "The Institutionalization of the U.S. House of Representatives," *American Political Science Review* 62 (March 1968): 144–168.
6. There are many accounts of contemporary political changes in the House. See, for example, Norman Ornstein, ed., *Congress in Change* (New York: Praeger, 1975); Norman Ornstein and Thomas E. Mann, eds., *The New Congress* (Washington, D.C.: American Enterprise Institute, 1981); Leroy N. Rieselbach, *Congressional Reform* (Washington, D.C.: CQ Press, 1986); and Polsby, *Congress and the Presidency,* 114–137.
7. See Joseph Bruce Gorman, *Kefauver: A Political Biography* (New York: Oxford University Press, 1971), 92.
8. Ibid., 106.
9. See Clem Miller, ed., with additional text by John W. Baker, *Member of the House: Letters of a Congressman* (New York: Scribner's, 1962), 123.
10. The most complete account of this battle, told mostly from Rayburn's point of view, is Neil MacNeil, *Forge of Democracy* (New York: McKay, 1963), 410–448.

11. Nelson W. Polsby, "Strengthening Congress in National Policy-Making," *Yale Review* 59 (Summer 1970): 481–497.
12. The best general discussion of the growth of congressional staff and its policy consequences is still Michael Malbin, *Unelected Representatives* (New York: Basic Books, 1980).
13. See John Hart, *The Presidential Branch* (New York: Pergamon, 1987).

Comment

Frank Freidel

Nelson Polsby's paper was rich in detail and implications. What I have to offer in response is a historian's point of view. I also want to take into account the presidency, since within our federal system, Congress and the executive branch have functioned like a pair of binary stars, orbiting each other faster and faster from the days of the Founders to the present.

I am fascinated with the question of modernization because, as Nelson Polsby suggests, there have been repeated modernizations since Congress began. He has analyzed the one that occurred in the previous thirty years. Because modernizations have been frequent in our history, a good bit of the functioning of Congress has been cyclical. The number of elements contributing to these cycles, however, is so considerable that it is impossible to calculate with any accuracy when the next cycle will occur.

At the end of Polsby's remarks, I almost expected a prophecy that a Republican Congress would again be elected, quite possibly because of the way in which political issues are evolving in the South. Abigail Thernstrom has demonstrated from a different point of view how liberal Democrats are being stifled in the South.[1] Few liberals are elected, most of the ones elected are from black districts, they are black themselves, and they have little chance of rising above the politics of their districts. So there are complications resulting from the extension of the franchise in the South.

If one looks at the relative power of Congress and the president in terms of cycles, one finds that from the beginning Congress has exercised enormous power; to a considerable degree that power has been negative, because Congress's check upon the executive was a safeguard the Founders intended. Overall, congressional leaders have been clever, even brilliant, sometimes more so than the presidents, and they have been responsible for a number of political innovations. The constitutional amendments have all come from Congress; sometimes presidents have recommended them and sometimes not. All Reconstruction legislation came from a Congress dominated by Radical Republicans, who temporarily took from the president almost everything except routine administrative power. Even in the case of Franklin D. Roosevelt, Congress helped shape several measures of the first New Deal program. It also produced the great TVA experiment in power production and regional development, which had been the dream of Sen. George Norris of Nebraska; the silver inflation amendment to the farm bill, which was the work of western senators; and, against Roosevelt's wishes, the notable establishment of the Federal Deposit Insurance Corporation. Congress made other modifications in Roosevelt's proposals during the first hundred days, in contrast to Republican lamentations that it was rubber-stamping its approval of whatever came over from the White House.

Generally, then, Congress has functioned as the drafters of the Constitution intended. Its role may be in part negative, but it performs an essential role in making emendations, changes, and improvements to administrative proposals. Some of the most creative work has come through cooperation between Congress and the White House. In the first New Deal Congress, Rep. Sam Rayburn of Texas, who would not be Speaker for some years, was already demonstrating his remarkable effectiveness. It was he, with the assistance of Thomas Corcoran and Benjamin Cohen, two bright young men Roosevelt assigned to him, who drafted the first federal securities legislation.

Despite the large role of Congress during the New Deal, Roosevelt, a strong president, was able to capture the headlines and shift the focus of public attention to the White House rather than to the Capitol. For much of American history the excitement was primarily over the deliberations of Congress. In the twentieth century, beginning with Theodore Roosevelt and Woodrow Wilson and continuing with other strong presidents, attention centered more upon the White House than on Congress.

Although the executive branch has grown enormously, Congress has by no means been eclipsed. It, too, has developed new techniques and machinery in recent decades. Yet, in terms of basics, Congress has changed less than the presidency. Today, as has been true since the legislature's eighteenth-century beginnings, outstanding senators and representatives have been powerful national figures in the center of great debates. Consequently, it has been possible for Merrill D. Peterson to define the politics of the period from 1820 to 1850 in terms of three men.[2] Peterson focused on Henry Clay, John C. Calhoun, and Daniel Webster. Not one of these men could have become president because the national views of each were well known and would have breached the tenuous political compromise between North and South. During the years of weak presidents before and after Lincoln, Americans ordinarily did not choose candidates identified with great issues. Leaders such as Clay could run for president, but they could not be elected because their views were repugnant in certain sections of the country. The country tended to elect military heroes or governors.

As late as the 1920s it was advantageous for a presidential aspirant to be a conspicuous governor rather than a senator. Franklin Roosevelt turned the adversity of his polio attack into an asset; it permitted him to decline to run for the Senate, to which he would probably have been elected had he run in 1922. In the Senate he would have had to take a stand on controversial matters that could have diminished his political allure. Rather, he aspired to the governorship of New York, where he could make a national reputation without having to commit himself on divisive national questions.

For those seeking the presidency since World War II, service in Congress has still been disadvantageous. Consider Robert Taft, "Mr. Republican," who took too many strong positions in the Senate, not all of them popular, for him to win the 1952 presidential nomination over a great military leader. Senators must do much juggling, primarily through television, to build national reputations and not lose out as contenders for the presidential nomination because of past controversial stands.

The information revolution has done much to bring Congress and the electorate to a national viewpoint. Americans have grown out of the parochialism in which their concerns were typically close to home: what counted most were local, then state, and only after that, national interests. Now almost the reverse is true. Except for being roused by increases in local or state taxes, Americans are most concerned with national affairs and figures. They think also in international terms, a profound change since World War II broke out.

The roles of members of both houses of Congress have increased in complexity. Previously, members were often not well informed on national issues, nor did they need to be since they spent most of their time with constituents rather than in Washington. Their staffs were minuscule, unable to provide much assistance. Furthermore, members of Congress were so poorly paid that they sometimes augmented their family incomes by placing their wives on their payroll as secretaries. A figure as distinguished as John Nance Garner of Texas, who was Speaker from 1931 to 1933, employed his wife. This practice was legal and open. Now congressional staffs are large and specialized, enabling members to be active in many areas. Most of them still function within a certain bailiwick, however, and are particularly active with the committee or subcommittee for which they serve as chairman or fill an important role. Much of this growth in staff size and power has been in response to similar growth at the White House. Countering the Office of Budget and Management, for example, is the Congressional Budget Office.

The United States alternates between periods of strong presidents and less effective ones and between strong Congresses, able to confront presidents successfully, and Congresses that, as in the first years of Lyndon B. Johnson's presidency, seem to enact almost everything that a powerful, persuasive president suggests would be good legislation.

NOTES

1. Abigail M. Thernstrom, *Whose Votes Count: Affirmative Action and Minority Rights* (Cambridge: Harvard University Press, 1987).
2. Merrill D. Peterson, *The Great Triumvirate: Webster, Clay, and Calhoun* (New York: Oxford University Press, 1987).

Comment

David Brady

Nelson Polsby argues cogently and thoughtfully that external factors—technology and demographics—have shaped change in the modern Congress. The result is a Congress that is still, to paraphrase Polsby, transformative of public policy and informationally more capable of dealing with the complexities of contemporary America than it would be without the changes. I agree with the broad outline of his argument; thus, I shall elaborate on certain aspects of it, focusing in particular on the relationships between committees, parties, knowledge, and power as they affect public policy.

An important question facing scholars of Congress is, what ultimately explains congressional policymaking? Contemporary research directs us to view public policy as a result of the interaction between the policy preferences of members of Congress and the internal structural arrangement of Congress as an institution. Put another way: Do congressional committees with their expertise (information advantage) dominate decisions in their policy domain in a way that is unrepresentative of members' preferred policy positions? For example, are there more agricultural subsidies than the nation and Congress in the aggregate would prefer? To approximate an answer to these questions, one needs to examine the critical relationship between committees and congressional parties. Polsby correctly asserts that the reforms of the 1970s strengthened the Speaker—and thus strengthened the majority party's ability to govern—and placed greater power in the subcommittees.

Committees and subcommittees are a primary, if not the primary, source of public information available to Congress. Congressional parties in the aggregate locate the centers of policy disagreement—for example, liberal versus conservative, North versus South. Polsby is right to claim that since the 1970s the parties have become more cohesive: Democrats are more liberal, Republicans more conservative. Thus, in the contemporary Congress, parties appear to be stronger than ever, and subcommittees are certainly stronger than they were in years past. What, then, is the relationship between parties, which loosely represent members' general policy preferences, and committees, which are Congress's chief source of information? It should now be clear that in order to pose this problem I have made a simplifying assumption: I treat committees as the component in the legislative division of labor that confers through specialization an informational advantage to committee members, while parties are treated as coordinators of aggregated policy preferences whose function is to give policy direction to congressional decisions.

The U.S. Congress, in large part, has solved its information needs by creating a committee system that allows members to specialize in policy areas of importance to them. As members acquire information, they have the opportunity to influence policy in their chosen areas. Does this committee arrangement distort the congressional policy process in such a way that members' policy preferences are not enacted? The dominant theory of Congress, the preference outlier theory, holds that committees are populated by members who are heavy demanders of particular committee goods. Members of the Agriculture Committee, for example, favor price supports and subsidies for farmers; Interior Committee members favor multiple use (timber cutting, mining, and grazing) of federally owned land; and so on across all committees. Each committee's policy position is therefore unrepresentative of floor, or general member, preferences. (The theory assumes that a committee's policy position is determined by the median member.) If this theory is true, why does the floor not simply override the committee and pass its own preferred position? For example, suppose the members of the Agriculture Committee favor an aid package of $40 billion because their constituencies are agricultural, while the House as a whole favors a $20 billion package because their constituencies are not farmers. Why is the final bill not at $20 billion since that is what the majority favors?

The answer, according to Kenneth Shepsle and Barry Weingast, is that *ex ante* the committee has agenda-setting powers and *ex post* the committee members serving on the conference committee protect the committee's preferred policy positions.[1] The rules also favor the committee's bills since the final vote on the conference committee report must be up or down—that is, it cannot be amended. In sum, because this arrangement allows public policy to be dominated by committees, it is unrepresentative of members' true policy preferences. The preference outlier theory assumes that there is an exchange across committees such that each committee gets more of its way than it otherwise would since other committees do not want their policies to be greatly compromised. The implication is that congressional policymaking is bent toward those interests that are organized or that can mobilize support around committee domains. Interests that are not organized and that cannot mobilize support for their policy preferences cannot influence policies. Purportedly, this argument explains why farmers, who make up about 2 percent of our population, get so much, while the poor, who outnumber farmers by at least six times, do not get favorable public housing policy or backing in other policies they support. This theory clearly indicates that knowledge and information are power and that they affect the direction of public policy.

An alternative approach to the preference outlier theory holds that legislative bodies such as Congress have a strong incentive to appoint committees that represent the policy preferences of the body as a whole. If Congress appoints such a representative committee, it will have the advantage of the committee's knowledge and expertise without paying a policy price for the information received. If, for example, Congress appoints an agriculture committee whose members favor market solutions as well as subsidies, the committee's policy choice (median vote) will be close to the floor's policy preference. The committee's knowledge does not dominate the process. Thomas Gilligan and Keith Krehbiel have argued that Congress does appoint committees that are representative of the body as a whole.[2] This point is in contradistinction to the preference outlier theory and interprets the relationship between information and policy very differently.

In the view of Gilligan and Krehbiel, for example, agricultural policy is what it is because a majority of members prefer it that way, not because of the structural elements emphasized in the Shepsle-Weingast theory of preference outliers. According to Gilligan and Krehbiel, reported legislation is a compromise between members with different views—liberal and conservative, Democratic and Republican, and northern and southern. Implicitly, if policy is more liberal than conservative, it is because Democrats have a majority and they are more liberal than Republicans. This line of inquiry has just begun and has yet to explain some important questions.[3]

The contrast between these two theories is dramatic and important. The Gilligan-Krehbiel theory essentially argues that public policy is reasonably representative in that it corresponds with the views of a majority of the elected representatives of Congress and thus, it is hoped, with the views of most American citizens. The Shepsle-Weingast theory holds that, because of the unrepresentativeness and power of congressional committees, public policy is dominated by organized interests. Determining which of these theories is correct will be one of the major research items for political scientists in the 1990s.

In conclusion, I want to point out that the history of Congress is replete with adjustments between committees and parties, members and constituents, and the president and Congress. Polsby attributes change in the modern Congress to external elements such as technology and demographic change. Members are affected by these changes in two ways: they are constrained by them, and they attempt to redesign the institution to accommodate change. Television affected senators' presidential opportunities, and members changed the Senate to take advantage of this opportunity by increasing the number of investigative committees. In the 1890s, as members' electoral careers became more stable, Congress as an institution was changed to accommodate members' congressional career goals. Parties were strong from 1890 to 1910, and committees were relatively weak. After the Progressive movement, parties were weakened and committees were strengthened.

Before Franklin D. Roosevelt, Congress was stronger than the executive; after him, presidents proposed and Congress disposed. In the post-Watergate era Congress appears to have regained some power. Unfortunately, we do not yet have a theory that explains the history of change in Congress; however, such a theory will have to account for how Congress as an institution organizes itself to process information and determine how asymmetries of information affect public policy. Polsby's paper raises crucial issues and takes us a step closer to answering this important question.

NOTES

1. Kenneth Shepsle and Barry Weingast, "The Institutional Foundations of Committee Power," *American Political Science Review* 81 (March 1987): 85–104.
2. Thomas W. Gilligan and Keith Krehbiel, "Asymmetric Information and Legislative Rules with a Heterogeneous Committee," *American Journal of Political Science* 33 (May 1989): 459–491. See also Krehbiel, "Why Are Congressional Committees Powerful?" *American Political Science Review* 81 (September 1987): 929–945.
3. One important question raised by this theory is why would members wish to serve on a committee if there is no policy payoff? That is, if the floor—the whole House—determines policy, what incentive is there for members to specialize on a committee or subcommittee?

4. Informed Legislation: Policy Research Versus Ordinary Knowledge

Allen Schick

The central concern of this volume, to paraphrase the famous question asked by Howard Baker at the Senate Watergate hearings, is, "What does Congress know when it legislates and when does it know it?" The simple answer is that Congress knows a lot and has the capacity to obtain needed information in a timely manner. Congress is a fragmented, permeable institution that takes in many thousands of pieces of information every working day. The legislative mind is a montage of many different influences. Advice and ideas flow in from diverse sources: news items and editorials published in state and district newspapers; constituent complaints or requests for assistance; reports submitted by government agencies; expert testimony at committee hearings; meetings with lobbyists or others who have privileged access. All these sources are grist for the legislative mill.

Congress is not just a passive receiver of information; it actively seeks out data and ideas. What Congress wants, it can usually get for the asking. Thousands of staff are available to committees and members; thousands more are a phone call away in congressional agencies. On demand, Congress can get executive agencies to open their files or to undertake in-depth studies. Committees have little difficulty getting the best and the brightest in relevant policy fields to proffer advice at hearings. The decentralized structure of Congress multiplies the points of access and makes it hard to keep information from entering. This structure also makes Congress's supply of information extraordinarily redundant, since ideas or data blocked at one point can penetrate at another.

It is appropriate to ask whether Congress has more information than

99

it can handle. Information overload is as serious a problem in legislative chambers as it is in executive suites. The problem is eased somewhat by a legislative division of labor that disperses interests and responsibilities among many committees and members. Collective action is facilitated in Congress when committees and members are expert in some matters and ignorant in others. The uninformed can act rationally by taking cues from party whips, senior members, or others whose judgment they value. (This specialization increases the possibility that Congress will be heavily influenced by the interest groups affected by its actions; this is an important concern that is beyond the scope of this paper.)

Despite the torrent of information and the division of labor, Congress may be ignorant in some important policy matters. On its own initiative and through information volunteered by others, Congress generally has little difficulty in identifying problems for which legislative action may be appropriate, but it may be unaware of the effect of its actions. In other words, Congress may know more about problems than about results, more about its own intentions than about the effects on others. For example, news reports and letters from constituents in the 1980s undoubtedly sensitized Congress to the problem of homelessness in America. Members may have been uninformed about the number of homeless persons, and they may not have fully understood why some people live in this desperate condition, but they knew enough to take action. After they have acted, as they did concerning the homeless, they are likely to have difficulty finding out what has been accomplished. If, pursuant to the McKinney Homeless Assistance Act of 1987, the problem persisted, they may not know whether this was because insufficient funding was provided, the funds were used ineffectively, or the program failed for some other reason.

The difference between knowing that there is a problem and knowing what has been accomplished is, in greatly simplified terms, the difference between ordinary knowledge and policy research. Policy research refers to systematic inquiry, typically using the tools of analysis, into the objectives and effects of government programs. Policy research strives for objectivity. It is careful about the methods used and emphasizes the systematic collection and interpretation of data. Policy research generally values data that can be expressed statistically and that are free of bias or subjectivity. Research is conducted into all areas of public policy, but the systematic evaluation of governmental intervention through social programs has probably garnered the most resources and attention. That is the area of research this paper primarily addresses.

Ordinary knowledge is, by contrast, unsystematic and biased. It is the perspective and attitude formed through everyday observation and interaction. Lindblom and Cohen refer to ordinary knowledge as knowledge that owes "its origin, testing, degree of verification, truth status, or currency ... to speculation and analysis. It is highly fallible, but we shall call it knowledge even if it is false." [1]

Not all knowledge can be compressed into these two categories, nor are the classifications airtight. Policy research plays a major role in identifying problems; it also redefines problems identified through ordinary knowledge. The common perception of why people are on welfare or of how recipients use food stamps may differ from the findings drawn from meticulous examination of the socioeconomic condition of needy Americans. Ordinary knowledge often contributes to assessment of results, as, for example, when parents write their representative about compensatory education programs financed by Washington but operated by local schools.

Policy research and ordinary knowledge sometimes reinforce one another, as, for example, when parents complain that their children are not being taught basic skills and researchers find that many youngsters entering the labor market lack sufficient skills to succeed. When the two streams of knowledge converge, policymakers can be expected to move in that direction. Often, however, research and ordinary knowledge tug in opposite directions, and the task of making effective policy is complicated. When, for example, the media report the seizure of a big cache of illegal drugs, the person in the street might conclude that the war on drugs is successful. Researchers sifting through the evidence may come to the opposite conclusion, that the flow of drugs evading detection is greater than ever before. Policy prescriptions are likely to diverge when the two kinds of knowledge diverge. Ordinary citizens may seek tougher law enforcement to cut down the supply; policy analysts may suggest means of discouraging demand. Clashes between the two kinds of knowledge can result in policy paralysis or, when the clamor for actions is great (as in the case of illegal drugs), in policies that respond to both perspectives. It is not surprising that the 1988 omnibus drug legislation (P.L. 100–690) had provisions seeking to constrain both demand and supply.[2]

Contradictions between ordinary and research knowledge are not uncommon. Researchers often boast that their findings are counterintuitive—that is, that they are the opposite of what common sense suggests. In legislating, committees and members of Congress cannot ignore ordinary thinking because their election success depends on garnering the votes of citizens who have no special expertise in policy matters. This paper first examines the influence of policy research and ordinary knowledge on Congress during the 1980s. It then discusses developments that have affected the capacity of Congress to use policy research. It is followed by several brief cases of legislative actions that reflect the interplay of ordinary knowledge and policy research. The paper concludes with a few suggestions for narrowing the gap between the two kinds of knowledge.

The Knowledge Base of Congress

My previous inquiry into the use of policy research by Congress was published in 1976.[3] The year in which that article appeared may have been a peak period in federally sponsored research.[4] In the 1980s major research organizations had to adjust to the Reagan administration's onslaught against social programs, a prolonged squeeze on discretionary expenditure from which most social policy research is funded, and the shrinking of the policy staffs and legislative initiatives of many federal agencies. The focus of research was narrowed somewhat by greater reliance than in the past on contracts rather than grants and by greater specificity in the terms of reference under which the research was sponsored. The policy research community weathered these stresses and was sturdier at the end of the 1980s than it was at the beginning of the decade.

During the 1980s there was a perceptible rise in the reporting of research by intermediaries such as news organizations and interest groups. These intermediaries have considerable influence on whether what analysts say is heard, because members of Congress do not get most findings firsthand. Instead, research is often filtered by journalists, who feature the material in an article or a telecast, or by lobbyists, who use it to bolster their arguments. Major newspapers seem to be giving more attention than before to policy studies, perhaps because today's reporters are better prepared to interpret findings and distill them into a readable article. An important channel for research has been opened by the spread of op-ed columns, which give experts in many fields a broader audience for their views on matters of current interest than they otherwise would have. As the principal source of news for most Americans, television is another disseminator of policy research. Although network documentaries have become almost extinct, much policy-relevant material is presented on news programs. The trade associations clustered in Washington have become adept in applying analysis in the service of advocacy. They are both sponsors and users of policy research, and they often find it useful to buttress their arguments with research findings. Although some researchers may disdain this exploitation of research, it attests to the importance of analysis in policymaking.

These developments have been spurred by the entrance of thousands of professional researchers into government agencies, think tanks, and many other organizations that produce or use policy research. Schools of public policy (the main training ground for policy researchers) were still in their infancy in the early 1970s; today they are well-established institutions that graduate, in the aggregate, more than a thousand researchers a year. Many of these graduates have landed jobs on congressional staffs or in one of the congressional agencies.

The market for research findings has been strengthened by the improved skill of analysts in addressing and communicating the policy implications of their work. Some researchers still hide behind methodology or are indifferent to what happens to their material, but many welcome the opportunity to present their findings in popularized formats such as congressional testimony and action memoranda. The relevance of research for policy has also been enhanced by several decades of investment by government agencies and research organizations in data bases and demographic models that can be drawn upon for comparing proposed options or for estimating the budgetary and program effect of pending legislation.

Many researchers are now sophisticated enough to address front-page issues without compromising methodological integrity or neglecting basic issues. In becoming more relevant, they have not surrendered objectivity or diminished the care with which data are gathered and interpreted. In the 1980s the Manpower Demonstration Research Corporation influenced welfare reform legislation in Congress and the research methods used in other institutions.[5] The Urban Institute, with which I was affiliated, integrated research and policy commentary in its Changing Domestic Priorities project. Many of the early publications in this series assessed the effect of Reagan policy changes on federal programs; later ones probed basic social conditions, such as the needs of the underclass and the changing structure of the American family.[6] This progression indicates that researchers do not have to forsake underlying problems when they strive for policy relevance.

The world of policy research mirrors the pluralism of the political process. There are now hundreds of competent research institutions; there is hardly a major university that does not have several of them. Many of these are as specialized as the policies with which they deal. Policy research has sprawled beyond the voluntary sector to the market economy; profit-making and not-for-profit institutions compete for contracts and collaborate on research. Once identified principally with liberal politics, policy research now spans the full spectrum of American political perspectives. In fact, right-of-center groups were among the most active and influential in the 1980s.

At the same time that policy research was maturing, ordinary knowledge flourished. An interactive society always has an abundance of popular ideas in currency. Political and technological developments have conspired to make these easily available to policymakers in Congress and in other influential institutions. Members of Congress are extraordinarily attentive to the common views and notions circulating about them. The following signs point in this direction.

• Polling has grown into a year-round means of measuring the attitudes of various segments of the population. Many regional and local newspapers (as well as television stations) conduct or sponsor polls on current policy questions throughout the year. Some of these may not pass scientific muster, but they provide members with clues to what voters are thinking. In addition, many members commission their own polls, not only as a part of their campaign strategy but also on a continuing basis.

• The convenience of jet travel and accommodating work schedules in the House and Senate enable most members to return home regularly during the session. Members use weekends and frequent recesses to meet constituents, stage town meetings, and maintain contact with local opinion leaders. The deployment of congressional staff has been adjusted to the reality that members are back home more than half of the year. The portion of House staff based in district offices escalated from 22 percent in 1972 to almost 40 percent in 1988. During the same period the share of Senate staff stationed in state offices climbed from 12 percent to 34 percent.[7] These back-home staff operate neighborhood offices, handle constituent requests, and maintain grass-roots contact with voters.

• Constituents now take more initiative than in the past in telling members what is on their mind. The annual flow of letters to the House rose from about 25 million in the 1970s to about 36 million in the 1980s; the volume of incoming Senate letters also has increased steeply.[8]

The attentiveness of members to constituent interests has bolstered their reelection prospects. The success rate of House incumbents seeking reelection is at an all-time high, more than 95 percent in the 1988 and 1990 elections. Significantly, as the number of "safe" House and Senate seats has increased, members have become more sensitive to their constituents. They have not taken advantage of reelection success to exercise more independence or to invest more of their resources and time on policymaking in Washington.

Competing for Attention: Policy Research Versus Ordinary Knowledge

With a robust policy research industry and the active dissemination of ordinary knowledge, Congress is awash in advice and information. Members must be selective in the matters to which they attend. Because their election prospects depend on responsiveness to what voters want, members cannot ignore the ordinary views expressed in incoming mail, local newspapers, and public opinion polls. In the competition for scarce congressional time, there is a strong possibility that policy research will lose out.

Some evidence that this is happening comes from the increased deployment of staff in state or district offices. The makeup of congressional staff has also changed. More caseworkers and fewer legislative aides are on the payroll these days than before. Casework is the meat and potatoes of congressional activity. It is the business of responding quickly to constituent requests for assistance. Most of the requests concern routine matters, such as a misplaced Social Security check or a denied disability claim. Staff members process cases in assembly-line fashion, usually under tight deadlines. Casework sometimes leads to broader policy questions, but the continuing flow of work and the emphasis on a fast response limit the scope of inquiry.

The work pace of congressional offices reflects the incessant demands on members' time. Members of Congress have more schedule conflicts and less opportunity for pause and reflection than ever before. There is nothing new about interruptions by roll calls, photo opportunities, and visits with influential persons. What is different is the sheer number of receptions at which their attendance is expected, the time diverted to fund raising, the number of "Washington reps" who call, and so on. The typical workday extends well into the evening.

Compression of the time available for reflection has been accompanied by the compression of the terms of debate. President Reagan's efforts in the 1980s to downsize domestic government and check the chronic budget deficit crowded out substantive issues and narrowed debate to financial concerns. Through most of the decade, legislative policy was dominated by budgetary matters. For example, the annual debate on defense policy was conducted in terms of percentages of real growth or decline, not in terms of force levels, defense objectives, or the role of the United States on the world scene.

This constriction of legislative debate has been forced by the protracted drive to reduce the deficit. The objective has become one of enacting (or fabricating) sufficient savings to satisfy that year's demand for deficit reduction. The principal vehicle for producing the savings is a reconciliation bill, a form of budgetary legislation that was not used before the 1980s. Just about everything associated with the reconciliation process drives out long-range or analytic considerations and emphasizes short-term savings.[9] Reconciliation is triggered by a directive in the congressional budget resolution instructing designated committees to recommend changes in revenue or spending laws. The form of the directive and the manner in which it is implemented emphasize money and diminish attention to substantive issues. For one thing, the directive specifies only the amount of revenue or spending change; it does not identify the programs to be affected. For another, response time by affected committees is usually limited to a few months at the most. Committees have a strong incentive to meet the savings target without making major program changes. Moreover, the frequency of reconciliation actions, particularly in the Medicare program, has spurred committees to meet the savings target through short-term adjustments (such as freezes on payment schedules), while ignoring program implications. Finally, the legislation recommended by committees is packaged into an omnibus deficit-reduction measure enacted by a Congress that is typically unaware of many of the provisions hidden in it.[10]

Heightened attention to budget issues has been accompanied by intensified conflict between the president and Congress over revenue and spending policies and a breakdown in congressional budget procedures. With the notable exception of the 1988 session, during the 1980s Congress failed to enact all regular appropriations on time, and it had to provide funding in an omnibus continuing resolution that was enacted under great time pressure. Some continuing resolutions became vehicles for enacting substantive legislation without consideration in committee or on the floor.

Restricting congressional attention to budgetary issues affected the Congressional Budget Office (CBO), which was launched in 1975 to provide Congress with budgetary data and analysis. At the outset CBO was organized, by Alice Rivlin, its first director, to be a channel for the application of policy research to legislative issues. It was to have a small corps of "number crunchers" and a large cast of policy analysts. Over time, however, the numbers work (such as estimating the cost of legislation or keeping score of congressional budget actions) became paramount, and policy analysis receded.

The diminished attention to policy issues is reflected in the decline in two important kinds of congressional activities: committee hearings and authorizing legislation. Hearings are the proving ground of legislation, the first stage at which policy research can have its fullest airing on Capitol Hill. Although most hearings do not directly draw on policy research, many call on experts to testify. Data on congressional workloads show that, after steeply rising in the 1970s and early 1980s, the number of House and Senate committee meetings fell sharply later in the decade. The number of House committee meetings peaked at almost 8,000 in the 95th Congress (1977–1979) and then fell to only 5,200 in the 99th Congress (1985–1987). Similarly, Senate committee meetings declined from a peak of 4,200 in the 94th Congress (1975–1977) to fewer than 2,500 in the 100th Congress (1987–1989).[11]

Congested congressional schedules may be one reason for this drop, but an additional consideration is the lack of funds for legislative initiatives. Without a strong market for new programs, committees appear disinclined to listen to witnesses and gather ideas for new legislation.

The drop in committee activity has a disappointing, but not altogether surprising, implication for policy research. Much research is directed at the assessment of ongoing programs; Congress, however, has only a weak interest in oversight, preferring instead to focus on opportunities for new legislation. To the extent, therefore, that program research examines past performance, interest in it may be limited on Capitol Hill.

Authorizing committees are the main consumers of policy research in Congress. Their responsibility goes beyond budget matters to the full range of program issues that may be examined in policy research. Most of the output of policy researchers fits into the jurisdiction of one or more of these committees. Authorizing committees were casualties of budget wars in the 1980s. Budget pressures led to a decline in the volume of authorizing legislation. Through most of the decade, some short-term authorizations, such as the annual defense reauthorization bill, were acted on, but it was difficult to get Congress to act on long-term, substantive matters. As a consequence, congressional use of policy research for authorizing purposes declined.

Authorizing legislation made a comeback in the last years of the Reagan presidency. Among other initiatives Congress enacted a housing authorization bill, reauthorized education programs, authorized aid to the homeless and a sprawling war-on-drugs effort, reformed welfare, and added a Medicare catastrophic program (which was later repealed). Some of this legislation was influenced by policy research.

How Competition Between Ordinary Knowledge and Policy Research Has Affected Legislation

In most areas of congressional activity, legislation is an amalgam of the two streams of knowledge. A perceived problem typically prompts congressional action. Policy researchers may enrich Congress's understanding of the problem, but by itself policy research rarely carries the day in Congress. Researchers recognize this limitation on their influence when they claim that the role of analysis is to weed out the worst alternatives, leaving to political actors the task of selecting among the satisfactory options.

One day's problem is another day's solution, and vice versa. In the 1970s many Americans felt cheated by a regulatory apparatus that made it difficult for airlines to establish new routes. This ordinary knowledge was reinforced by policy researchers, who provided strong arguments that competition would increase, service improve, and fares drop if airlines were deregulated. By the late 1980s many Americans believed that a lack of competition was driving up airfares and compelling them to fly through congested hubs. Policy researchers will undoubtedly have something to say on this subject if Congress decides to review airline deregulation. Whether they have as much influence this time will depend to a considerable degree on whether their advice is in accordance with ordinary knowledge.

In this section I examine the interplay of ordinary knowledge and policy research in several legislative actions of the 1980s. The case studies are brief and do not consider all factors impinging on congressional action. Their purpose is to suggest that the relation between the two kinds of knowledge takes various forms. Four kinds of action are reviewed here:

program termination, retention, enhancement, and reform. I shall examine one program in each of the categories. The four programs are public service employment (PSE), food stamps, Medicaid, and Aid to Families with Dependent Children (AFDC). They share a common objective of assisting low-income persons, but they have fared differently in the legislative process.

Program Termination

The conventional wisdom is that once a program is established, it remains in the federal budget forever. The reality is somewhat different, however; Congress occasionally abolishes programs. The roster of programs terminated in the 1980s included PSE, urban development action grants, and revenue sharing. Although terminations are exceptional, they shed light on the interaction of policy research and ordinary knowledge. I will concentrate on the first of these programs, PSE. When Congress acted, a formidable body of evaluative data was available.

Why PSE? The simple answer is that Ronald Reagan wanted the program eliminated. But he also wanted Congress to terminate dozens of other federal programs, which survived the budget axe. In fact, Reagan's final budget, submitted to Congress in January 1989, proposed the termination of more than eighty federal programs. Most of those proposals had been made in previous Reagan budgets but were ignored by Congress.

The likelihood of a program being abolished is greatly strengthened if ordinary knowledge and policy research render similar verdicts. When the two forms of knowledge diverge, a program can have remarkable staying power. The food stamp program, discussed shortly, is an example of just this divergence.

PSE began in the mid-1970s as a countercyclical program to provide the unemployed with jobs and training. As it evolved, PSE emphasized the hard-core unemployed, persons who would not otherwise get jobs. The expectation was that by giving these persons work experience and training, PSE would equip them with the skills to make it on their own. Although PSE was part of the Comprehensive Employment and Training Act (CETA), the training component was not adequately funded and almost all PSE dollars went for the salaries of those employed by the program.

The ordinary knowledge of PSE made it an easy target for Reagan's claim that it provided dead-end jobs rather than meaningful employment. There were news stories of persons paid for make-work such as leaf raking and accounts of individuals getting PSE jobs through political connections.

The unions were wary of PSE because of concern that it took jobs from their workers and depressed wage levels. Local governments liked PSE at the start, but their enthusiasm diminished when eligibility standards were tightened to discourage substitution of PSE workers for regular municipal employees. Franklin and Ripley reported that "it became conventional wisdom by the late 1970s that PSE was wasteful." [12]

Researchers had a somewhat more positive view of the program, but they too were hard-pressed to defend it. The direct cost of each PSE participant was much higher than for any other CETA program—$8,000 per PSE participant in 1976, compared to only $2,600 for on-the-job training and $1,400 for classroom training.[13] Researchers found that PSE had "probably not been cost effective. This provides support for the Reagan administration's position that federal funds should be spent on training rather than employment." [14] PSE was caught in a political vise. To prevent alleged abuses, the program targeted economically disadvantaged persons. In 1976, 45 percent of the participants were from this group; by 1980, 93 percent were drawn from this segment of the population. Rather than enhancing support for PSE, however, this change had the opposite effect. Hard-core disadvantaged persons had a difficult time "graduating" from the program and getting their own jobs. With "the enrollment of persons who were less competitive in the job market . . . placement rates declined between 1978 and 1980." [15] Although part of the difficulty in placing PSE enrollees was due to a deteriorating economy, support for the program was undermined and PSE was terminated.

Program Retention

PSE was not the only federal program facing budget pressures and adverse public opinion in the early 1980s. Food stamps also came under attack, but the outcome was different from that of PSE.

The food stamp program is expensive and reaches many more persons than PSE ever did. When Reagan took office in 1981, the food stamp program provided approximately nineteen million persons with benefits at an annual cost of more than $10 billion. Because it is among the most visible federal programs—shoppers at a checkout counter can readily notice others paying with food stamps—the program has long been the butt of countless stories of fraud and abuse. One popular version is of shoppers buying dog food with food stamps; another is of them purchasing steaks; a third is of well-dressed individuals wheeling grocery carts to their late-model cars. Although the details differ, the various versions share a sense of disapproval, that undeserving persons are ripping off the government at the expense of hard-working taxpayers.

Policy research added some blows of its own. It seems that food stamps, which were ostensibly established to enrich the nutrition of low-income persons, do not do much for nutritional quality.[16] Despite the bad press and negative findings, the food stamp program survived. The main reason is undoubtedly political. The program is usually considered as part of omnibus farm legislation. Logrolling representatives from farm areas and urban centers put together deals in which the former get price supports and the latter get food stamps.[17] This is not the whole story, however. Although the food stamp program gets relatively low marks as a nutritional program, it gets very high grades from policy researchers, who view it as an income-support program. Many researchers regard food stamps as the closest thing the United States has to a universal income-support program. Approximately twice as many people benefit from food stamps as from AFDC. When the purchase requirement was removed in 1977, the character of food stamps as an income-transfer program became more apparent. The food stamp program has a number of strengths as an income prop. Benefit and eligibility rules are, unlike AFDC, uniform throughout the country, and the program is available to all persons who meet the income and asset criteria; the program is highly sensitive to changes in the economic circumstance of recipients; and it is effectively targeted to the very poor. In the early 1980s more than 90 percent of the households receiving food stamp benefits had gross incomes below the poverty level. None of these benefits went to households with incomes in excess of 125 percent of the poverty level.[18]

The food stamp program presents a clash between ordinary knowledge and policy research. In preserving the program, members of Congress have heeded research findings, but they have not been able to ignore outcries that the program is rife with waste and fraud. In response to complaints, they tightened eligibility requirements and enacted legislation requiring the Department of Agriculture to penalize states that have error rates above a certain target.[19] In this way, members have protected a successful program while trimming costs slightly and demonstrating that they are doing something about the perceived fraud.

Program Enhancement

During expansionary periods, such as the Great Society boom in the 1960s, Congress does not need much inducement to initiate or expand programs. When budgetary stress sets in, however, and the emphasis is on conserving resources, Congress is aware that spending to enhance some programs will require it to make offsetting cuts in others. For this reason, not many program increases were voted during the 1980s. But a few expansions occurred, and Medicaid was one of the more notable ones.

Like PSE and food stamps, Medicaid is targeted at low-income persons and was cut back during Reagan's first year as president. Because of the way Medicaid operates, the cuts were not due principally to adverse ordinary or policy research knowledge but to changes in eligibility for AFDC. (Approximately 80 percent of Medicaid beneficiaries are eligible by virtue of their participation in AFDC or Supplemental Security Insurance. Hence, restrictions on AFDC eligibility, especially for the working poor, automatically removed a substantial number of persons from the Medicaid rolls.)

The ordinary knowledge of Medicaid has generally been more favorable than that of PSE and food stamps. Stories of Medicaid "mills" have made the rounds, but most of the bad press has been directed at providers ripping off the program, not at recipients. A patient using Medicaid in a crowded emergency room does not have as much notoriety as a shopper using food stamps in a crowded supermarket.

During the 1980s the public appreciation of Medicaid improved. Stories of children living in poverty undoubtedly had an effect, as did growing awareness that approximately 15 percent of the population was without medical insurance all or part of the year. Concern about the fairness of the Reagan revolution and its effect on vulnerable groups translated into more favorable attitudes toward Medicaid. In 1987, 61 percent of those surveyed in a *Washington Post*/ABC News poll favored an increase in Medicaid spending, compared with 44 percent six years earlier. Only 6 percent thought that Medicaid spending should be decreased.[20]

Policy research contributed directly to this upturn in public opinion. One contribution was identifying the uninsured population and finding out why individuals were not covered. Another was analyzing changes in Medicaid and showing that a growing percentage of children living in poverty were not covered by Medicaid. A comprehensive evaluation of Medicaid by a team of sixty researchers from eleven institutions gathered compelling evidence of critical gaps and deterioration in Medicaid protection. One finding was that in 1978 more than 980 children received Medicaid assistance for every 1,000 children in poverty; the number had declined to about 735 children for every 1,000 children in poverty by 1983.[21] Another finding was that only 35 percent of the poor children living in two-parent families were enrolled in Medicaid. The erosion in coverage meant that "although poor families and children make up a growing proportion of the poverty population, the proportion of Medicaid resources directed to poor families and children . . . [was] declining." [22]

Despite these findings, Medicaid was being injured by AFDC's unfavorable image. The solution devised by Congress was to enhance Medicaid protection by allowing states to sever the eligibility ties between it and AFDC. In a series of enactments, mostly reconciliation bills in the late 1980s, Congress extended Medicaid coverage to low-income pregnant women and children who were not eligible for AFDC. In this way, the ordinary knowledge that tainted AFDC no longer impeded Congress from responding to the needs identified in policy research.

Program Reform

Genuine reform is rare in American politics because it is redistributive. Some interest groups are made better off when important characteristics of a program are changed; others are made worse off. Reform is most likely when there is consensus on what is awry and what should be done to correct the situation. The consensus has to operate at both levels of knowledge discussed in this paper.

One would think AFDC to have been among the least appropriate candidates for successful reform. It is welfare, the program that Americans have in mind when they rail against welfare cheats and others who avoid work by living off the public dole. There was growing dissent in the research community as to whether public assistance was an effective response to those in need. A coterie of conservative scholars, led by Charles Murray, vigorously argued that welfare (which they took to mean the whole gamut of assistance to low-income persons, not just AFDC) operated to the detriment of those it purported to benefit.[23] AFDC's low esteem was reflected in the fact that it was left off the list when other programs (such as aid to the disabled, blind, and elderly poor) were federalized. The federal government permitted AFDC payments to be as low as states were willing to make them.

Like seventeen-year cicadas, welfare reform emerged in the mid-1980s after a long period underground. The previous major effort—Richard Nixon's family assistance plan (FAP)—had come to naught in the early 1980s. It had foundered on deep divisions between liberals and conservatives over benefits and other issues. The outcome was different in 1988, however, the year that Congress passed welfare reform legislation. This measure and the route it took to enactment were complicated, and the approved version fell considerably short of what reformers had in mind when they launched the effort. What concerns the discussion here are not the details of the legislation but how welfare managed to overcome adverse public opinion and disagreement among policy researchers to build a consensus for reform.

Public opinion on welfare (and other poverty programs) is a maze of ambivalent and often conflicting attitudes. Americans generally believe that government should aid those in need, but they also believe that many of those receiving assistance are malingerers. These perceptions have made proposals combining work and welfare politically attractive. The work component satisfies public opinion that welfare recipients should be assisted only to the extent (if they are able) that they are productive. In the first half of the 1980s many states, acting under authority provided by Congress, established work-welfare programs. As these experiments progressed, they were closely evaluated by policy researchers, who generally found them to be effective in upgrading the skills and the labor market experiences of participants. These findings narrowed the policy gap between liberals for whom mandatory work was anathema and conservatives for whom welfare was an invasion of individual responsibility.

Policy researchers transformed work from an ideological issue into a practical question: For which part of the welfare population was work an appropriate requirement? Researchers contributed to policy consensus in still other ways. Pioneering studies by Ellwood and Bane found that welfare recipients were divided between two very different groups: those who had inadequate income and were typically on welfare for a brief period of time and those who had a wide range of social deficiencies and were usually on welfare for an extended period.[24]

In the second half of the 1980s a remarkable policy consensus formed around the distinction between those who were "income dependent" and those who were "behavior dependent." [25] A series of wide-ranging reports "revealed a surprising degree of consensus," Robert Reischauer found. "Liberals, moderates, and conservatives generally agreed about what is wrong with the current welfare system and what general directions reform should take. This consensus . . . has allowed Congress to move forward with reform legislation." [26]

As things turned out, the consensus was little more than a veneer that masked longstanding policy rifts. Old fissures opened as the measure moved through Congress, and the enacted legislation delivered much less reform than had been hoped for.[27]

The Interaction Between Ordinary Knowledge and Policy Research

In each of the four cases outlined in this paper, Congress responded to both kinds of knowledge. It terminated PSE, which had an unfavorable public image; it retained food stamps but took modest steps to curtail fraud and abuse; it enhanced Medicaid when public opinion supported that move; and it sought to meld work and welfare in correspondence with the prevailing view that recipients should be made to contribute to society.

Congressional action also made substantial use of policy research in each of the cases. Researchers found PSE to be less cost-effective than other job-training approaches; they rated food stamps as highly effective in reaching the needy population; they identified widening gaps in Medicaid protection for low-income mothers and children; and they gained fresh insights into the problems and characteristics of those on welfare.

As oversimplified as the cases undoubtedly are, they suggest that policy action depends on a convergence of ordinary knowledge and research. The two streams of knowledge do not have to be in perfect harmony—they are not in the case of food stamps—but Congress has to accommodate both streams when it acts.

Policy Research in the Service of Ordinary Knowledge

The cases discussed in the previous section suggest that policy research is not cordoned off from ordinary knowledge. Ideas flow from the one into the other. In the 1980s Americans became increasingly aware of big holes in medical insurance. Was it because more of them experienced situations in which they lacked coverage, or was it because research, filtered through the media and other intermediaries, reported on the more than thirty-five million Americans lacking protection? Probably both forces were at work.

Social science researchers differ in the extent to which they play to a public audience. Some seek opportunities to write op-ed pieces or to appear on talk shows. Others prefer to let their work speak for itself. Yet the very business of social science is one of dealing with everyday behavior. Relevance can never be far away for those studying public policy.

In view of the importance of policy research to the quality of public programs, it would not be untoward to suggest that the scope of this research be broadened to make it easily usable by elected policymakers. The two modest ideas I offer in this concluding section owe more to my conviction that the terms of research are unduly parochial than to any convincing evidence that if it were broadened research would be more appreciated. The first suggestion is that research be qualitatively concerned with the sequencing of events and with the plain facts that every policy has a past and that the past influences both what is now and what might be. The second suggestion is that policy research give greater prominence to the full range of the social sciences.

Policymakers and policy researchers treat the past and the future differently. Their methods impel analysts to write off the past and to discount the future. All that matters are the decisions to be made today and the present value of those decisions.

The concept of "sunk" costs—costs that have already been incurred—reflects the analytic treatment of the past. Researchers are taught to ignore sunk costs and to take into account only the opportunity to use new resources. Ordinary knowledge is a stream of thought that flows from the past to the present. Today's attitudes depend on what was experienced yesterday. What we "know" about the poor depends, for example, on the attitudes formed when we were growing up, ideas filtered through the media, and the like. Politicians have a similar respect for the past. For them, sunk costs are an important, often decisive, influence. If a facility has been built, they deem it prudent to authorize additional funds so that it may be operated.

The more researchers delve into today's problems, the more they are driven to recognize the heavy hand of the past. The critical distinction in poverty research between those who lack adequate income and those who lack a broad range of social capacities reflects this trend. When poverty was viewed predominantly as an inadequacy of income, the past could be ignored and attention directed to ways of providing supplemental resources. Now that hard-core poverty is viewed as a behavioral problem, we cannot ignore past developments that led to the problem. Broken homes, teen-age pregnancy, lack of basic education, school drop-out rates—all are failures that occurred before young people were added to the welfare rolls. To assist these youths in gaining independence, we must know from where they came.

To avert a transmission of dependency to the next generation, policy-makers might want to intervene through enrichment activities in early childhood programs. The present value of preschool assistance is small indeed if the measurable benefits do not accrue until the child nears adulthood. Yet ordinary knowledge tells us that if we fail to educate the pre-schooler, we may forgo the opportunity to do so in the future. Ordinary knowledge looks at the future as dependent on current policy; researchers look at current policy as dependent on future return.

Discounting is part of an approach to research oriented to economics. Despite the influences of political, sociological, psychological, and other social forces, too much attention is still paid to economic and related quantitative factors. This bias is reflected in the hold that "random assignment" has as the method of choice for the study of policy interventions by government. Whatever its considerable virtue in fostering objective research, random assignment strips the "subject" from the institutional environment in which the policy intervention occurs. These considerations are often decisive in determining the efficacy of the policy. The ways in which a school is managed—the classroom setting, the motivation of teachers, the role of the principal, the situation in the corridors—are among the institutional arrangements that spell the difference between educational success and failure. This research finding will come as no surprise to adults who recall their own student days.

Policy researchers would do well to model the ways ordinary knowledge accumulates. They should do this not because conventional wisdom is right—it often is not—but because an understanding of this kind would enrich the value that research adds to society.

NOTES

1. Charles E. Lindblom and David K. Cohen, *Usable Knowledge: Social Science and Social Problem Solving* (New Haven: Yale University Press, 1979), 12. Lindblom and Cohen also refer to "professional social inquiry," which has some affinity to what is labeled "policy research" in this paper.

2. Among its many provisions, the omnibus drug bill enacted in 1988 authorized more than $1 billion for drug abuse treatment and prevention and more than $400 million for education. In addition to these "demand side" provisions, the legislation sought interdiction of supply through cooperative efforts with other countries, strengthened law

enforcement and detection, and imposition of the death penalty for certain suppliers.

3. Allen Schick, "The Supply and Demand for Policy Analysis on Capitol Hill," *Policy Analysis* 2 (Spring 1976): 215–234.

4. The National Academy of Sciences identified $1.8 billion spent on social knowledge production and application in 1976. See Richard P. Nathan, *Social Science in Government: Uses and Misuses* (New York: Basic Books, 1988), 188–189.

5. See Nathan, ibid., chap. 5, and, among other reports, Barbara Goldman et al., *California: The Demonstration of State Work/Welfare Initiatives: Final Report* (New York: Manpower Demonstration Research Corporation, February 1986).

6. The early volumes in the Changing Domestic Priorities series, published by the Urban Institute, Washington, D.C., include John L. Palmer and Isabel V. Sawhill, eds., *The Reagan Experiment* (1982) and *The Reagan Record* (1984). Later publications include John L. Palmer, Timothy Smeeding, and Barbara Boyle Torrey, eds., *The Vulnerable* (1988) and Andrew J. Cherlin, ed., *The Changing American Family and Social Policy* (1988).

7. Norman J. Ornstein, Thomas E. Mann, and Michael J. Malbin, *Vital Statistics on Congress, 1989–1990* (Washington, D.C.: Congressional Quarterly, 1990), tables 5–3 and 5–4.

8. Ibid., table 6–9.

9. The reconciliation procedures are explained in Allen Schick, *Reconciliation and the Congressional Budget Process* (Washington, D.C.: American Enterprise Institute, 1981).

10. See Allen Schick, *The Whole and the Parts: Piecemeal and Integrated Approaches to Congressional Budgeting*, prepared for the House Committee on the Budget, 100th Cong., 1st sess. (Washington, D.C.: U.S. Government Printing Office, 1987).

11. Ornstein, *Vital Statistics*, tables 6–1 and 6–2.

12. Grace A. Franklin and Randall B. Ripley, *CETA: Politics and Policy* (Knoxville: University of Tennessee Press, 1984), 209.

13. See Laurie J. Bassi, *CETA—Has It Worked?* (Washington, D.C.: Urban Institute, June 1982), 15.

14. Ibid., 3.

15. William Mirengoff et al., *CETA—Accomplishments, Problems, Solutions* (Kalamazoo, Mich.: Upjohn Institute for Employment Research, 1982), xv.

16. J. S. Butler and Jennie Raymond, *Knowledge Is Better Than Money: The Effect of the Food Stamp Program on Nutrient Intake* (Madison: University of Wisconsin, Institute for Research on Poverty, January 1987).

17. See John Ferejohn, "Congress and Redistribution," in *Making Economic Policy in Congress*, ed. Allen Schick (Washington, D.C.: American Enterprise Institute, 1983), 131–157.

18. See *The Effects of Legislative Changes in 1981 and 1982 on the Food Stamp Program* (Washington, D.C.: Urban Institute, May 1985), 28.

19. U.S. General Accounting Office, *Food Stamp Program: Refinements Needed to Improve Accuracy of Quality Control Error Rates*, Washington, D.C., September 1986.

20. *Washington Post*, January 27, 1987, A4.

21. Department of Health and Human Services, Health Care Financing Administration,

Medicaid Program Evaluation: Final Report, Washington, D.C., December 1987, III-16.

22. Ibid., III-29.

23. Charles A. Murray, *Losing Ground: American Social Policy, 1950–1980* (New York: Basic Books, 1984).

24. David Ellwood and Mary Jo Bane, *Slipping Into and Out of Poverty* (Cambridge, Mass.: National Bureau of Economic Research, 1983).

25. See the Working Seminar on Family and American Welfare Policy, *The New Consensus on Family and Welfare* (Washington, D.C.: American Enterprise Institute, 1987).

26. Robert D. Reischauer, "Welfare Reform: Will Consensus Be Enough?" *Brookings Review* 5 (Summer 1987): 4.

27. The breakup of the consensus is discussed in Robert D. Reischauer, "The Welfare Reform Legislation: Directions for the Future," in *Reforming Welfare Policy,* ed. Phoebe Cottingham and David Ellwood (Cambridge: Harvard University Press, 1989).

Comment

Carol H. Weiss

Information comes streaming into Congress—from FBI reports, constituent complaints, and special pleadings of interest groups. But, as Allen Schick observes, the big change in the past ten or fifteen years is that an increasing amount of the information that reaches Congress is policy research.

I agree with Schick that the news media are one of the channels through which policy research flows. In an investigation of media coverage of social science, I found that the media give a high level of attention to social science research, particularly to issues on the public agenda.[1] Some news stories report the release of a new study and describe the findings. Other stories cover current events, such as congressional action on welfare reform, and bring in research findings to illuminate the discussion. A third kind of story does not refer to research findings but quotes a social scientist. Quoting a political scientist or economist has become a well-established way to bring in a different point of view, to enlarge the discussion, or to legitimate a perspective.

The media are becoming an important avenue by which ideas from research reach members of Congress. Members and staff tend to pay particular attention to the media, because the media serve Congress as a proxy for public opinion. The media serve other functions, too. They are the "house organ" for government, telling appointed officials, bureaucrats, and legislators who is doing what and what each of them is trying to get on the agenda. Congressional offices carefully screen the media, and when policy research findings turn up, they take notice.

Schick says that interest groups convey policy research to Congress. That certainly was true in a study I did of congressional subcommittees.[2] Some subcommittee staff rely heavily on interest groups for information, and almost all of them listen to lobbyists as part of the job. There is nothing very new in that. What is new is that lobbyists increasingly support their policy claims with data. A convincing argument is no longer good enough; now an argument requires research evidence as warrant. To make their cases, competing interest groups each advance their own arguments,

with the accompanying research and analytic support. In the process committee members and staff are exposed to a variety of research information.

Members of Congress often seem to prefer to obtain their research
from interest groups rather than from "objective" policy researchers. They
doubt that any researchers are really objective; they suspect that everyone
has a political bent and a political axe to grind. With academic analysts,
they do not know what values are being advanced and therefore do not
know how to compensate for them. With lobbyists, they know precisely
what position is being promoted, and they can judge what "correction
factor" to apply.

When members of Congress and staff hear about policy research from
lobbyists, they know it is relevant. It has already been interpreted, merged
with politics, and applied to legislative provisions. It is directly linked to
measures before the committee. This is policy research in its shirt sleeves,
ready to get down to business.

Of course, the research and analysis that come in from different sources
are inconsistent, sometimes even contradictory. Since each lobby highlights
information that supports its own cause, discrepancies abound. To sort
out the rival claims, members will occasionally ask for an independent
judgment from a neutral body, such as the National Academy of Sciences
or the Congressional Research Service. Sometimes they will question all
the claimants, asking each group to comment on the evidence supplied
by others. Often they will sift through the evidence themselves. As experienced politicians, they believe they understand each group's biases.
Their usual premise is that all sides exaggerate and that the truth lies
somewhere in between. They try to ferret out enough about the strengths
and weaknesses of each side's arguments to get a good purchase on the
situation. One subcommittee staff member said, "The political process
tries to get at the truth, if we have time, by sorting through the claims
and counterclaims.... [A]s long as you have liberals and conservatives
and some sort of balance, you can generally get at the truth." And that
is the basis on which many staff and members operate.

The thrust of Allen Schick's argument is that policy research and ordinary knowledge compete in the legislative process. His examples are
illuminating, but the competition he discusses is only part of the story.
The main competition is between policy research and political interests.
We all know that political interests matter. Schick discussed their importance in a 1976 paper.[3] Whatever the new-found salience of policy analysis,
we should not lose sight of the primacy of politics. Members are elected

to Congress to represent their constituents, to mediate the interests of lobbies and groups, and to follow the ideological proclivities that appealed to the voters in the first place. They are not in Congress simply to follow the direction implied by the latest policy study.

In fact, policy research can seem fundamentally dangerous. Edward Banfield thought it was dangerous because it keeps turning up new problems for government to solve, thus fostering increased government intrusions into daily life.[4] On the other hand, Henry Aaron thought that policy research has conservative effects. Because it demonstrates how little is really understood about the causes and solutions of social problems, it slows down efforts at reform.[5] Some analysts of government programs think there is a potential danger in showing how little most programs achieve, because the news might discourage Congress from further initiatives. But there is another danger. Policy research can be dangerous to the extent that it purports to provide one right answer to a problem—or people believe that it does. Believing that one has the single right answer can promote a hardening of positions and thus make compromise difficult. For a legislative body whose mission is to negotiate among diverse interests and values and reach accommodations, policy research has costs as well as benefits.

Schick concentrates on the relatively new element on Capitol Hill, the increasing receptivity to policy research, rather than the obvious fact that politics dominates. Although values and interests are the essence of congressional action, members of Congress now recognize that government is more and more complicated and that they need good information to see that the right things are accomplished and the wrong things avoided. They need research and policy analysis to help them translate their values and interests into the outcomes they desire.

Members of Congress and their staffs, particularly those on authorizing subcommittees, use policy research and analysis in four main ways. First, they use it to support their existing policy positions. When they find data that agree with what they want to do, they can use the data to reinforce their sense that what they are proposing is right and to convince supporters that they are on the side of good and reason. They use research findings to attack their opponents' case and to persuade waverers to come over to their side. The effect of using research can be to mobilize and strengthen their coalition.

A second use of policy research is to serve as warning. Policy research can show that a situation is worsening. More children are in poverty; AIDS cases are multiplying; high-tech computer companies are losing out to foreign competition. Similarly, evaluations of existing programs can show that current efforts are having little effect on the problems that they were meant to solve. Certain tax write-offs are not stimulating investment; job training programs are not getting the chronically unemployed into jobs. Such research signals that a problem needs attention, and members can use the findings to advance the issue on the congressional agenda.

A third use of policy research is to provide guidance for action. Analysis demonstrating that one strategy works better than another can provide direction for specific provisions that should be adopted. Evaluations that identify successful programs can provide guidance for the kinds of activities to be funded. When members use policy research as guidance, they incorporate this kind of information into legislative provisions and amendments.

A fourth use is to confer enlightenment. Research provides not so much direct advice for action as new ways of thinking about an issue. Research offers new constructs, a new frame within which to consider the problem. As the ideas from research come into currency, they can alter the ways in which people formulate the questions: what aspects they see as fixed and inevitable and what aspects they see as amenable to change. Research can settle some points that people used to argue about and raise the level of discussion about remaining uncertainties. Above all, it can recast the parameters of policy debate. People need not do anything different at the time, but they address the issue in different terms.

In the study of congressional subcommittees, I found that the most common use of policy research was to support preexisting positions.[6] This was not always a matter of staff members digging into research reports for a few supportive nuggets to use as evidence. Sometimes it was a sophisticated ploy, with research leading to extension, fine-tuning, and revision of elements of legislation to make it better fit the situation as revealed.

The second most common use was to attend to the warnings that research displayed. When research, statistics, and evaluations signaled that a situation was deteriorating or that current activities were making insufficient headway, committees took note.

Third in frequency was the use of research to provide guidance. This was not guidance in the sense of what goals or broad directions to pursue; it was more likely to concern detailed provisions, such as eligibility criteria or formulas for disbursement of funds. In several cases, however, research gave direction for important measures, such as cost-containment schemes in health care. Sometimes the guidance was negative guidance: research suggested the avoidance of a strategy that most people until then had favored.

Least often mentioned was the use of research to reconceptualize issues, the use I call enlightenment. In studies of executive branch agencies, enlightenment was commonly cited, but on Capitol Hill the reformulation of policy issues seemed to take place off-stage and at some remove, almost as an echo of debates waged in other arenas. The reason may be that recent Congresses have met in times of financial duress, and few new legislative initiatives are being considered. Without the money to mount new programs, there is little call for rethinking the contours of policy issues. Furthermore, Congress seems to absorb much of its policy research in predigested gobbets. The package that Congress considers is often a policy prescription into which research ideas have already been incorporated. Congress ingests the new ideas without recognizing their provenance in policy research. Important conceptual shifts have taken place over the past several Congresses, but even when the ideas have come from policy research, few people in Congress seem to identify research as the source.

Three aspects of the current state of affairs are most interesting. First, more well-trained professionals, with enough analytic training to understand and want policy research, work on congressional staffs than ever before. A host of fellowship programs bring trained people to Washington to serve a year in Congress, and many fellows stay on. Some have come from the support agencies. Some are graduates of schools of public policy. So there is a growing audience for policy research, particularly on committee and subcommittee staffs. Second, analysts working for Congress are more savvy about anticipating problems of interest to Congress and, later, in presenting information in ways that make sense to the congressional audience. The fit with Congress's needs seems to be improving. But third, the deluge of research information has overwhelmed Congress's capacity for screening and interpreting data. Information overload is a mild term. With all the new technologies of information transfer, research often manages to get through and be heard. The big task for Congress, however, is to interpret it responsibly.

The congressional support agencies can help, but they have to maintain a politically neutral position. Many outsiders are eager to lend a hand, but they often have special causes to promote. Interpreting and applying policy research to politically charged issues are tasks that members and staff are reluctant to delegate to anyone else; those tasks are truly their responsibility. For all the recent improvements in the relevance of policy research to Congress's problems, its dissemination to appropriate users, and Congress's receptivity to its messages, this block remains. Congress's internal capacity to review research critically and to interpret its implications has not caught up with demand.

NOTES

1. Carol H. Weiss and Eleanor Singer, with Phyllis Endreny, *Reporting of Social Science in the National Media* (New York: Russell Sage), 1988.
2. Carol H. Weiss, "Congressional Committees as Users of Analysis," *Journal of Policy Analysis and Management* 8 (Summer 1989): 411–431.
3. See Allen Schick, "The Supply and Demand for Policy Analysis on Capitol Hill," *Policy Analysis* 2 (Spring 1976): 215–234.
4. Edward C. Banfield, "Policy Science as Metaphysical Madness" in *Bureaucrats, Policy Analysts, Statesmen: Who Leads?* ed. R. A. Goldwin (Washington, D.C.: American Enterprise Institute, 1980), 1–19.
5. Henry J. Aaron, *Politics and the Professors: The Great Society in Perspective* (Washington, D.C.: Brookings Institution, 1978).
6. Weiss, "Congressional Committees."

Comment

David E. Price

Allen Schick's opening observation is a pertinent one: In Congress we know more about problems than about results. We know more about our intentions than about the effect of what we do. In part, that is because it is more difficult to get and to analyze information about results and effects than about problems and intentions. In part, it is because the political incentives to get information about results are far weaker, as David Mayhew pointed out years ago in his essay on Congress's "electoral connection." [1]

Schick's distinction between policy research and ordinary knowledge is useful as far as it goes. Although these two categories are not necessarily exhaustive, his arguments about the advantages of ordinary knowledge in the policy arena are persuasive.

In many other works Schick has stressed that the terms of policy debate in the United States have been narrowed since the beginning of the 1980s. [2] Substantive issues have been crowded out, and budget and fiscal issues have become the main focus. The evidence for what he calls the "fiscalization" of policy debate abounds. He might have mentioned the irony of this situation, given the analytic aims of those who instituted the budget process in the 1970s and who put the Congressional Budget Office in place.

Schick convincingly describes the dependence of policy action on the convergence of ordinary knowledge and research. Welfare reform is a good example. The bill enacted in 1988 to strengthen the work component in welfare assistance represented a convergence of conservative and liberal ideology in certain respects, but it also reflected a convergence of ordinary knowledge and values with the conclusions of policy research. Other good examples come to mind: the WIC supplemental food program for women, infants, and children and the Head Start program. Politicians on the stump sometimes say about these kinds of programs, "Even if I cared about nothing but the economic bottom line I would back these programs; they more than pay for themselves." Programs, such as these, that most people support out of compassion or a sense of social responsibility also demonstrate a sound bottom line. Policy analysis feeds effectively into the more eclectic kinds of arguments used in defending those efforts.

Schick rightly emphasizes the need for a broadened approach to policy research. He is correct in suggesting that historical, psychological, sociological, and political perspectives can usefully be added to the economic modes of analysis that generally prevail. When public policy programs were founded in our universities in the 1970s, policy analysis generally meant economic analysis. Belatedly, we have realized that the historical analysis of public policy has much to contribute and that policy analysis should incorporate other social sciences.

The main objection I have to Schick's dichotomization of knowledge is that it leaves much out. The kind of knowledge that members of Congress are most familiar with, as they operate day to day, does not neatly fit into the categories that he has conceived. A major body of knowledge with which members are concerned comprises the needs and interests of particular groups and communities; it incorporates knowledge about the effects of existing and prospective policies on those groups and communities. This particularistic knowledge is not "ordinary" in the sense of being common-sensical or universally shared. It is usually not the product of careful, objective, systematic research. But this particularistic knowledge is more than just an unreflective expression of interest: it has content; it puts forth claims and arguments; it is what representatives typically encounter as we meet with various groups in our offices each day.

Schick's point is still valid, however, even if the categories are more complicated than he suggests. The mutual reinforcement of various modes of knowledge is a potent force, and members of Congress understand this very well. Particularistic appeals are frequently combined with the invocation of broader themes and values and with more systematic claims of public benefit.

A good example from my experience is the House Banking Committee's debate in 1988 of the expansion of bank powers, which included the repeal of the Glass-Steagall Act and the rationalization of banking regulation. The argument for expanded powers was much stronger when it was expressed not only in terms of bank interests but in broader terms of public benefit—the lowered cost of capital, for example, and the well-being of various regions of the country that could have expected new sources of capital from this kind of expansion. The public interest argument was strengthened by impressive studies such as that of Gerald Corrigan, head of the New York Federal Reserve.[3]

The initiative to expand bank powers is perhaps not the best example because in the end it fell victim to a clash of jurisdictional claims on Capitol Hill and to contending interests in the financial community (and thus is back on the agenda in the 102d Congress). It is still true, however, that the case for legislation of this kind, particularly complex legislation that entails severe conflict, is far stronger if the various modes of knowledge can be effectively combined than if they do not converge.

Schick mentions lobbyists as another source of information. When I think about effective lobbyists, I do not think of people who simply tell me what they want and ask where I stand. Rather, I think of those who appreciate my position, who are able to talk about the intersection between their perspective and the broader issues that I must consider. In other words lobbyists, too, need to go beyond the particular and combine different modes of argument.

Finally, I want to suggest some ways that these categories of knowledge apply to congressional operations. How, we might ask, is ordinary knowledge invoked? I think immediately of John Kingdon's work on congressional voting decisions and of Richard Fenno's study of how members of Congress relate to their constituencies.[4] Central to both studies is the concept of "explanation." Both Kingdon and Fenno looked very carefully at how members of Congress explain their votes and actions and how they calculate "what will fly" with their constituents. Members might cast a certain vote only when they are confident they can justify it in terms of widely held perceptions and values back home. Members must constantly explain themselves and their actions in terms of ordinary knowledge. A decision that does not lend itself to such an explanation often has a heavy burden of proof against it.

In the era of television journalism, of thirty-second ads and negative advertising, a *defensive* deference to ordinary knowledge has probably become more important in congressional behavior than it was before. Members have to consider whether the canons of ordinary knowledge furnish the context for an effective attack against them if they cast a certain vote or engage in a particular activity.

It would be useful also to consider how congressional staff use these different modes of knowledge and to look at their role in transmitting and combining them. The job of congressional staff members is to combine objective knowledge with policy entrepreneurship, drawing on policy research and combining this knowledge with an entrepreneurial search for policy gaps. They must stimulate initiatives that fill those gaps and, at the same time, fill the member's need for recognition at home and for enhanced stature within Congress. Schick argues persuasively that policy research should be deepened and broadened. The enduring challenge for members and their staffs is to translate that knowledge into serious and effective policy initiatives. This requires strategies to achieve convergence with the canons of ordinary knowledge and with the particularistic views of those who have a stake in the policy. It demands a willingness to push, to educate, and to expand the limits of political consensus. And it requires constant attentiveness to the realities of politics and power.

NOTES

1. David R. Mayhew, *Congress: The Electoral Connection* (New Haven: Yale University Press, 1974).
2. See, for example, Allen Schick, *Reconciliation and the Congressional Budget Process* (Washington, D.C.: American Enterprise Institute, 1981), 35.
3. Gerald Corrigan, *Financial Market Structure: A Longer View* (New York: Federal Reserve Bank of New York, 1987).
4. John Kingdon, *Congressmen's Voting Decisions*, 3d ed. (Ann Arbor: University of Michigan Press, 1989); Richard F. Fenno, Jr., *Home Style: House Members in Their Districts* (Boston: Little, Brown, 1978).

5. Rational Ignorance, Professional Research, and Politicians' Dilemmas

Mancur Olson

No analysis of the knowledge that grows out of scholarly research, and its relationship to political power, can be complete unless it faces up to a sad and inescapable reality: rational ignorance. This seemingly oxymoronic phrase, rational ignorance, is not a contradiction in terms. In some circumstances that are important for politics and government policy, the typical citizen serves his or her individual interests best by allocating relatively little time to the study of public affairs, even though this leaves the citizen ignorant of many matters that are important for the country.

The paradox becomes clear when one examines the situation of an average citizen who is deciding how much time to devote to studying the public policy choices facing the country. The more time the citizen spends studying public affairs, the greater the likelihood that a vote will be cast in favor of rational policies. The typical citizen will, however, receive only a small share of the gain from the more effective policies and leadership. In the aggregate, the other residents of the country will get almost all the gains, so the individual citizen has no incentive to devote much time to fact finding and to thinking about what would be best for the country. Each citizen would be better off if all citizens spent more time than they now spend finding out how to vote to make the country better serve their common interests.

This point is particularly evident in national elections. The gain to a voter from studying issues to determine the vote that is truly in his or her interest can be expressed as a formula: the gain is the difference in the value to the individual of the "right" election outcome, multiplied by the probability that a change in the individual's vote will alter the outcome of the election. Since the probability that a typical voter will change the outcome of the election is minuscule, the typical citizen, whether a physician or a taxi driver, is usually rationally ignorant about public affairs.

Occasionally, information about public affairs is so interesting or entertaining that it pays the citizen to acquire it for these reasons alone. Similarly, individuals in a few vocations can receive considerable rewards in private goods if they acquire exceptional knowledge of public goods. Politicians, lobbyists, journalists, and social scientists, for example, may earn more money, power, or prestige if they have more knowledge of public business relevant to their respective vocations. Sometimes exceptional knowledge of public policy can generate exceptional profits in stock exchanges or in other markets. Nevertheless, the typical citizen will usually find that his or her income and life chances will not be improved by the zealous study of public affairs or even of any single collective good.

This fact—that the benefits of individual enlightenment about public goods are usually dispersed throughout a group or a nation rather than concentrated upon the individual who bears the costs of becoming enlightened—explains many other phenomena as well. It explains, for example, the "man bites dog" criterion of what is newsworthy. If people watched television newscasts or read newspapers solely to obtain the most important information about public affairs, aberrant events of little importance would be ignored and patterns of quantitative significance would be emphasized. Since the news is, by contrast, for most people largely an alternative to other forms of entertainment, intriguing oddities and human-interest items are in demand. Similarly, the media fully cover sex scandals among public figures or events that unfold in a suspenseful way, whereas the complexities of economic policies or quantitative analyses of public problems receive only minimal attention. Public officials, often able to thrive without giving the citizens good value for their taxes, may fall from power because of an exceptional mistake that is simple and striking enough to be newsworthy. Extravagant statements, picturesque protests, and unruly demonstrations that offend much of the public are also explicable in this way: they make gripping news and thus call attention to interests and arguments that might otherwise be ignored. Even some acts of terrorism that are described as senseless can from this perspective be explained as effective means of riveting the attention of the public to demands about which it otherwise would remain rationally ignorant.

The Difficulties of Collective Action

The rational ignorance of the typical voter is an example of the general logic of collective action. This logic is readily evident when one considers organizations that lobby a government for special-interest legislation or that cooperate in the marketplace to raise prices or wages. Some examples are professional associations, labor unions, trade associations, farm organizations, and oligopolistic collusions.

To understand these organizations, one must be aware of the difficulty of collective action that arises because the benefits these groups win for their clients go automatically to everyone in some group or category. If an association of firms wins a tariff, the price will rise for every firm that sells the commodity or product in question, regardless of whether the firm contributed to the effort to win the tariff. Similarly, if one group of workers strikes to bring a higher wage in some factory or mine, all of the workers in the factory or mine will receive the benefit of the higher wage, regardless of whether they paid dues to the union or walked in the picket lines that made the strike successful. The same reasoning applies to the firms or workers in any kind of cartel.

Because the benefits of collective action go to everyone in a category or group, it is not rational for an individual to work voluntarily to obtain collective goods in the interest of his or her group or class, at least in large groups. The individual will get the benefits of whatever actions others undertake in any case, and, in large groups, the single individual or firm is not alone able to bring about the desired results.[1]

Individuals in large groups do not voluntarily, in the absence of special arrangements I will consider below, contribute time and money to organizations that would lobby or fix prices or wages for the same reason that the typical citizen remains rationally ignorant about many aspects of public affairs. An individual will receive only a minuscule share of the return, whether it is benefits from a group organized for collective action or gains from research about which way to vote.

In the case of large organizations that lobby or combine to fix prices or wages, there are special arrangements that explain why they are able to attract dues-paying members. In all large and lasting organizations for collective action there are always some special gimmicks, which I call "selective incentives," that account for most of the membership in these organizations.[2] The selective incentives are individualized benefits or punishments that induce firms or people to participate in or to help pay the costs of collective action. One example of a selective incentive is the element of compulsion inherent in the closed shop, the union shop, and the coercive picket line, but this is only the most obvious example. All large organizations for collective action that survive have some analogous arrangements. These arrangements are usually very subtle and often provide those who join and participate in the organization with individual benefits while denying these benefits to those who do not.

When the beneficiaries of collective action are few in number, members of the organization may voluntarily take rational action to obtain collective goods without selective incentives. To illustrate this, think of the small number of large firms in a relatively concentrated industry. If, say, three large firms of about the same size operate in an industry, each firm will tend to obtain about a third of the benefits of any action to get political favors or to raise prices for the industry. This third of the benefits will usually be a sufficient incentive for each firm to take considerable action in the interest of the industry. When the numbers in a group are small, each participant will also have a noticeable effect on how well the common interest of the small group is served; this will affect the likelihood that the others will contribute. Thus small groups will often bargain until all participants agree to act in the group interest. This organizational advantage of small groups, and particularly of small groups of large firms, has, as I will show, important implications for public policy.

Rational Ignorance Strengthens Ideologies

The rational ignorance of the typical citizen arising from the logic of collective action suggests that simple ideologies and political slogans will play a gargantuan role in political life. As Anthony Downs has explained, ideologies are in part substitutes for detailed research and sustained reflection about public affairs.[3] If a citizen subscribes to one of the familiar ideologies, he or she will have some guidance on how to vote and on what to say when engaged in political arguments. If it is not rational for the typical citizen to spend a lot of time doing research on public affairs, but a left-wing or right-wing ideology can be acquired at little or no cost, it is understandable that many people will let ideology play a large role in determining how they vote. The ideology will indicate, or at least will appear to indicate, what general policy or what political party is best for people in their category or social class. Clearly, most of the votes cast by ordinary citizens are greatly influenced by ideology (or by party affiliation, which usually amounts to much the same thing).

The rational ignorance of the typical citizen is not the only reason that ideology plays a large role in modern life. Some social scientists, journalists, and politicians, who have strong professional incentives to be particularly well informed about public affairs, are also highly ideological. There are apparently psychological attributes that make some people highly ideo-logical even when they are well informed. Although I will not examine these attributes in this paper, I suggest that they interact with the rational ignorance of the typical citizen to give the familiar ideologies and slogans an extraordinarily large role in modern society.

In this paper I will endeavor to show that "supply-side economics" and "industrial policy" are mainly outgrowths of right-wing and left-wing ideo-logies, respectively, and thus are also outgrowths of the typical citizen's rational ignorance about public affairs. To understand how supply-side economics and industrial policy became politically influential, one must first consider the right-wing and left-wing ideologies that inspired them.

Examining the Ideologies

The centerpiece of political debate today is the dispute over the proper role of the government, particularly the extent to which government ought to aid those of slender means. From the right, particularly the classical liberal, or laissez-faire, right, the main argument is that the growth of government intervention impairs economic performance and individual freedom and that overgenerous welfare-state programs have reduced the incentive of low-income people to work and to save. From the left the most common argument is that modern society must not be fearful of using the resources and plans of democratic government to ensure that the society develops in a desirable direction and particularly to ensure that compassionate provision is made for the needs of those for whom the market does not provide an adequate income. The ideological debate just described is commonplace not only in the United States but also in all other developed democracies as well. It attracts the serious attention of scholars as well as of politicians and journalists.

Given the overwhelming preoccupation with this ideological debate, it is surprising that little careful study has been given to the question of how well each side in the debate succeeds or fails in explaining economic performance in different countries and historical periods. If the right, or classical liberal, side of the argument is correct, we ought to find that societies that are growing most rapidly and have the highest per capita incomes are the ones in which the role of the government is the smallest and the redistribution of income in the direction of low-income people is the least. Conversely, if the left, or democratic socialist, side of the argument is correct, we ought to find the most impressive economic performance and the highest standard of living, at least for the poor, in the societies in which the role of government is relatively large and the redistribution of income to the poor is relatively generous. We can test the familiar ideologies by looking at changes across various historical periods when the role of government and the extent of income redistribution by government have differed.

David Smith is one of the few people to look at the evidence on this central debate of modern democratic societies.[4] In 1975 he looked at the percentages of the gross domestic product (GDP) that were spent or transferred by governments in developed democracies and tested the relation between this variable and the rate of economic growth in the society. As I see it, Smith found only a weak and questionable association. This association was a negative one—societies having a larger role for the government had a slower rate of growth. The relation was so fragile, however, that, if one omitted Japan—a special country in many ways—from the statistical test, the relationship disappeared. Japan has a smaller public sector and a faster rate of growth than the other major developed democracies, and it was largely responsible for the relationship Smith found.

Using somewhat more recent data than these, Erich Weede also found a negative relation between the share of national output taken by government in taxes and the rate of growth of per capita income. His results were also crucially dependent on observations of Japan.[5] Weede also tested whether a Socialist party in the government or in the governing coalition affected the rate of growth, but he found no statistically significant relationship.

In a major book entitled *Theories of Comparative Economic Growth,* Kwang Choi explored whether any relationship exists between the spending and transfer by government and the rate of economic growth, the level of investment, and some other variables.[6] He found no strong relationship between the role of government and the rate of economic growth.

One of the relatively few other studies on this issue is an article by Samuel Brittan, the distinguished economic journalist for the *Financial Times* of London. Brittan has been one of the most influential advocates of monetarism and free markets in the United Kingdom. As a visiting professor at the University of Chicago in 1978, he published an article on the "British disease," the slow economic growth of Great Britain.[7] He argued, no doubt to the surprise of most of those who share his general approach, that the surprisingly poor performance of the British economy during the years after World War II cannot be explained in terms of the role of the state in Great Britain or the extent of income redistribution to low-income people. The United Kingdom, compared with its European neighbors, Brittan pointed out, is not greatly different from the average of the European countries in the proportion of the nation's resources that are consumed by or handled by the government. In fact, the proportion is usually lower in Great Britain than in Holland, Sweden, Norway, and West Germany, but the latter countries have enjoyed a far better postwar economic performance than Great Britain has. This observation alone makes it unlikely that the role of government in Britain is the main explanation for its poor economic performance.

Brittan's case becomes still stronger when he considers the historical pattern. The British economy, he observed, began to fall behind the rates of growth of comparable European economies in the last two decades of the nineteenth century. This was the very time when Great Britain and the British empire had the closest thing to ideal laissez-faire government that the world had ever seen. The relatively slow British growth, I would add, continued through the interwar period and became all the more noticeable in the post-World War II years, when the United Kingdom was often under democratic socialist governments and the welfare state came into being. Great Britain, then, has grown relatively slowly under laissez-faire government and labor or democratic socialist government alike.

Periods of Economic Growth

In this section I look at the historical periods with very different rates of economic growth and then examine the relative size of government and the extent of income redistribution in each of these periods.

In the nineteenth century Great Britain, to some extent the United States, and to a lesser extent the European continent had policies that were closer to laissez faire and free trade than at any other time in human history. Great Britain and its huge empire followed not only laissez faire in domestic policy but also free trade. Apart from large subsidies to the railroads, the United States had something resembling laissez faire internally, although it certainly did not have free trade. Nor did many of the continental European countries. Yet, taking all the evidence together, the world as a whole in the nineteenth century came closer to laissez faire and free trade than it has at any other time. The nineteenth century was also a period of impressive economic performance. These facts, taken by themselves, argue on the side of the conservative or classical liberal argument that seeks to limit the role of the state and emphasizes the adverse effect of redistribution on the incentives to work and save.

The record in the interwar period was quite different from that before World War I. Although the period between World War I and World War II did not see the establishment of substantial welfare states—in general, that occurred after World War II—it saw an incomparably higher level of protectionism and economic nationalism than the years before World War I. Protectionism and high tariffs were the most striking features of the economic history of the interwar period (with even the British empire abandoning free trade). The interwar period was in general a period of poor economic performance and, above all, of the Great Depression.

Developments in the United States during this period are perhaps a little simpler to describe than in other countries. At the same time they are instructive from the point of view of the issues under consideration. In the 1920s the United States had a conservative and probusiness government under the presidencies of Harding, Coolidge, and Hoover. These presidents were not only conservative Republicans, but they also wanted to keep the role of the government and the transfers to the poor at a minimal level. At the same time, protective tariffs were extremely high and rising, with the Fordney-McCumber tariffs and then with the Smoot-Hawley tariff passed just as the Great Depression set in. The American economy did fairly well under Harding and Coolidge and in the first months of President Hoover's administration.

Then began the deepest depression that the United States—or the world—had ever seen. A substantial period of conservative and probusiness, though protectionist, government thus culminated in a catastrophic depression. This depression was not really cured, although it was somewhat ameliorated, under the New Deal administration of Franklin Roosevelt; only with World War II did the American economy fully recover.

From the end of World War II until about 1970 two facts of economic history stand above all others. The first striking fact is that in all major developed democracies the welfare state reached its full development and began to manage a significant proportion of the national income. The second important fact is that these major developed democracies grew more rapidly during this period than they ever had before. Some, like Germany and Japan (and for a time Italy), grew with incredible speed; even the slowest growing among these countries, like Great Britain and the United States, grew more rapidly than they had ever grown before. So the welfare state, on the one hand, and unprecedented economic growth, on the other, came to the major developed economies of the West at essentially the same time. Indeed, the postwar era was the period of the greatest increase in the peacetime role of the government, the largest effort to redistribute income to the poor, and the most rapid economic growth the world has known.

Was there a causal connection between the large governments and the welfare state and rapid economic growth? From the first quarter-century after World War II, it would seem so, but this observation does not fit with the experience of the nineteenth century; nor does it fit with the experience of the 1970s, when the welfare state in most developed democracies became larger than ever and the economic performance turned sour. If the relationship between the welfare state and economic performance were considered in more detail, many more contradictory observations would be apparent.

Perhaps the detached reader will agree that no clear picture emerges from the aggregative and historical evidence about the role of the state and the rate of economic growth. Given the almost universal preoccupation with the role of the government and the extent of income redistribution to low-income people, one would expect that—if either side of the ideological debate was correct—there ought to be clear and conspicuous evidence of an association one way or the other. Given the widespread interest in the issue, one would expect that someone would have shown a compelling association between the role of government and the rate of growth, but (to the best of my knowledge) no one has. If people feel strongly, as most of them do, about how large the role of government should be in a democratic society, one would suppose that those strong convictions rested on some clear and unambiguous finding about the role of the state and economic performance. That clear and conspicuous evidence is not there, and the evidence usually is not even systematically examined.

It is possible that the size and ideology of governments strongly affect the standards of living of low-income people, even if they have no clear effect on the rate of economic growth or the level of per capita income. Since generally less data exist on the standards of living of relatively low-income people than on rates of economic growth, one must be extremely cautious in drawing any conclusions. So far as one can tell from the available studies, however, there is no strong evidence, if any at all, that the ideology or size of government is related to the standard of living of relatively poor people.[8]

Thus one may assume, at least provisionally, that something else must be crucially involved in determining the rate of economic growth and the standard of living of low-income people besides the issue around which the ideological debate revolves. If governments of right-wing and left-wing ideologies do not achieve what they claim they will achieve, one has a right to suspect that their actions and choices are often not those that their ideologies and slogans might lead us to expect. When we see what else is involved, and why both the left and the right are often unfaithful to the ideologies they espouse, we will be able to come back to the familiar ideological debate and understand it better. And this in turn will yield a fresh perspective on the debates on supply-side economics and industrial policy.

The reader may ask, if something else is involved besides the role of government and the extent of income redistribution, what is it? What is the something else that must be there, obscuring or denying us a clear connection between the role of government and the speed of economic growth and making governments behave in ways that are not predicted by their ideologies?

Special Interests

My candidate for the role of the "something else" is a topic already discussed, the nature of collective action in society. The difficulties of collective action may seem unrelated to the determinants of the rate of economic growth or the standard of living of low-income people, but a close relationship will be evident when one considers the incentives that organizations for collective action confront. Let us suppose that some group has accomplished the very difficult and problematic task of organizing for collective action and that the group is organized to lobby the government or to act as a cartel in the marketplace to influence prices or wages.

What is the incentive facing this organization? One can see the answer best by considering an organization that, although it might have many members, is still only a small part of the whole country or society in question. For the sake of simple arithmetic, one can assume it is an organization that represents 1 percent of the income-earning capacity of a country. Suppose it is a labor union whose members' wages are in the aggregate 1 percent of the national income of the country in question. Or suppose it is a trade association of business firms that in the aggregate earn 1 percent of the national income.

Could this organization, representing 1 percent of a country, serve its members by increasing the efficiency and productivity of the country of which it is a part? In general, it is better to be part of a rich and efficient society than of a poor and inefficient one, so this is a logical possibility to examine. A lobbying organization could, for example, lobby for measures that would make the society in which its members live and work more productive and successful than formerly. Would it have an incentive to do this?

An organization that represented 1 percent of its society would receive on average only 1 percent of the benefits from increasing its society's productivity. If the national income of the United States rises by a billion dollars because some special-interest group that is organized for collective action wins more efficient public policies, the members of the special-interest group that represents 1 percent of the country will receive, on average, 1 percent of the benefits resulting from their action. But they will have borne the whole costs of their lobbying to improve the country. If they obtain 1 percent of the benefits of their action and bear the whole costs of their action, it will pay them to try to increase the society's efficiency and prosperity only if the benefits of that action to the society as a whole exceed the costs of that action by 100 times or more. Only if the cost-benefit ratio is better than 100–1 will an organization for collective action that represents 1 percent of the country serve its members best by trying to make the society more prosperous and efficient.

How then can a special-interest group best help its clients? By winning a larger slice of the pie—or the national income—that the society produces.

But, the reader may ask, if groups lobby for favors from government or if their members combine in the marketplace to obtain monopolistic prices or wages, will the economy not become less efficient and productive? Will the members of the special-interest group bear part of the reduction in the national income that comes from the inefficiencies brought about by their effort to capture a larger proportion of the national income? The answer is yes. In general, when cartelization occurs the efficiency and prosperity of the society are reduced. A combination or cartel will produce and sell less, and charge more for it, and that will make the society less productive and efficient. Similarly, special-interest lobbying will induce resources to crowd into the particular areas favored by the lobby-inspired legislation. So the special-interest organization's contribution to the national income—its marginal social product—is lower than it would have been in other areas, and the efficiency of the economy is reduced. In general, both cartelization and special-interest lobbying will reduce the society's efficiency and productivity.

The special-interest group, it will be recalled, represents 1 percent of the society, and its members will bear only 1 percent of the loss in national income or output that occurs because of the inefficiency that its activities bring about. The group's members will receive the whole of the amount redistributed to them—the whole of the increase in the size of their slice of the pie—but they will bear only 1 percent of the losses from the shrinkage of the pie. It pays this hypothetical special-interest group to seek to redistribute income to its own members even if this reduces the national income by up to 100 times the amount redistributed!

A society dense with organizations for collective action then is like a china shop filled with wrestlers battling over the china and breaking far more than they carry away. A society in which the difficult task of organizing collective action has been overcome in many sectors will be a society full of organizations that have little or no incentive to produce anything of value to the society. But these organizations will have great incentives to struggle to increase their share of what society is producing and to persevere in that struggle even when it reduces the output of the society by many times the amount that each group gains through distributional struggle.[9]

If the organization of collective action is difficult and problematic, and if only some groups have small numbers or access to the necessary selective incentives, it will take a long time for societies to organize for collective action. It will, in other words, take quite some time before many groups will have had the good luck and the good leadership needed to organize for collective action. Older and long tranquil societies should then be expected to be less efficient and dynamic than otherwise similar societies that have had less time to accumulate organizations for collective action. Accordingly, we have the testable implication or prediction that the long stable societies ought to be doing less well economically than would in general be expected.

The Theory Fits the Facts

Evidence abounds that long-stable societies are indeed not doing as well economically as would be expected. The society that has had the longest period of stability and immunity from invasion and institutional destruction is Great Britain. And, as the theory predicts, Great Britain has the poorest economic performance of all the major developed democracies.

The theory also predicts that if totalitarian government, revolution, or defeat in war destroys the institutional fabric of a society, including its special-interest organizations, that society will grow surprisingly rapidly, after a free and stable legal order is established. It will be relatively innocent of special-interest groups. Any such groups it will have are also likely to be relatively "encompassing" and therefore less of a problem for economic development than narrow special-interest groups.[10] Thus societies that have suffered the institutional destruction that eliminates special-interest groups ought to grow more rapidly than they would otherwise be expected to do.

The economic miracles of Germany and Japan after World War II are precisely consistent with this implication of my argument. In Italy, the institutional destruction in World War II, though considerable, was less complete than in Germany and Japan. The economic miracle in Italy, though there definitely was one, was correspondingly shorter and less sizable than those in Germany and Japan. This again is in accordance with the theory.

The theory also predicts that the parts of the United States that have been settled longest and have never been defeated in war would have poorer economic performance than those parts of the United States that have been settled most recently and have had less time to accumulate special-interest organizations. These areas perform less well than the recently settled West and the South, which was, of course, defeated in the

Civil War and has only lately seen the end of its turmoil over what policies should prevail with respect to race. The South, like the West, is growing far more rapidly than the Northeast and the older parts of the Midwest. Thus the most striking and anomalous examples of remarkable growth and of surprising stagnation since World War II are consistent with the theory.

So are the most striking examples of economic growth since the Middle Ages. Consider Germany's rapid economic advance after the Zollverein was established in 1834 and after German unification in 1871. Or the growth of Japan after the Meiji Restoration of 1867–1868, the growth of the United States in the nineteenth century, the growth of Britain during the Industrial Revolution, the growth of Holland in its golden age in the seventeenth century, or the commercial revolutions in England and France in the sixteenth century. All these examples involve what, in *The Rise and Decline of Nations*, I call "jurisdictional integration." [11] That is, they all experienced the creation of a wide market within which free trade prevailed. At the same time a new jurisdiction or government was created that changed the location of the capital and required lobbying on a scale quite different from what was necessary to influence the parochial small jurisdictions that existed before.

After the creation of the much larger jurisdiction and the wider market, rapid economic growth always followed. A detailed examination of the matter shows that this growth was in large part because the jurisdictional integration undercut the special-interest groups of the day. The special-interest groups of earlier centuries were called guilds in Europe and *za* in Japan. When people were freed of the tariffs and economic restrictions that surrounded each feudal fief or walled city, they could purchase goods from other parts of the jurisdiction and thereby obtain better value. Thus the new competition from other parts of the newly integrated jurisdiction undercut the guilds or *za*, which had organized monopolies behind the tariff walls that kept outside competitors away.

Once jurisdictional integration occurred, textile production—the main kind of manufacturing at that time—shifted to the rural areas of Europe. Production in rural areas had to be organized under the cumbersome "merchant-employer" system, whereby merchants brought the raw materials to countless separate cottage producers and later returned to pick up the finished product. This was done in part because the rural areas were not under the control of guilds and therefore had lower production costs.

After jurisdictional integration abolished the local trade restrictions that had supported the guilds, production shifted to suburbs and to new towns as well as rural areas. The Industrial Revolution grew up mainly in new towns or suburbs of old towns in which the rules of guilds did not apply.

There is then much evidence, only a small part of which I have offered here, to show that the creation of common markets and large jurisdictions for setting economic policy brought startling changes in the pace of economic performance. There is, moreover, every reason to believe that the impressive economic performance that occurred in the cases noted above was possible in part because jurisdictional integration undercut the special-interest groups that thrived behind the protectionism, particularly in small jurisdictions.

Why Neither Ideology Explains Economic Performance

So there is "something else" that explains more of the variation in economic performance than does the scale of the government or the extent of income redistribution to the poor: the level of lobbying and of cartelization. Earlier, in discussing the proportion of the national income the government was consuming or handling in various countries, I pointed out that this proportion had no strong relationship with the rate of economic growth or the level of per capita income.

The first reason the size of government is insufficient to explain the variation in growth rates and income levels is that it overlooks an important force that impedes economic development. This is the force of cartelization, or the combination of firms and individuals in the marketplace that can maintain noncompetitive prices or wages, obstruct the free flow of resources, and slow the innovation that brings economic growth. In focusing on the role of government alone, the laissez-faire ideology is guilty of what I call monodiabolism, or singling out one enemy of the market as though it were the only enemy. Some cartelization can take place without the aid of government, as I claim to have shown with examples from China and India in *The Rise and Decline of Nations*.

The second reason the traditional ideological arguments do not explain the variation in economic performance across countries is that they neglect variations in the ways that governments operate. What a government does depends in large part on the extent of lobbying. Although a lobby-free democracy will not operate perfectly, it is likely to operate much more efficiently than one that is under the thrall of special-interest groups. Variations in the ways governments operate also depend on whether government policies are dominated by coalitions that have an incentive to redistribute income rather than to produce it. To the extent that governments are dominated by lobbies seeking policies to redistribute income to themselves, the government will have a more adverse effect on economic performance than it would have had if it had been free of these lobbies.

The third reason that neither of the traditional ideologies is successful in explaining economic performance cannot be understood until we analyze the connection between prior income and status, on the one hand, and the capacity to organize and collude, on the other. One aspect of this connection emerged from the earlier account of how small groups, and particularly small groups of large firms, can organize with less difficulty than large groups. This suggests that industries with a small number of large firms will be among the first and best organized segments of society and that big business and the wealthiest people will normally be better organized than most of the rest of society. This point did not escape Adam Smith's attention, but it is often overlooked today.

Another factor works in the same direction: the selective incentives that large groups need to organize are more readily available to those with established positions and high incomes than to entrants or those with low incomes. This is evident from even a glance at the histories of special-interest groups. The professions organized long before workers in practically every society. Similarly, skilled workers organized unions long before unskilled workers did. The first unions represented skilled workers in England, and during the first half century of organized labor in the United States, unionized workers were called the "aristocracy of labor." Even among unskilled workers, those who already have jobs, not the unemployed or new entrants, are most likely to be organized. In no society anywhere are the poorest people or the unemployed effectively organized. Those who already have jobs in a factory or mine can often set up a picket line or a dues checkoff that will enable them to engage in collective action, but the unemployed and the poor are scattered throughout society and normally do not even gather at any one location at which their behavior might be coordinated. Thus both the organizational advantages of small groups and the access to selective incentives ensure that the nonpoor, and particularly the established and prosperous elements in society, have disproportionate capacities for organized and collusive action.

The correlation between income and status, on the one hand, and organizational power, on the other, suggests that most redistribution of income brought about either by lobbying of the government or by cartelization will not be redistribution to the poor. In fact, most redistribution is not toward the poor. The value of the money and goods transferred through the welfare system and other programs for the poor is only a tiny part of the government budget. Transfers in the forms of cartel prices or wages, tariffs, tax loopholes, and government subsidies are overwhelmingly directed toward the nonpoor. This is true in the United States and in many other societies as well. Such social expenditures as are directed toward the poor are not due mainly to the lobbying or political pressure of the poor but rather to the willingness of the nonpoor to allow such expenditures. The main sources of effective support for programs for the poor are the compassion of most people and their awareness that programs for the poor provide a measure of social insurance against personal and family catastrophes that could strike anyone.

Thus the third reason that the ideology of a government and the extent of its redistribution of income to low-income people are not closely correlated with economic performance is that most redistribution, and most of the distortions in market incentives due to such redistributions, do not involve the poor in any case. There is much argument about fairness and about how much should be done for the poor, but this argument has only a marginal effect on what societies do and on economic performance. Most redistributions are from the unorganized to the organized, and these redistributions are not closely related to the ideology of the government.

The fourth reason the familiar ideologies fail to explain economic performance is that redistributions to the poor usually damage incentives less than do redistributions to the nonpoor. This is true even when the redistributions are of similar size. The reason is that the poor are, on average, less productive than the nonpoor; they are likely to be people who have disabilities or who lack marketable skills; and they often are aged or are mothers without husbands. Although transfers to the poor and the taxes that pay for them have some adverse effect on incentives, these transfers usually reduce efficiency by less than do subsidies to the nonpoor.

When nations subsidize the nonpoor, they channel the time and energies of some of their most productive people and assets into less productive pursuits and thereby reduce social efficiency. Institutional arrangements that misallocate the labor of healthy males in their prime working years are damaging to the efficiency of a society, yet such institutional policies are common. Professional associations and public policies that control the practice of law and of medicine, for example, are costly to the society, because the time of some of the most highly educated and energetic people in the society is being misdirected, yet few areas of modern society are so rife with cartels, self-serving regulation, and other redistributions as the law and medicine. Tax loopholes that induce people to become tax accountants and lawyers divert some of the most able and aggressive people in the society from socially productive pursuits and induce much of the productive capacity of the society to move into tax-favored activities that are relatively unproductive for society. Yet such loopholes are becoming more numerous over time. Tariffs, tax concessions, and bailouts to major corporations divert or enfeeble some of the most productive enterprises in the whole economy, yet such schemes are increasing with each passing year.

The fifth reason the traditional ideologies fail to provide a good basis for predictions about economic performance is that the ideological rhetoric of parties and politicians does not reveal much about what they actually do. The right wing often advocates free enterprise and free markets. In doing this it performs a useful public service, since the advantages to society of competitive markets are usually underestimated by those who have not studied them seriously. Similarly, the left wing often advocates compassion and fairness. In so doing it strengthens the nobler side of human nature and makes our civilization more decent and sensitive to misfortune than it would be otherwise.

The problem is that most right-wing parties and politicians do not spend most of their time freeing up markets and that most left-wing parties and politicians do not spend most of their time aiding the needy. In long-stable societies such as the United States most political activity on both the right and the left is devoted to the purposes of the organized interests rather than to free markets or to the needs of the poor. The organized interests that support right-wing parties are usually from business and from the professional and prosperous classes. These organized interests will normally be rewarded when a right-wing politician is victorious. The distortions of market incentives that result when such groups are rewarded with tax loopholes, tariffs, and monopoly rights for the professions are particularly damaging to economic efficiency precisely because the beneficiaries of these rewards often possess unusually valuable abilities and assets. Similarly, when the left is victorious, the payoffs will usually be to the organized interests that have been the sources of the campaign contributions and lobbying pressures. Most politicians on the left spend much of their time working for their paying clients. These include cartels of workers, teachers, and other public employees and frequently special interests from the most prosperous segments of the society that have made campaign contributions, often to both candidates on both sides of the ideological divide. Thus the ideological debates do not give us a good basis for understanding economic performance because they are an imperfect guide to what either right-wing or left-wing governments mainly do.

If what I have said here is true, the ideologies of both the left and the right, with their untiring emphasis on the role of government and on redistribution of income to those with lower incomes, are insufficient to guide modern society. They focus almost exclusively on problems and issues that, although significant, cannot explain the main variations in the fortunes of different societies or the fluctuating progress in different periods. They also obscure other problems that may even prove fatal to modern society. Worst of all, these ideologies leave the impression that the great trade-off is between equity and efficiency. Although occasionally there can be tension between these goals, as between any others, they are not often in conflict today. The resources our society diverts to those with organized power go mainly to those who are already well off.

Rational Ignorance and Fads in Public Policy

This paper began with the idea that the typical citizen, because of the logic of collective action, is rationally ignorant about many aspects of public affairs. Given the cost of acquiring information about public policy, it is understandable that many citizens use the familiar and simple left- or right-wing ideologies for making decisions about public affairs. The limited explanatory power of each of the familiar ideologies is entirely consistent with the notion that they are more often devices for avoiding careful research and reflection rather than embodiments of detached observation and careful thinking about the experience of nations and peoples. The attraction that one or the other of the familiar ideologies holds for many professional students and participants in public affairs shows that rational ignorance cannot be the whole explanation of the attraction of the familiar ideologies, but it is part of the explanation.

There is further evidence of the role of rational ignorance in explaining beliefs about public policy in two fashionable additions to the familiar ideologies in the 1980s: supply-side economics and industrial policy. I shall argue in the next two sections that these two extensions of the right-wing and left-wing ideologies, respectively, are better evidence for rational ignorance than the ideologies themselves.

Supply-Side Economics

Occasionally, the label supply-side economics is used in such a broad way that it encompasses what essentially all competent economists, whether on the right or the left, have known since Adam Smith: that the pattern of incentives in a society has a great effect on its efficiency and level of production. In the 1980s, however, this label was used to identify a much narrower doctrine than this. It was the novel notion that, in the United States, cuts in overall tax rates would so greatly increase the amount of labor and saving that tax collections would increase. This notion was, on more than one occasion, explicitly accepted by President Reagan; in large part it inspired the tax cuts he advocated and obtained early in his administration.

Statistical and econometric evidence about the response of labor and saving to changes in posttax wages or interest rates is not the kind of information that the typical citizen would acquire because of its entertainment value. Complex econometric information and economic theory are not presented even in economic newspapers such as the *Wall Street Journal*. If they were, the editorial board of the *Wall Street Journal* would not have expected tax cuts to be self-financing, but that newspaper would no longer have a wide circulation.

Thus a huge democracy and its communications media can largely ignore information that is essential to rational policymaking, even about issues of surpassing importance. This happens even when almost all competent specialists, whether on the right or the left, agree about the evidence. The majority of competent economists never expected that the Reagan tax cuts would be self-financing. Even most economists who were strongly identified with the right-wing agreed that supply-side economics was not consistent with the quantitative evidence about the supply of labor and of savings. The tax cuts were nonetheless passed, and the nation is now burdened with a huge and harmful structural deficit. Experience has confirmed that supply-side economics was as baseless as almost all economists had said it was, yet even now it retains some journalistic and political support. This is mainly a consequence of rational ignorance. Rational ignorance also explains the power of lobbies and cartels; if all citizens had complete information and understanding of all public issues, lobbying would have no effect and cartels would not be tolerated.

Industrial Policy

Industrial policy, like supply-side economics, means different things to different people. The publications I have seen advocating industrial policy are vague. Some are so vague that they invite the response that industrial policy is neither a good idea nor a bad idea but no idea at all—that it is the grin without the cat. Nonetheless, most of the proposals for an industrial policy with which I am familiar have three common features.

The first feature is a tripartite board with representatives from business, labor, and government that would determine, or at least make influential recommendations about, the industrial policy. The second feature is a bank—in some proposals explicitly compared to the old Reconstruction Finance Corporation—that would have access to government-guaranteed or government-financed credit and thus could make subsidized loans. These loans would be combined with temporary protection against imports or other government subsidies that the tripartite board could recommend or establish. They would serve as an incentive to persuade the firms and unions singled out by the board to adopt the reforms recommended by the administrators of the industrial policy. The third feature of the proposals is that the tripartite board would focus on industries in trouble, often because of foreign competition, or it would seek out high-technology industries deemed to be especially promising, or it would take both of these approaches.

I turn first to proposals to help industries in trouble. In the United States today these industries most conspicuously are the ones that have been around a long time. Often they are important in the old industrial regions of the country. Clearly, the steel and automobile industries are among those in trouble. These industries have been around a long time; indeed, the United States was for quite some time the world's leading producer of steel, and it once manufactured four-fifths of all the world's automobiles. The apparel, textile, footwear, and farm machinery industries are also having trouble competing with imports. These industries too have a long, often illustrious, history.

By contrast, new industries in the United States are doing relatively well. America has a significant lead over the rest of the world in computers and in most high-technology fields, and it is doing well in relatively new industries such as aircraft and jet engines.

As already noted, older societies and regions that have had long periods of stability in which they have organized distributional coalitions tend to do less well than newer or recently stable regions that have had less time to accumulate institutional sclerosis. This suggests that similar processes may be at work differentiating old and new industries and firms.

A closer examination reveals that this is precisely the case. The U.S. steel industry, for example, has a long history during which it became accustomed to high levels of collusion and cartelization, among both the firms and the workers. For a long time the "Pittsburgh plus" system of cartel pricing prevailed. Under this system the cartel enforced its price for steel by requiring that all firms charge the same price. Discounts that could be hidden by variations in transport costs were prevented by the rule that all steel sold had to include the cost of transportation from Pittsburgh, even if it was produced elsewhere. The "big three" automobile companies similarly appear to have avoided all-out price competition for extensive periods, and their labor force also enjoys a monopoly wage one-half to two-thirds above the average of wages for American manufacturing. Similar examples could be cited in many other industries and firms.

It should be obvious from observations of the American government as well as from the foregoing argument that existing organized interests will greatly influence the selection of the members of any board or agency that implements an industrial policy. Indeed, some proposals for an industrial policy institutionalize and magnify the influence of established lobbies by stipulating that the governing board be composed of representatives of business and industry as well as of government; they propose that the very foxes that have been stealing the strength of our economy should be put in charge of the chicken coop. It is no coincidence that some proposals for an industrial policy have drawn powerful support from established business and labor leaders. These proposals would protect the established interests that are the main source of our economic problems from competition with new firms, new workers, and new countries.

Those proposals for an industrial policy that would allocate capital on preferential terms to promising new firms in emerging industries must explain how they would ensure that the lobbying power of established and often declining industries and firms would be kept at bay. The "sunrise" industries and firms cannot lobby until some time after they have been established, and they cannot compete politically with established interests.

Advocates of industrial policies should also explain why a government board or agency would allocate capital more effectively than the people and firms that are investing their own money. A vast amount of evidence indicates that it is precisely in areas of high uncertainty and risk that governmental bureaucracies are least useful. Some of the most promising ventures and technologies will fail, and the official who lends public monies to an undertaking that fails will risk notoriety. Even the rationally ignorant may learn of a spectacular failure, but they may not take the trouble to note that investment plans that exclude innovations risky enough to have a significant chance of total failure are unlikely to generate any major advances. The official who bets on the risky venture will not receive the profits if the venture succeeds but will normally be in trouble if the venture fails. Government investment programs therefore are almost always too conservative. It is in the areas of uncertainty (such as high technology and new industries) that private venture capital has the greatest advantage. The government can best promote science and technology by providing the public goods of pure research that the market will not provide and by creating an environment that is open to every kind of new enterprise and innovation, foreign or domestic.

Rational Ignorance Means Nonsense Is Taken Seriously

Thus the left-liberal advocacy of industrial policy is distressingly similar to its right-wing counterpart, the notion that tax cuts are self-financing. Like the better-known versions of supply-side economics, the industrial policy proposals are mainly manifestations of the difficulties that the rational ignorance of the typical citizen generates for modern democracy.

The examples of supply-side economics and industrial policy illustrate a great obstacle that limits the use of the knowledge generated by professional research in public policymaking. Because of rational ignorance, the ideas that will have the most political appeal are by no means necessarily those that will have the greatest value to society. Rather, they will often be ideas that are appealing on casual examination. The typical citizen has no incentive to engage in the sustained research and hard analysis that is often necessary to see through unwise policy proposals or to understand the case for the best available proposals. The average citizen also has no incentive to undertake inquiries that would reveal how much he or she may lose from special-interest legislation or cartelistic pricing. Many of the average citizen's ideas about what is in the national interest are derived indirectly from the propaganda of organized interests.

Politicians, no less than the rest of us, are normally interested in career advancement and job security. They are, like the rest of us, usually sincere in hoping that all will be well for their fellow citizens. Politicians accordingly often face a dilemma. Since they are professionally concerned with public affairs, they have much more incentive to acquire information about public affairs than the average citizen does; it is not usually rational for them to be ignorant. Yet they are elected, or defeated, mainly by those who are rationally ignorant. Thus decent politicians face a dilemma. They can work hard at finding good policies and trying to get them adopted. But this may not serve their career interests, which would sometimes be better served if they sought campaign contributions from organized interests and presented superficially attractive policy proposals.

Although there are no panaceas that will solve the foregoing problem, there are some ways of making it less serious. But diagnosis precedes prescription, and the treatments needed for this chronic ailment must be left for another paper.

NOTES

1. For a full statement of this logic and supporting evidence, see Mancur Olson, *The Logic of Collective Action* (Cambridge: Harvard University Press, 1965).
2. Ibid., 51 et passim.
3. Anthony Downs, *An Economic Theory of Democracy* (New York: Harper and Row, 1957).
4. David Smith, "Public Consumption and Economic Performance," *National Westminster Bank Review,* 1975.
5. Erich Weede, "Democracy, Creeping Socialism, and Ideological Socialism in Rent-Seeking Societies," *Public Choice* 44 (1984): 349–366.
6. Kwang Choi, *Theories of Comparative Economic Growth* (Ames: Iowa State University Press, 1983).
7. Samuel Brittan, "How British Is the British Sickness?" *Journal of Law and Economics* XXI (October 1978): 245–268.
8. Many relevant studies on the relation or lack of relation between the ideology of governments and the distribution of income are summarized in Erich Weede, "The Effects of Democracy and Socialist Strength on the Size and Distribution of Income," *International Journal of Comparative Sociology* 23 (September-December 1982): 151–165. See also Simon Kuznets, *Modern Economic Growth: Rate, Structure, and Spread* (New Haven: Yale University Press, 1966); Malcolm Sawyer, "Income Distribution in the OECD Countries," OECD Occasional Studies (Paris: Organization for Economic Cooperation and Development, July 1976); and Sridar Hajra, *Trends in Income Distribution: A Comparative Study* (New Delhi: Economic and Scientific Research Foundation, 1971).
9. The argument I have just put forth is casual and incomplete. It is stated completely and

carefully in Mancur Olson, *The Rise and Decline of Nations* (New Haven: Yale University Press, 1982). The skeptical reader is invited to check every step of the logic of my argument in that book. What has been set out here should be sufficient to call attention to some testable implications or predictions of the argument that can be compared with reality.

10. Ibid., 47–53.
11. Ibid., chaps. 5 and 6.

Comment

Newt Gingrich

Reading Mancur Olson's paper, I could not decide whether to respond as a politician, a citizen, a historian, or a "showboat," taking cheap shots. It was tempting to respond as a showboat, but I could not help but think about Lucky Jim and the whole American professorate and the degree to which I would like to challenge the paper.[1]

At the outset, however, let me say that I agree strongly with Olson's central thesis: there are structures of organized power that over time strangle the opportunity to innovate. In a world of change these structures are extraordinarily destructive. Olson is right. Some of us in Congress will continue talking about a corrupt, liberal welfare state and using language similar to his. Books such as *City for Sale*, about New York City, and *Honest Graft*, about the U.S. Congress, elaborate on the points that he makes—correctly, I think.[2] Nevertheless, I disagree with him at several levels.

First, he writes as an economist, and I think that is a major error when one is trying to understand how humans function. I have to confess my bias. Until I dropped out of college to manage a congressional campaign, I was a political science major. I dropped political science and became a historian. The reason was that, in politics as practiced, I found the social sciences to be too narrow in the slices of life with which they deal. To give an example, Olson refers to econometric projections of supply-side economics. In fact, one of the principal arguments of supply-side economics is that econometric projections are irrelevant; therefore, it should not be surprising that economic projections do not show exactly what supply-side economics produces. The reason is simple: at the core of supply-side economics is the idea that human beings tend to be motivated by exceptional changes in their culture and psychology and therefore behave differently in reaction to those changes. Using econometrics is somewhat like taking a slice of tissue, looking at it under an electron microscope, and trying to describe a frog. Econometrics tells us about the slice under the microscope; it does not explain the frog. The frog is alive. The microscope is an apparatus with which to study things that are dead. The principal argument of the supply-siders is a social studies or humanities argument, not an economic argument, and most economists will admit that.

My second objection is that no current economic theory relates to the world financial market; therefore, all models of gross national product are irrelevant. The reason the economists were wrong throughout the 1980s is that they tried to apply nation-state models to global financial systems. They were consistently wrong because one cannot talk about liquidity or capacity being pushed when dealing with world capacity. In any country with a relatively open economy, and, say, a 90 percent rate of factory utilization, that country will be increasing imports from Hong Kong. This will not necessarily create an inflationary spiral. Use of all the underlying global models is similar to having somebody trained on a DC-3 jump into a 747 and yell, "I'm ready!" It is not the same business; it is not the same technology; and the equations are not the same.

Third, the main lesson I have learned as a politician goes back to something I had experienced but had not understand intellectually until I read Gary Wills's book, *Inventing America*.[3] To paraphrase Wills, no modern historian can explain George Washington because all modern historians are rational in their attempts to explain how people function. Washington's effect on the country was outside the rational. It was mythic—a function of who he was, of how he behaved, and of how he communicated belief, stability, and authority.

As a historian studying leaders such as Mao, Lenin, Washington, Jefferson, Lincoln, and Theodore Roosevelt, I have concluded that the underlying power of human will and imagination, the power of what is forged by experience, is closer to poetry and fiction than to fact and reason. To give an example, the best study of Lincoln, in my judgment, is Gore Vidal's *Lincoln*.[4] Although it is a novel, it gives the practicing politician a sense of the frustration and the difficulties that Lincoln experienced. He operated in a world not of rational linear projections nor of logical steps but in a world that resembled a complex ballet in which events happened simultaneously. That is what politics was and is all about.

We do not have language to explain that reality. In fact, most academics beat to death those with enough creativity and breadth of vision to try to talk outside rational speech. Those faculty members who do not fit the mold will not get tenure; they will not be promoted.

Politics and Economics

This brings me back to Olson's three major topics: rational ignorance, industrial policy, and ideological shifts. I would like to consider each of them.

Rational Ignorance

Olson's term "rational ignorance" is arrogant. People are not rationally ignorant; people are rationally informed. I know precisely as much about my next car as I need to know to buy it because I do not value cars. My brother-in-law knows infinitely more about the car I did not buy than I know about the car I did buy because he likes cars. We are both informed to the level we need to be to achieve the purpose we want.

That has always been true. The Founders wrote the Constitution in secret. They believed in limited, indirect voting because they thought one could not inform many people. Any notion that we ever had a golden age of literate people who thought rationally is held only in faculty gatherings. The truth is—and this is the great genius of the Founders—that they were very human. They assumed that people would not spend much time studying foreign policy, and they did not want them to.

From my experience in Washington I believe the Founders were right. Every time the State Department briefs Congress on a crisis, it presents us with a new set of names. As soon as we have digested the information well enough to ask questions, the crisis is over and we are asked to turn our attention to yet another new place. Members of Congress soon discover that we can learn almost as much from the Sunday *New York Times* as from official briefings. Sometimes we learn more from the *Times* than from the briefings, and we can ask questions the briefer cannot answer.

There is then an academic preciousness, as though tons of knowledge matters. Most of the time, in most of history, being wise and being smart are not the same. Wisdom is knowing what is necessary to be known. Being smart is knowing many things. Adolf Hitler, for example, was smart about some things, but he was wrong about attacking Russia. Winston Churchill was uninformed about a surprising number of things, but he was right about one very important thing.[5]

Members of Congress are not stupid. We recognize our ignorance. We must make decisions in real time, with limited knowledge of what is going on, with limited awareness of what the implications will be, and with a bureaucracy that will not function perfectly.

A good example is the U.S. Navy's entry into the Persian Gulf in February 1987. The major question then was whether the Iranians would use Chinese shore-to-ship missiles. That was not the right question, however, because the Iranians never intended to use those missiles. Mines were their first line of defense. The U.S. Navy did not send to the Persian Gulf mine sweepers or helicopters that could sweep for mines. The Navy was mesmerized by high technology and ignored the low end of the fight. Those of us in Congress who were knowledgeable about the Navy anticipated what would happen. We did not necessarily know that Iran would use mines, but we knew that it operates in clumsy ways.

People who study the way life really works understand that it is better to overpower by sheer mass and effort. The West was won with great sloppiness, with massacres and starvation. It was not won elegantly by nine people from the Kennedy School of Government. During the invasion of Normandy it was necessary for the Allies to apply so much force because victory was uncertain. I mention these examples as background because our academic and intellectual environments have withdrawn from the fundamental realities of life. Life is sloppy and hard and complicated.

I am not sure then that it is fair to say people are stupid because they consciously get only the information they need to trigger the checkoff mechanism they want. (Those who doubt that should try reading every label the next time they walk through the grocery store.) Everybody exists in a world of selective information, not of rational ignorance.

I would argue that we will achieve a high voter turnout when we learn to send signals, in brief bites, that use code words that matter. Lincoln's "splitting the rails" and McKinley's "full lunch pail" and the "war hawks" of 1812 are good examples of our great tradition of using political code words. People have always communicated in short slogans. "I love you" is a short slogan. It may have a long marital contract behind it if you live in California, but it is a short slogan.

Industrial Policy

I agree with Olson that the supply-side model, as he describes it, does not work. Nor does the industrial-planning model. I am not convinced, however, that their failure leads to his ultimate conclusion. I believe that we do have an industrial policy. Olson cites two areas dominated by the United States—computers and jet engines. We are strong in these areas, frankly, because the U.S. government cheated, giving money without contracts through agencies such as the Defense Department. And that department (and its antecedents) has had an industrial policy at least since the 1890s. The reality is that this country has always cheated. What we said to other countries is, "We will spend massively on research and development. You, however, should not spend anything on research and development, and then let's have fair trade."

If one reads the German critiques of Adam Smith from about 1820, one will discover that the Germans, who tried to build up industry in competition with Great Britain, understood exactly what the British were doing. The British, with their greater capitalization, established leadership, and efficiency in manufacturing, also had access to raw materials from their empire; they were well positioned to take advantage of a free-trade European economic organization.

In the twentieth century, for example, say, the United States invents the computer and mass produces it through the Defense Department. This is not an industrial policy, you understand. Or, say, the United States produces the B-47, the B-52, and so forth, and then tells Boeing, "If you want to use the same technology, we do not object." Who is kidding whom?

Of course, we have a high-tech industrial policy. It does not figure in a model because it is obscure and outside the norms, and nobody can figure out how to turn it into pork barrels. The minute it is turned into pork barrel, it will become exactly what Olson describes: a defense of the past rather than an invention of the future. The reason for this is that the only people who can get organized are those who already exist, and they tend to crowd out those who come later. I agree with Olson's analysis on that point. But the United States does have an industrial policy, and it works. Only in the 1960s did the United States begin to decay. But that is the topic for another discussion.

Ideological Shifts

I think the United States is in a period of ideological shifts. In a Hegelian sense, it is moving toward synthesis.

On the right we have been arguing that we have to move from an opposition conservatism, largely characterized by its definition of what went wrong with the Great Society and afterwards, to a governing conservatism. That is to say, "If we conservatives had absolute control, what would we do?" Let me give an example. People will say, "I am a Jeffersonian conservative," a code phrase, in the South at least, that means agrarian, small government. Nonsense! Thomas Jefferson sent a scientific expedition to the Pacific, he sent the Marines to the shores of Tripoli without congressional permission, and he bought half a continent without telling Congress the details. I tell my friends, "I am happy to limit myself to Jefferson's scale: we will do nothing larger than the Louisiana Purchase."

An activist conservatism can be nonbureaucratic. The reason I say this is that since the late 1950s, because of the way the left has defined government, the argument has been—as Olson describes it—between big government and small government. As a historian, I think this argument is nonsense. For example, one cannot explain the rise of eastern Asia without Confucian culture. The combination of the Confucian focus on learning and extended family values with hard work and discipline explains why every single one of the eastern Asian countries is working. The People's Republic of China will grow rapidly in the next thirty years. The more the Chinese allow the market to direct their energy, the more rapidly they will grow. Their cultural values are ideal for the information/industrial age. Confucian China created the right cultural framework for a world in which knowledge matters.

In New York Asian families open grocery stores. In California they send their children to Cal Tech. Because they invest in the future, they reap huge benefits. Their sense of the past and the future is a cultural phenomenon. The great failure of nineteenth-century Britain, which led to its collapse, is a cultural phenomenon. The British aristocracy and the cultural snobbishness that worked during the beginning phases of industrialization could not be broken up at a class level to produce the kind of education that originated in Germany. The German system, which entered the United States through Johns Hopkins University and the University of Chicago, gave us the modern system of industrial engineering and science. At that point the British began a decline that was interrupted under Margaret Thatcher, which is why Thatcher is, more than anything else, a cultural politician. *Mrs. Thatcher's Revolution,* a critical but serious study of what she tried to accomplish, demonstrates that she is a cultural phenomenon more than a political phenomenon.[6]

What the United States needs is a synthesis. I mean by this a synthesis of a governing conservatism. We need to shift from a corrupt, liberal welfare state (corrupt in the sense that Olson describes it because it has lost the purposes that legitimized its creation) to an honest, conservative, opportunity society—from corrupt to honest as a fundamental standard. This would be a fundamental change comparable to the shift that occurred from Regency England to Victorian Britain. It would be a change comparable to the switch from living as a dandy in a ribald society to living in a staid, middle-class society.

We are seeing a shift from liberalism in the post-World War II sense of the word. This was the sense of the word epitomized in Lyndon Johnson's Great Society. Liberalism achieved two great things after World War II (other than keeping us involved in the world). It decolonized the Third World and it ended segregation in America. Liberals should be proud of those enormous achievements. Liberalism also did some very unintelligent things. The worst was bringing about the inner-city welfare system, which has nearly destroyed the poorest third of our country's black population and created an underclass, a great tragedy in human suffering. We must continue the shift from liberalism to conservatism in its broadest sense. (For example, schools should give diplomas only to students who can read them. We need very fundamental changes in education.)

Another recent shift is the result of a recognition of core American values that predate 1965. We must shift governmental focus from welfare, which is designed to prop up the weak, to opportunity, which can strengthen the ability of the weak to climb. Consider the nonbureaucratic activism of Theodore Roosevelt. He could be extraordinarily inventive. He could go on a hunting expedition to benefit the American Museum of Natural History as surely as he could expand the Smithsonian Institution, and he thought both were legitimate activities. He saw the presidency as a "bully pulpit" from which the president could arouse the entire nation.

The Failure of Politics

The failure of American politicians, the intellectual elite, and the news media since the late 1960s has been a failure of our elites to work hard enough, to think long enough, to do the job. We ought to be asking ourselves, "Why have those of us in charge done such a poor job at thinking through and creating a political atmosphere that results in 50 percent of the American people failing to vote?"

Politics is the only industry in America where, in 1988, when only 51 percent of eligible Americans voted, we blamed the people who did not show up. Can you imagine a McDonald's meeting after 51 percent had rejected the Egg McMuffin? Would the managers have asked why the consumers were so stupid?

What we are seeing is the collapse of politics as an art form. Politics, I would argue, is the most difficult art form in a free society other than fighting a civil war. When the great political machines died, we lost the apprenticeships that teach this difficult art. The result is that because our political leaders are anemic in practicing their art we are not able to create a product line, an agenda, that says to average Americans that voting is worth an hour of their time, that their ballot will sufficiently change the lives of their children and of their own and their neighbors' families that it is worth an hour of time. I think a strong civic discourse is the duty of the elite. We need people who aspire to public service and are willing to subordinate their time and energy to learn the trade. Anybody can play, but they have got to be willing to pay the dues.

Three groups should be taken to task: the politicians (not just people in politics, but all who participate), the news media, and the intellectuals. These three groups have failed the American nation. Their job should be to create an ideology that gives the nation a clear direction worth gambling with for a generation.

NOTES

1. Kingsley Amis, *Lucky Jim* (Garden City, N. Y.: Doubleday, 1954).
2. Jack Newfield and Wayne Barrett, *City for Sale* (New York: Harper and Row, 1988); Brooks Jackson, *Honest Graft* (New York: Knopf, 1988).
3. Gary Wills, *Inventing America* (Garden City, N. Y.: Doubleday, 1978).
4. Gore Vidal, *Lincoln: A Novel* (New York: Random House, 1984).
5. The most useful book I have read on Churchill is Robert Rhodes James, *Churchill: A Study in Failure, 1930–1939* (London: Weidenfeld and Nicolson, 1970). It argues that if Churchill had died before 1939, or if Hitler had not attacked Poland, Churchill would have been considered deranged and few would have paid attention to him.
6. Peter Jenkins, *Mrs. Thatcher's Revolution: The Ending of the Socialist Era* (Cambridge: Harvard University Press, 1988).

Comment

Jodie T. Allen

I agree with the substance, if not every detail, of what Mancur Olson has so eloquently written. Rather than taking issue with particular points, I want briefly to consider whether Congress can improve upon "rational ignorance." It is true that Congress is under pressure from lobbies and advocacy groups—groups with a penchant for gain at the expense of loss for the larger body politic. And, yes, the press and other media feed the public's appetite for the titillating—and senators and representatives must respond to their demands. But, I shall argue, Congress can and should build a sounder basis for policy than the self-pleadings of well-heeled lobbies and the sound-bite opportunities offered by the network news. Congress does, in fact, build such a rational basis more frequently than its many critics would concede. Let me offer a few examples.

My first example has to do with welfare reform, a subject in which I have dabbled for more than two decades. Welfare reform was one of the first nonmilitary issues to which the techniques of modern economic analysis were methodically applied. During the late 1960s and the 1970s would-be welfare reformers in the former Department of Health, Education, and Welfare, the Office of Economic Opportunity, and private research organizations built microsimulation models to measure costs, caseloads, and even feedback effects of various welfare program structures. Ultimately, these models became very sophisticated.

Even more innovative than those measures were the large-scale controlled field experiments that sought to measure behavioral responses—how people changed their work effort, family structures, living arrangements, and patterns of consumption under a variety of income maintenance schemes. Some systematic exploration was undertaken to determine how different ways of administering transfer programs affected their results. A lot was learned from those studies, too.

For a while it looked as if all this study was in vain. Throughout the 1970s welfare reform stayed deadlocked over issues that had much more to do with politics, pressure, and prejudice than with science. In the early 1980s politicians simply lost interest in the subject. Ken Bowler, who served so ably for many years on the House Ways and Means Committee staff and who is an astute consumer of good policy analysis, at one point became so discouraged that he concluded gloomily that maybe all this research was a waste of time because nobody paid any attention to it.

In sober retrospect it is clear that was not the case. Welfare reform, as it was then conceived by most academicians, did not pass. But that was not just because the standard prescription of extending welfare benefits more broadly over all poor people ran afoul of public distaste for welfare caseloads. The very research that grew up around the reform effort suggested that there were some negative side effects of transfer payments, not big ones but effects that were large enough to be worrisome to policymakers rightly concerned about strengthening families and work effort.

The direction that welfare reform has taken since the late 1970s has been quite different from what was envisioned by the reformers of the 1960s. The emphasis on work effort and personal responsibility is for the good. The research techniques and even some of the substantive and administrative findings from the welfare reform studies have been applied to reforms of other transfer programs, such as food stamps and unemployment insurance. Good research knows no party: these findings have been useful to policymakers in both Republican and Democratic administrations. Joe Califano drew on them under Jimmy Carter, but so did David Stockman under Ronald Reagan.

Science and technology cannot always triumph over superstition and ignorance. An even more potent foe can be good intentions. The Agent Orange case pops to mind. I spent a great deal of time exploring and editorializing about this issue in the early 1980s. It caused me anguish because, this time, science did not support the original idea of where the equities lay.

Agent Orange was a defoliant used by the Army to make it harder for the Viet Cong to hide in the thick underbrush of Vietnam. From a P.R. standpoint Agent Orange was a disaster: It was used in an unpopular war; it was produced by an unpopular industry; it raised the ugly specter of chemical warfare; and some batches of it contained traces of dioxin, a deadly poison.

But, as I discovered when I dug into the issue, dioxin, contrary to most of what has been written, is not an ingredient in Agent Orange. It is merely an unwanted byproduct of the production process, produced in minute quantities in some batches when quality control was sloppy. Moreover, dioxin is quickly dissipated in sunlight, especially when present in an airborne spray. It has never been known to cause organic damage in humans without first inflicting them with chloracne, a disfiguring skin ailment that, it turns out, only a handful of Vietnam veterans have ever suffered.

No hard scientific data suggest that even the GIs most directly involved in handling the defoliant suffered from Agent Orange exposure. Like the rest of us, Vietnam veterans suffer from many war-induced ailments and many non-war-induced ailments. But as a group they and their offspring are measurably healthier than the general population. Even as the scientific studies piled up showing no Agent Orange effect, sympathy for the veterans and their families—some of whom, just like families of nonveterans, had a variety of genetic and acquired disorders—poured in. Finally, the chemical companies set up a fund under a settlement presided over by a judge who frankly admitted there was no scientific basis for the claims. So science cannot necessarily emerge victorious on a highly emotional issue. In this case at least some rough justice was served.

Rational study and analysis can have their triumphs over special interests as well. The biggest score of the late 1980s was the 1986 tax bill. It is true that the bill was far from perfect. The "bubble" tax schedule that put people earning between roughly $50,000 and $150,000 in a higher tax bracket than those earning $5 million was a shameful political compromise and an affront to every principle of equity known to tax analysis. The bubble was shifted upward somewhat in the 1990 tax and budget bill, but it persists. The big failure of the 1986 bill was that it did not raise enough revenue. But it was certainly a triumph over the well-heeled special interests that had set up housekeeping in the tax code over the years.

How, then, can Congress obtain more of this good analysis and, even more important, how can it learn to heed it? Although there is no magic formula, I offer three rules of thumb for members of Congress.

Learn the rudiments of analysis. Learn how not to be fooled by shifting bases in charts that make climbs seem sharper than they are; by percentage comparisons in which it is the absolutes that matter, or vice versa; by figures that look large or small only because the numbers they are being compared to have grown or shrunk. There are many tricks, but not so many that you cannot pick them up in an afternoon or two.

Do not believe everything you read in the newspaper. At least, do not believe everything in the nonspecialist press. Particularly, do not pay attention to stories that pretend to touch all the bases in the name of "balance" and "fairness." Remember that reporters, at least those at any decent paper, are under pressure from their editors to give both sides of an issue. Unless they are specialists in the subject (and covering an issue for a couple of months does not necessarily make anyone a specialist at anything other than how to get a quick, playable quote), reporters may dutifully consult any readily accessible source on the "other side" and give the same credence to the most crackpot analysis as to the most carefully considered and researched.

Seek out both sides of an argument. Talk to the best people on both sides, and make an honest effort to hear and understand the other side. Herb Stein, Council of Economic Advisers chairman under Nixon, once said that the hardest, almost impossible, thing he tries to teach his policy analysis students is to lay out all the options honestly rather than putting the option they like best in the middle and surrounding it with two losers. If I learned anything as an editorial writer—where writers daily face the brickbats of anyone who feels offended or misrepresented—it is that proponents of the other side are always worth listening to. Often, they will change your mind at least on some point. And sometimes, if you listen carefully and ask the right questions, you will even change theirs.

II

Issues Before Congress

6. Knowledge, Power, and National Security

Ernest R. May

Knowledge, power, and national security are obviously linked. So are ignorance, weakness, and national insecurity.

If a nation does not understand threats from outside—and its own strengths and shortcomings—it lives either in clouds or in terror. Before the Second World War, Americans knew relatively little about the rest of the world; they wished it away. With President Roosevelt's backing, Congress in 1937 passed a "permanent neutrality" act. There were only six dissenting votes in the Senate and thirteen in the House.[1] After the war Americans knew little about communism, less still about the Soviet Union—both suddenly menacing. One result was the hysteria we commemorate as McCarthyism.

Knowledge Versus Power

Knowledge and power are reciprocals. The less raw power a nation has, the greater its need for knowledge, and vice versa. The legend of David and Goliath conveys this moral. So does the history of David's heirs in the state of Israel—they never skimp on knowledge.

The more power a nation thinks it has, the less it is likely to seek knowledge. The extreme example is the Qing dynasty in China. The emperors and their mandarins assumed that they needed to know only their own kingdom. A committee could handle "barbarians" such as the British. It took a series of losses, including destruction of China's army and navy by the despised Japanese, to shake this illusion.

The United States today has relatively less power than it once had.

Americans have correspondingly greater need for knowledge. To say this is not to draw an analogy with nineteenth-century China. It is not even to endorse the notion of the United States as a "nation in decline." It is a simple statement of fact about the world of the 1990s.

Power and national security are both relative. A nation has absolute resources—land, water, people, minerals, machines, money, and so on. These resources count as power in comparison with the resources of other nations. Security is a function of power and of danger. A relatively weak nation can be secure if it has few enemies. Costa Rica, for example, has been comparatively secure even though it keeps no army at all. A relatively powerful nation can be insecure if it has many enemies. That was the lot of the German empire established by Bismarck.

The United States began as a weak and endangered alliance. The Articles of Confederation were created by the equivalent of a North American Treaty Organization. The Constitution made the arrangement something more than a security pact. Slowly, a nation emerged; over time it became less weak. Meanwhile, coincidentally, Europeans kept busy at home. Britain, which could have been America's enemy, preferred to trade. Other powers had to reckon with the British fleet. Americans increased and prospered. After the Civil War, when national unity ceased to be in doubt, the United States economically began to outstrip all potential rivals. Americans enjoyed almost complete security. They saw little need for knowledge.

The End of "Free Security"

Franklin Roosevelt and the senators and representatives who voted for "permanent neutrality" in 1937 were trying to recapture the country's earlier safety. They failed.

The Japanese war commencing at Pearl Harbor shocked Americans almost as much as the Japanese war of the 1890s had shocked the Chinese. The Pacific fleet was sunk in an American port! For a time Californians had blackouts and air raid drills. As the tide of the war turned, Americans saw endless film footage of bombs raining on Hamburg, Berlin, Dresden, Tokyo, and other cities. Although no bomber of the time had intercontinental range, Americans had no trouble imagining bombs falling on New York, Chicago, or Los Angeles. After Hiroshima their vision included mushroom clouds.

For a short time after the war Americans had reason again to feel both powerful and secure. The American economy boomed. The United States accounted for half of the world's production. Japan had become a ward, and so had Germany—or most of it. The other prewar powers were all enfeebled. As Charles de Gaulle put it, "In the Second World War, all the nations of Europe lost. Two were defeated." [2] Although Walter Lippmann wrote as early as 1947 of a "cold war," Russia had little capability for military action outside its immediate neighborhood.[3] It had no navy and no long-range air force. The United States had a monopoly on the atomic bomb.

That period of power and safety was short. By the end of the 1950s other industrial nations had recovered. The United States accounted for only about 35 percent of the world's production. By the end of the 1960s the U.S. share had fallen to 30 percent; in recent years it has dropped to about 25 percent. Absolute numbers, of course, ran in the other direction. The U.S. gross national product in 1980 was almost ten times what it had been in 1950. But relative power was less than it had been.

The relative security of 1945-1950 gave way to often terrifying insecurity. The Soviet Union exploded its first nuclear device in 1949. Before a decade had passed the Soviet Union and the United States both had large arsenals not only of nuclear weapons but of thermonuclear weapons that were hundreds of times more destructive than the atomic bomb. The Soviet Union had an ocean-going fleet and a long-range air force. In the late 1950s it began to show off long-range ballistic missiles. By the end of the 1960s it had hundreds of missiles able to place thermonuclear warheads, in a matter of minutes, on any stationary target in the United States.

The sense of insecurity that had spread in the United States by the end of the 1960s is suggested by snatches of Senate debate quoted by Spencer Weart in his book *Nuclear Fear:* "There comes a time when the tens of millions of casualties are so enormous that civilization is destroyed, and if there are a few people living in caves after that, it does not make much difference." [Joseph Clark, D-Penn.] "If we have to start over again with another Adam and Eve, then I want them to be Americans and not Russians." [Richard Russell, D-Ga.][4]

Today "America in decline" is announced as if it were a sudden discovery. It is not. The identical theme played loudly in the late 1950s after *Sputnik*. John F. Kennedy's speeches echoed it. "Only a small fraction of our high school graduates," he protested in 1958, "have had even one year of chemistry. An ever smaller proportion have had one year of physics. . . . Our lag in mathematics is even more shocking." Accepting nomination in Los Angeles in 1960, Kennedy spoke of "a change—a slippage—in our intellectual and moral strength." [5]

The same theme was heard at the end of the Vietnam War and yet again at the end of the Carter administration. When Ronald Reagan accepted the Republican nomination at Detroit in 1980, he sounded much like Kennedy in Los Angeles twenty years earlier: "Who does not feel rising alarm when the question in any discussion of foreign policy is no longer, 'Should we do something?' but 'Do we have the capacity to do anything?' " [6]

Periodically, Americans have noticed their lessening power and have vowed to do something about it. Sometimes they took action. Then they became distracted or forgot. Something like *Sputnik* or Vietnam or the Teheran hostages or a plummeting trade balance or Iraq's invasion of Kuwait startled them back into a mood of concern. The national rhythm was a little like that of a chronic dieter or a person who intermittently strives for fitness.

On occasion the American reaction involved some effort to make up for the comparative loss of economic power or of physical security by adding to the knowledge account. The shock of the Korean War led to much increased spending on the Central Intelligence Agency and other intelligence agencies. The federal government and private foundations and universities invested in scholarships and research fellowships for study of the Soviet Union. *Sputnik* brought yet another outpouring of funds for the intelligence community, particularly for reconnaissance satellites and other collection systems. The federal government provided temporary massive support for science education and foreign language education. Foreign area research centers proliferated.

In the 1970s there was not much comparable effort to enlarge knowledge about the outside world. Vietnam provoked introspection. At both ends of Pennsylvania Avenue and in editorial offices and research centers, attention was focused on American affairs. Americans asked how Lyndon Johnson could have committed the nation to war in Vietnam, not what had happened or was happening in Vietnam. The public was more interested in the Nixon administration's burglaries and wiretaps than in the nations with which it had been dealing abroad.

In the 1980s, after the humbling events in Iran, the Reagan administration and the congressional oversight committees added heavily to the intelligence community's human and analytical resources. Little happened, however, outside the intelligence community. Post-*Sputnik* initiatives seemed to have lost most of their momentum. Reports during 1988 highlighted shortcomings in almost every area that the education acts of the 1950s had sought to strengthen. In February 1989, announcing its acceptance of most of these findings, the National Governors' Association declared, "We do not know the languages, the cultures or the geographic characteristics of our competitors." [7]

It should be noted, at least parenthetically, that the Soviet Union, once the most threatening U.S. competitor, went through a process of acknowledging, then ignoring, then rediscovering a decline in power. Joseph Stalin called for forced-pace industrialization in part, as a slogan went, "to catch up with and surpass the United States." Nikita Khrushchev set a similar goal in the 1950s, when he acknowledged that not all had gone well under Stalin. Leonid Brezhnev and Aleksei Kosygin did the same in the 1960s.

From word-of-mouth *shutki* shared with Westerners, we know that some elements of the Soviet public saw greater weakness than the leaders before Mikhail Gorbachev would ever admit. At about the time Senators Clark and Russell had their exchange about Adam and Eve, Muscovites were asking one another, If there were an Adam and Eve, what would their nationality have been? Answer: Russian. They had no clothes. They had nothing to eat but an apple. And they were told they were in paradise.

Gorbachev's admissions about the Soviet economy are far more candid and far less doctrinaire than those of his predecessors, but they are not entirely novel. What is novel, among other things, is his evident determination to develop and apply knowledge. The significance of *glasnost* lies in the promise that the Soviet people may more freely acquire and exchange information about the outside world and about the Soviet Union than ever before. The hope is that, long before free markets loosen the flow of goods and services, free learning will give Soviet society the equivalent of a jump start.

In the United States it remains to be seen whether revived concern about national power will translate into active concern about the state of knowledge. Although I hope that it does, I want to voice two cautions. I then want to put forward three suggestions.

Two Cautions

The first caution is against confusing knowledge with information. Past efforts have often emphasized the latter. America's capacity to collect photographic and signal intelligence has grown at a fantastic rate. It is not apparent that the United States has achieved anything like a comparable rate of increase or improvement in its capacity to analyze these pictures and intercepts.[8]

Outside government, too, there has been some tendency to treat knowledge as bits of information or at least to measure knowledge by volume or weight. No American institution, as far as I know, carries this tendency as far as did Georgi Arbatov's Institute for the Study of the USA and Canada in Moscow. There, I am told by a former associate, junior researchers had to meet a quota of twenty written pages a week. Senior researchers had a quota of twenty-five. "Publish or perish" operates similarly but more loosely in the United States. (In our country there are usually no quotas for professors with tenure.)

The point should be obvious but is easily forgotten. Remember Pearl Harbor. The United States had ample information and was reading Japan's most secret coded messages, but the government did not know what to make of them. Few Americans understood Japan. Those who did were not in a position to say to the president of the United States or the secretary of state, "You must imagine a country in which what happens is what would happen here if decisions were made—and only made—by agreements between Douglas MacArthur and Ernie King!" Panama is another example; there are few countries about which foreign affairs analysts in the United States have more information per capita or per square inch. Yet it was manifest in 1988–1989, in confrontations with Gen. Manuel Noriega, that no one—certainly no one in a position to act on it—possessed knowledge about how, if at all, to influence events in Panama City.

I might also cite a positive example. The U.S. government acted in an extraordinarily sensitive and constructive manner in facilitating the transition in the Philippine Islands from the regime of Ferdinand Marcos to that of Corazon Aquino. Rep. Stephen J. Solarz, D-N. Y., and Sen. Richard G. Lugar, R-Ind., played crucial roles. Representative Solarz chaired a subcommittee that investigated Philippine affairs after the 1983 murder of Benigno Aquino. Its hearings and reports repeatedly focused U.S. public and executive branch attention on questions that might otherwise have been noticed only deep within the bureaucracy. Senator Lugar observed and passed judgment on the 1986 election that Marcos attempted to steal. He then led in urging President Reagan to tell Marcos that the time had come for him to step down.[9]

What enabled American leaders to act as they did was, to be sure, timely information. Even more important was understanding. It was sophisticated, knowledgeable analysis performed at the right times by the right people—that is, by experts who were known by Solarz, Lugar, and other American decision makers for their good information and reliable judgment.

The second caution is against assuming that the way to translate knowledge into power is through organization charts and dollars. This is not to speak against organization charts. It is certainly not to speak against money being spent for knowledge. The caution, based on looking at history, is against assuming that it takes only organization and money to create knowledge.

After World War II the United States wanted to prevent another Pearl Harbor. To that end, the U.S. government built an elaborate "intelligence community." Every time thereafter that the intelligence community failed to foresee some important occurrence, it was reorganized. It was reorganized after the first Soviet atomic device; after the Korean War and China's intervention; after a failure in Indonesia in the late 1950s; after the Bay of Pigs; during and after the Vietnam War; more than once after Watergate; after the fall of the shah of Iran; and after the Iran-contra affair. This is not to mention reorganizations accompanying changes in agency directors.[10] Other parts of the community, such as those within the Department of Defense, suffered reorganizations almost as frequently. Meanwhile, as I have already observed, reorganized and usually expanded agencies received additional money.

The record, insofar as it can be read by the public, does not encourage belief that this tendency to reorganize was a perfect formula for improvement. If the intelligence community improved its performance (which there is some reason to believe), the government did not. Richard Betts is surely correct in saying that America should expect surprises. When they occur, they are usually products of well-laid plans involving both cover and deception.[11] But if reorganization and new wads of money achieved what they were supposed to achieve, the United States should not have repeatedly deceived itself. Yet it did. Within many Americans' memory were the "bomber gap," the "missile gap," and the Berlin Wall; the advent of Castro, the Bay of Pigs affair, and the Cuban missiles crisis; and the illusion, surviving through four administrations from Kennedy to Ford, that South Vietnam would somehow reform itself and that North Vietnam would somehow come to our heel. Americans also remembered with dismay when SALT I did not slow Soviet ICBM modernization, when Egypt attacked Israel, when OPEC hiked oil prices, when the shah tumbled, and when Noriega did not, until captured by U.S. invading forces.

A Historical Warning: 1940, France

One of the most instructive examples of the need for quality intelligence comes not from U.S. history but from that of Germany and France in the early part of World War II.[12] In 1940 Germany was inferior to the Western allies by almost every measurement—personnel, training, and equipment. The German army had much less artillery. It had fewer tanks, and most of its tanks were not as good as France's. Although the German air force had a superior fighter bomber (the *Stuka*), it did not have much else. German generals prepared an offensive against the French and British only because Hitler demanded it. Many of them expected to lose. After study, they concluded that, despite material inferiority, they might bring about a victory if they surprised the allies by running a Panzer-led offensive through the Ardennes Forest.

The German offensive was, of course, a total success. The French and British were taken by surprise. Their troops in the low countries were cut off from reserves and supplies. After six weeks of fighting, France surrendered. The British army evacuated via Dunkerque.

The Germans accomplished this feat not only with inferior military forces but with less well organized intelligence services and less good information than the Allies had. The German General Staff had a twenty-nine-man Foreign Armies unit. They had no other resources for assembling and analyzing intelligence. The central intelligence organization, Adm. Wilhelm Canaris's *Abwehr*, worked for Hitler, whom most of the generals regarded as an enemy. Signal intelligence came under Deputy Führer Hermann Göring and was used mostly for internal security (and internal politics). The Foreign Armies unit had no human agents in France. It had trouble even locating the headquarters of the group of French armies that the Germans would be fighting.

The French, by contrast, had a superb intelligence organization—perhaps the best in history. The French army's Deuxième Bureau controlled or had access to all human and technical sources, including bugging devices and other police sources within France itself. It had agents at the heart of the Third Reich. When Hitler gathered his generals in the Reich Chancellery to harangue them, the Deuxième Bureau would have a verbatim account within seventy-two hours. Before the Germans attacked in 1940, French intelligence had not only predicted an attack through the Ardennes but had come close to naming the exact date.

The key difference was the experience and knowledge of the German intelligence officers and their personal relations with the generals making strategic decisions. The experts on France in the Foreign Armies section of the German General Staff judged subjectively when they predicted that the Ardennes attack would take the Allies by surprise. They had for years been studying French military publications, the French military education system, and French military leaders. They thought France's generals too old and too inflexible to depart from long-prepared plans. The operational planners in the German General Staff knew these intelligence officers. They had learned over the years to calibrate what they said. They trusted their judgments and acted on them.

On the French side, intelligence officers were expected to provide planners with their own best estimates and with evidence supporting other estimates. Planners and commanders then formed their own opinions, relying on their own knowledge and experience. French generals concluded that their German counterparts would not be so rash as to risk everything on a dash through the Ardennes. No one whose opinion commanded sure respect was prepared to say to the generals: "But do not forget Hitler. Do not forget that the Third Reich is not the Third Republic. German generals may be as inclined to prudence as are French generals, but they may be less able to obey their inclinations."

This example—in which the quality of the knowledge was not a function of resources or formal organization—leads to my three suggestions.

Three Suggestions for National Security

The first suggestion is that, in thinking about how knowledge can contribute to national power and national security, the emphasis should be on people. The chief comparative advantage of the German intelligence officers was the length and depth of their study of the French. They did not have an advantage in IQ. Their leader, Col. Ulrich Liss, was more admired for his skill as a horseman than for the sparkle of his mind. Some of the officers of the Deuxième Bureau, by contrast, could have been professors at the Sorbonne. But the German experts were informed to a degree unmatched on the French side. They spoke French. They had spent a lot of time in France. The generals knew what they were talking about. French generals did not have the same conviction about their intelligence officers.

In thinking about how to build knowledge, Americans ought to adopt several assumptions. One is that they cannot foresee what parts of the world will be important to them in the future. Who could have predicted in the 1950s that by the 1980s there would be an urgent need in America for knowledge about Islamic fundamentalism, Armenian nationalism, or the geography of Grenada? Or that by the 1990s Americans would want to know as much as possible about the Kurds and Azerbaijanis? Another assumption to be adopted is that the lead time involved in developing human repositories of knowledge is longer than the lead time for developing and producing any military system or intelligence collection system, no matter how complicated. The men and women whose judgments will affect U.S. national security in the year 2020 are already college students. If they have not already begun to learn the languages and study the cultures of the areas about which they will have to form judgments, it may be too late. The national attitude ought to be that of the English squire admired and often cited by John F. Kennedy. When told that a tree he wanted to plant would take two hundred years to mature, he responded, "Then we must plant it at once."

A second suggestion is that the United States itself should have more *glasnost*. Of course, it is important that the executive and legislative branches be able to conduct some of their business in private, and there are secrets that ought to be kept. Intelligence agents obviously ought to be protected, and so should some of the techniques of intelligence gathering. But most information generated by or within the U.S. government needs protection for only a short period of time. A survey of government records conducted in the early 1980s found that only one-third of 1 percent of current files in executive agencies were ever consulted.[13] Most documents in filing cabinets (or on filed-away disks) are not useful for current government operations. If they have any value, it is probably for scholars. They remain locked up, useful to no one. The officials with power to release them (including members of the House and Senate) have no time to look at old files. They have no incentive to risk letting out one stray document that contains an actual secret or that embarrasses someone or invades someone's privacy.

I do not argue for wholesale application of the Freedom of Information Act principle. In fact, I do not think the existing act helps much in building knowledge. It is useful to journalists and lawyers. Through them it is useful to the Republic. Inquirers can ask for and obtain specific documents, such as an inspector general's report or someone's FBI file. They can thus expose wrongs or safeguard rights. The act is much less easily used by scholars, because scholars usually want scattered documents relating to a specific subject, say, nationalism among Soviet minorities or factionalism within the Palestinian National Congress.

What I do urge is a serious effort in all branches of the federal government to share information with scholars and students. It would be hard to have a less serious effort than at present. So far as I know, no operating executive agency devotes the equivalent of a single worker's time to review and release documents other than those requested under the Freedom of Information Act and related procedures. The State Department may count as an exception. Some of the personnel in its Historical Office produce the documentary series *Foreign Relations of the United States*, initiated by Secretary of State William H. Seward in the Lincoln administration. The Historical Office releases files for public use once it has made extracts for its series and has published its volume. The office has begun bringing out volumes for the second half of the 1950s. The State Department also has a Classification/Declassification Center, customarily staffed by retired Foreign Service officers. Abetted by other cautious bureaucrats on the National Security Council staff and elsewhere, officers in this center have succeeded in postponing or preventing release of most material of any later date.[14]

The State Department example suggests that there is not much promise in looking to agencies to serve the interests of scholarship and thus of knowledge. Possibly, Congress and the executive branch should consider some arrangement providing for automatic transfer of records to the archivist of the United States. As it is, official records do not come into the hands of the archivist until agencies choose to release them. Perhaps the archivist should receive all records of more than a certain age and be enjoined by statute to release records for public use at the earliest point consistent with national safety and the protection of individual rights. The British employ a system somewhat like this. Perhaps we should imitate it. But my aim here is not to argue the merits of particular formulas. It is to argue the general point that while secrecy is often necessary for national security it is an enemy of knowledge. If we believe that knowledge is also important for national security, we should do more than we are now doing to reduce the number of secrets and shorten their lives.

My final suggestion is that we should give much more thought to the question of how knowledge is used than we do now. At Harvard, under an open and completely unclassified contract with the CIA, scholars are collaborating with various elements of the intelligence community to study how to improve interaction between intelligence analysis and decision making. The enterprise is overseen by a council and steering committee that includes several members of the legislative branch.

The scholars at Harvard are looking at several cases, including some I have mentioned here. The fall of Marcos and the fall of the shah are among them. So are Germany and France in 1940. What is striking is the thinness and the rather casual anecdotal base for most existing opinion about this relationship, whether on the side of the analysts or on the side of decision makers.

Improving this base requires intensive and time-consuming interaction between scholars willing to think about the subject and analysts and appointed and elected officials willing to take time from their schedules to reflect on their experiences. Such an interaction is not easily arranged, but it is worth arranging. Much can be learned—and not exclusively about the arcane worlds of intelligence and foreign or defense policy. If rules or principles come to light, they are likely to apply to any set of connections between possessors of knowledge and users of knowledge. I hope progress can be made. I think it will.

NOTES

1. These were each house's votes on its version of the legislation. The conference report favored the House version. The House accepted it with the same vote as before. The final vote in the Senate was, however, 41–15, with some of the nays coming from ardent isolationists such as William E. Borah of Idaho, who argued that the House version left too much discretion to the executive branch. See Robert A. Divine, *The Illusion of Neutrality* (Chicago: University of Chicago Press, 1962), 186–193.

2. Quoted in Richard Nixon, *The Memoirs of Richard Nixon* (New York: Warner, 1979), I:461.

3. Walter Lippmann, *The Cold War* (New York: Harper, 1947).

4. Spencer R. Weart, *Nuclear Fear: A History of Images* (Cambridge: Harvard University Press, 1988), 236.

5. John F. Kennedy, *The Strategy of Peace* (New York: Harper, 1960), 170; and Kennedy's

acceptance speech quoted in Arthur M. Schlesinger, *A Thousand Days: John F. Kennedy in the White House* (Boston: Houghton Mifflin, 1965), 60.

6. See William Schneider's essay in *Eagle Defiant: United States Foreign Policy in the 1980s*, ed. Kenneth A. Oye et al. (Boston: Little, Brown, 1983), 33–66.

7. *New York Times*, February, 26, 1989, 22.

8. The best-informed published accounts of these developments are James Bamford, *The Puzzle Palace: A Report on America's Most Secret Agency* (Boston: Houghton Mifflin, 1982); William E. Burrows, *Deep Black: Space Espionage and National Security* (New York: Random House, 1986); and Jeffrey T. Richelson, *The U.S. Intelligence Community* (Cambridge: Ballinger, 1985).

9. Sterling Seagrave, *The Marcos Dynasty* (New York: Harper and Row, 1988), is a good summary account. It, however, misses much of the story that I emphasize here. It mentions Solarz and Lugar only briefly and, except for Frederick Brown of the Senate Foreign Relations Committee staff, says nothing about analysts, such as Marjorie Niehaus of the State Department, who shaped the judgments of decision makers. At Harvard, a Kennedy School of Government draft case, "The Fall of Marcos" (C16-88-794.0), elaborates the argument given here.

10. The best published account is John Ranelagh, *The Agency: The Rise and Decline of the CIA* (New York: Simon and Schuster, 1986).

11. Richard Betts, *Surprise Attack: Lessons for Defense Planning* (Washington, D.C.: Brookings Institution, 1982).

12. A brief account of this appears in Ernest R. May, ed., *Knowing One's Enemies: Intelligence Assessment Before the Two World Wars* (Princeton: Princeton University Press, 1984), 510–519. I am working on a longer version.

13. Report of the Committee on Government Records (Washington, D.C.: American Council of Learned Societies and Council on Libraries, 1983). This report was reissued by the American Academy of Public Administration.

14. See "Report of the Advisory Committee on Historical Diplomatic Documentation, February 1988," *Newsletter of the Society for Historians of American Foreign Relations* 19 (June 1988): 40–45.

Comment

Stephen J. Solarz

I concur with Ernest May's recommendations. Our government should prudently anticipate future surprises. It is useful, however, to distinguish between different kinds of surprises. There are "surprise initiatives" for which secrecy is considered essential. Foreign governments will attempt in various ways to keep from us knowledge of the initiatives that they are contemplating. Obviously, we have an interest in trying to penetrate the veil of secrecy, but, as May says, we will not always succeed.

Other kinds of surprises are the result not of calculated decisions designed to deceive the United States or to lull it into a false sense of security but of the interaction of complex social, economic, political, cultural, and historical forces. Some of the most significant geopolitical developments of our times, which have had profound implications for vital American interests, were unpredicted. Analysts inside and outside government who were recognized experts in the politics and problems of other countries failed to predict the Sino-Soviet split, the fall of the shah of Iran, the Soviet withdrawal from Afghanistan, the emergence of *perestroika* and *glasnost* in the Soviet Union, or the modernization program in China. Several years before the emergence of these developments, few, if any, of the leading experts in the country had predicted them. I can recall vividly the Soviet invasion of Afghanistan in 1979. If one had assembled the nation's hundred leading Soviet specialists and asked them what were the chances that a decade later the Red Army would be leaving with its tail between its legs, I do not think any of them would have predicted that a retreat was likely to occur. And yet it did.

The lesson to be learned from such events is that, although obviously we need to increase our knowledge, we need to do the best we can to minimize the possibilities for these grand surprises. Moreover, we need to approach the future with a little humility. If we can be certain of one thing, it is that a century from now new surprises will have taken place that nobody could have predicted.

Looking at May's example of the Philippines, I think it is important to avoid the mistake that people often make in analyzing political campaigns.

The tendency is to assume that any successful campaign, in which the candidate wins, is a brilliantly managed campaign and that any losing campaign, in which the candidate is defeated, is by definition a poorly managed one. That conclusion is not logical. Losing campaigns can be brilliantly managed, and winning campaigns, miserably managed. The true test of an effective campaign is not whether an office seeker wins or loses, but whether he or she maximized the potential in the situation. A candidate can win by 1 percent who should have won by 25 percent, and one can lose by 1 percent who should have lost by 50 percent.

In the Philippines, the major reason for U.S. success there was luck, not government analysis. Only at the 59th minute of the 24th hour of the 365th day of the year did we decide upon a policy. If the minister of defense, Juan Ponce Enrile, and the chief of staff, Eddie Ramos, had not decided to break with Ferdinand Marcos (because Enrile concluded that Marcos was about to arrest him), Marcos might well have remained in power for some time. High-ranking people within the Reagan administration, even after the elections, even after it was clear that Marcos had declared himself the winner on the basis of massive fraud, thought that the United States would be wrong to cut its links with Marcos. I argued for cutting our links. The administration opposed a break, contending that it might demoralize the Philippine army and government and create a vacuum that might be filled by the communist-dominated New People's Army.

A number of us on the Hill felt that Marcos would ultimately fall and that the communists would be the major beneficiaries. Therefore, we believed, it was in the American interest to speed his departure by severing our links to him. The administration resisted that analysis until Enrile and Ramos broke relations with Marcos. At that point our government made the right decision and deserves credit for it. But if that fortunate circumstance had not taken place, such a happy ending might not have occurred.

How can we maximize the benefits of knowledge for our policymakers and for our country so that we can minimize surprises and act in ways that truly promote the national interest? In conclusion, I would like to offer three suggestions.

First, it is important that we build competitive analysis into the policymaking process—particularly into the collection and assessment of intelligence within the responsible agencies—so that fundamental assumptions can be challenged. With the institution of competitive analysis, we are more likely to avoid decisions that do not take into account all the relevant information than if we had not done so.

Second, it is necessary that we keep the collection and assessment of intelligence separate from policymaking. Policymaking should not drive intelligence. In the 1980s we suffered from this interference in the case of Nicaragua. On several occasions, while being briefed by government agencies, I had the uneasy feeling that the views of intelligence analysts were being driven by those who were making the policy. When that happens, when intelligence is consciously or even unconsciously shaped to satisfy the prejudices of policymakers, we do not serve our country well. Although there must be a connection between intelligence analysts and policymakers, it is vital to keep the two components institutionally separate.

Third, it might be useful to establish an Office of the Historian in every government agency and department. Most of the federal agencies or departments that currently have this office collect and collate internal memoranda and materials for publication. The historian's office, in essence, maintains an institutional history of the agency. But there is a case to be made for requiring the establishment of such an office in every agency of the government, not simply to compile data for purposes of history but also to require agency officials to consult the records of the historian's office before making major policy decisions. Given the enormous turnover among decision makers at high levels of the bureaucracy, administrators may overlook institutional history. By bringing to bear the institutional history of the agency, decision makers could benefit from reviewing analyses of similar proposals or initiatives from the past. They could take into account previous reactions, problems, and achievements in formulating their proposals and recommendations. Legislation along these lines would enable us to benefit significantly from the kind of historical analysis that can inform contemporary decision making.

7. New Directions in Economic Policy

Lawrence H. Summers

Policymakers today must cope with an increasingly integrated world economy. By almost any index the world has become a smaller and more integrated place than ever before, especially during the past twenty-five years:

- Ten times as many Americans traveled abroad in 1988 as in 1960.
- The dollar volume of trade has increased in the world economy fifteenfold since 1965.
- Multinational corporations now carry out more than half of U.S. imports and exports.
- The total volume of cross-border bank accounts that were denominated in foreign currencies in 1963 was $7 billion; by the end of the 1980s that number was $2 trillion.
- On the average day in 1988, $350 billion in foreign exchange changed hands.

These figures all indicate huge changes from the pattern of the past, and it is not difficult to see why international economic integration has increased so rapidly.

Explaining the Rise in Economic Integration

Two coequal forces drive this integration. The first is the influence of technology. As transportation and communications technologies improve, more and more transactions in goods, services, and factors of production become economically feasible.

A single 747 airplane can ferry more people across the Atlantic in one day than the *Queen Mary* could in a year. The current cost of round-trip airfare from Boston to London is less than the 1960s price for airfare from Boston to New York. These statistics illustrate how sharply transportation costs have declined. This trend also affects the way we work and live. On several occasions a colleague of mine, who is conscientious about his teaching responsibilities, had speaking engagements in Europe on Saturday and the following Tuesday. Without much hesitation he gave his speech on Saturday, returned to the United States on Sunday, flew back to Europe just in time to give his speech on Tuesday morning, and returned home Tuesday afternoon so that he could teach on Wednesday.

Communications technology has also improved dramatically. Today it costs half as much to call London from Boston as it cost to call Chicago in 1965. Sending a document instantaneously from Washington to London would have been impossible in 1965 but is effortless now. There is every reason to believe that this kind of technological progress will continue. By one estimate the cost of transmitting information across the Atlantic is likely to fall by 90 percent within the next twenty-five years.

The second force responsible for the increasing integration of the world economy is the reduction of political and military conflict. Although it is true that since 1960 capital flows and international trade have increased relative to the size of the world economy, the level of economic integration was higher in the late nineteenth and early twentieth century than in 1960. Obviously, the two world wars that were fought in the first half of the twentieth century interfered with the forces of economic integration. If the current harmony among nations prevails, the pace of integration should quicken—a process that should accelerate in light of recent developments in Eastern Europe.

What does this increased integration, brought about by peace and technological progress, mean for economic policy? The United States has had extensive experience with economic integration, but at the state level rather than the federal level. Governors and state legislatures have sought to design and implement economic policies that will promote the goal of high and rising standards of living in a setting in which capital, goods, and labor move freely across their borders. Although the challenge of integration is not entirely new, it is new at the national level.

Five Lessons for an Interdependent World Economy

The analogy of the U.S. federal system suggests five lessons that will be important for policymakers to understand in an interdependent world economy: (1) Economic integration is beneficial, (2) the definition of what is "American" becomes ambiguous, (3) international policy coordination of economic activity is important, (4) investment in what is distinctively American should be pursued, and (5) the United States must maintain prudent macroeconomic policies.

The Benefits of Economic Integration

It is vital that we maintain free trade and continue this trend of increased integration. Unquestionably, the confederation of the original thirteen colonies spawned the greatest free trade area in the history of the world. Clearly, if the United States were suddenly to be split at the Mississippi River, the prosperity of both halves of the U.S. economy would decline.

Free trade increases the prosperity of all by permitting specialization and a division of labor based on comparative advantage. It may, in the short run, result in some dislocation, but on balance it is clear that integration is mutually beneficial to all parties. The U.S. government should attempt to promote this integration, not to interfere with it.

The Redefinition of "American"

It was once said that what is good for General Motors is good for America, and what is good for America is good for General Motors. It makes less sense to say that what is good for Delaware is good for Du Pont, and what is good for Du Pont is good for Delaware. In a world in which more than half of IBM's profits are earned abroad, in a world in which more than half of Taiwan's trade surplus represents exports by American multinational corporations, the divergence between "American" corporations and American interests becomes an important one. This will have a number of important implications in areas such as tax and antitrust policy.

In the earlier part of this century states levied corporate income taxes on the profits earned in their jurisdictions. It soon became clear that these taxes were not feasible, however, since corporations could use transfer pricing to move all profits to the state with the lowest tax rate. To address that problem, "formula apportionment" was used. For example, if a firm had 5 percent of its employment, sales, and facilities in a particular state, it would pay taxes on 5 percent of its profits to that state. I predict that a similar principle will guide the taxation of multinationals, an area of the law that has become complex and difficult to administer.

We may also have to revise our antitrust laws, which are currently aimed at preserving competition in the American market. It is not clear how one defines the domestic market when American firms are subject to intense import competition. When it is clear that there will be a high-definition television industry abroad, it may not make sense to worry about the possibility of the industry being monopolized in the United States. First, only a small number of American companies are involved in it, and, second, American companies engage in joint production.

The Importance of International Policy Coordination

In the future it will be necessary or desirable to increase international coordination to the extent that nation-states want to tax, regulate, and affect economic activity. Here again the experience of the states is instructive. States that are generous in offering the corporate charter provisions that managements prefer attract all the corporations. Capital mobility puts pressure on states to engage in similar competitions in other regulatory and tax issues.

Whether this dynamic is desirable or not depends on one's attitudes toward the rules that are at issue. If one thinks that any taxes on profits or capital income are undesirable, one can only be pleased that mobility and competition across jurisdictions will make it impossible for states to tax profits. If decision makers believe that certain forms of regulation and taxation are desirable, even in the context of capital mobility, the case for international coordination of economic activity and regulation is strengthened.

The tax policy debates of the late 1980s provide an example of this phenomenon. Although I do not endorse this point of view, the argument is often made that the deductibility of interest should be limited because the current tax code has stimulated an excessive number of leveraged buy outs and acquisitions. One of the counterarguments is that limiting the deductibility of interest will simply give foreign companies an advantage in acquiring American firms. It may or may not be desirable to curb acquisitions, but if it were, clearly, international coordination of regulatory and tax policies would be the most effective way to do so.

The Need for Distinctively American Investments

In an integrated economy it is important to invest in factors that are relatively immobile and distinctively American. In a global economy it is important to make investments yielding benefits that are relatively confined to the United States.

This is exactly the kind of economic policy challenge that state and local governments must confront. The state of Massachusetts would not benefit greatly from a policy that encouraged its households to save more money than they had previously, since most of the savings would eventually flow into national or even international capital markets. Similarly, investment in basic research would yield some local benefits, but most would not be captured by firms within the state. That does not mean that these investments are undesirable, but state and local governments have realized that the two kinds of investments that give the highest payoffs are investments in infrastructure and education.

In a world in which technology and capital are mobile, only the skills of the American people are distinctively American. That is why the deterioration of the American educational system over the past twenty years is so alarming. There are innumerable horror stories: many children cannot read train schedules, and about 75 percent of American high school students cannot find France on a world map. Policymakers do not know how to reform our educational system. Money alone is not the answer. One fact that is worth remembering, however, is that the average verbal SAT score of a student going into teaching is only 420. Since half the teachers in the United States will be retiring by the end of the century, this low score suggests some of the steps we must take to improve our educational system.

Recent data also indicate that higher education has become increasingly important for our society's economic well-being. In 1976 Richard Freeman wrote a book called *The Overeducated American*.[1] In this book he observed that the difference in income between college and high-school graduates had declined from approximately 30 percent to 20 percent during the 1970s. That situation has changed dramatically. Between 1979 and 1987 the average income differential between twenty-six-year-old males with and without college degrees increased from 29 to 57 percent, a trend that is continuing today. This is the largest and most rapid change that has been observed since such data have been collected; it indicates that the demand for highly skilled personnel is rising relative to supply. For these reasons increases in the level and efficiency of our investment in education are essential if the United States is to meet the needs of the new workplace and compete in an increasingly integrated world economy.

A similar argument (with somewhat less certainty than for education) can be made with respect to investments in infrastructure. Unfortunately, since the 1960s net investments in infrastructure as a share of the federal budget have declined by more than 75 percent. As a result the efficiency of our economy is reduced as bridges crumble and roads and airports become congested. Infrastructure, too, is distinctively American, not something that is likely to be moved overseas.

Maintenance of Prudent Macroeconomic Policies

It is tempting to take the position that economic integration eliminates the need for the United States to address its budget and trade deficits and low savings rate. After all, no one worries about the trade deficit between New Jersey and California. If the United States runs budget deficits, but can borrow from abroad to finance investment, the budget deficit is not really a problem. William A. Niskanen made an argument along these lines in the early 1980s, when he explained why budget deficits had not crowded out investments to the extent that many observers had expected.[2]

This line of reasoning is dangerous if taken to extremes. Consider, for example, the case of a small, open economy engaged in heavy external borrowing to allow consumption to rise faster than income. This economy watched its interest rates rise, saw the relative price of its goods on world markets increase, and eventually experienced a financial crisis. I am not describing Mexico, Argentina, or Brazil. I am describing New York City between 1971 and 1975, when it pursued all of these policies. At some point borrowing to finance consumption became untenable because creditors began to wonder whether the city had the will to repay its debt. The city's eventual adjustment was extremely painful. I do not think the United States is at that stage now, but neither did the people of New York City in 1973. Several warning signs have emerged. One sees proposals to restrict foreign investment. There is the very real possibility that financial markets will accept the projection that the dollar will fall to 90 to 100 yen. When this happens, the prophecy will become self-fulfilling, and capital, both domestic and foreign, will flow out of the United States just as capital left New York City.

As long as economic integration is incomplete, it is not likely for the richest country in the world to be able to rely on foreign capital to finance half its net investment. This situation, which threatens the stability of the U.S. and the world economy, could derail the process of integration. The United States should not take the willingness of foreigners to extend credit in the short run as a signal that it can live beyond its means in the long run.

In conclusion, I believe that these five lessons and the challenges they present—maintaining an open trade and financial system, redefining what "American" is, coordinating policies that affect transnational economic activity, investing in what is distinctively American, and maintaining macroeconomic balance—will define the international dimension of economic policy.

NOTES

I am grateful to Thomas Kalil for assistance with this paper.

1. Richard Freeman, *The Overeducated American* (Orlando: Academic Press, 1976).
2. William A. Niskanen, Remarks presented during the opening panel of Public Policy Week, sponsored by the American Enterprise Institute, Washington, D.C., December 1981.

Comment

Isabel Sawhill

A s always Lawrence Summers is creative and thoughtful in the way he lays out the issues. Since I do not disagree with him, I would like to consider some slightly different topics.

During the past two hundred years the United States has clearly made accomplishments in its economic policy. In particular, the economy is less susceptible to financial panics and major depressions than it once was. That is in part due to institutional changes and in part due to advancements in economic understanding and economic policy.

But the United States could still do a lot better than it does. The major problem is that it does not have a well-considered and well-coordinated economic policy. As a result we as a nation are, to use Sen. Daniel Patrick Moynihan's words in the 1989 report of the National Economic Commission, "slouching, not marching toward the 21st century." [1] There are many reasons for the absence of an overall economic policy. Some of them are related to the nature of U.S. political institutions, which Americans may or may not want to change. But we should at least be debating these matters.

What should be the major goals of economic policy? I would certainly include reducing inflation, lowering unemployment, promoting growth, and, a little more controversially, ensuring a fairer distribution of income than we have now. One could also argue for the inclusion of a fifth goal—improving our competitiveness—which links back to Lawrence Summers's observations. I omitted competitiveness because the problems the United States has in that area are symptomatic of its failure to achieve the basic goals enumerated above. If the nation were able to achieve these other goals, our international trade balance and our competitiveness would not be major issues.

These goals, as stated, are not particularly controversial, but rhetoric does not constitute a policy. One must specify one's objectives. This is something politicians generally have been unwilling to do. There is a danger in setting specific goals. They may turn out to be unrealistic and will then be ignored. This was the fate, for example, of the Humphrey-Hawkins legislation of 1978 and the Gramm-Rudman legislation of 1985. It remains to be seen whether it will be the fate of the balanced budget legislation of 1990.

Given the aforementioned problems, I do not favor embedding specific numerical objectives in legislation, but I do support an explicit public debate about U.S. economic objectives.

Reducing inflation is the first goal on my list. Is the national objective to reduce the inflation rate to zero, that is, to eliminate inflation? Or is it simply to contain inflation at its present level? The de facto policy in recent years has been one of containment. The goal, at least since 1983, has been to prevent an acceleration of inflation above approximately 4 percent a year. I do not think that was a bad policy, but some would argue that we missed an opportunity to eliminate inflation entirely. In the midst of a recession few people worry much about inflation, but it is a major constraint on the Federal Reserve's actions. Inflation hawks are willing to accept a longer or deeper recession to achieve their goals; inflation doves are not.

Economists are divided over which is the better policy. Some believe that high unemployment, even for a few years, does more damage to the economy than a moderate level of continuing inflation. But they would also admit that it would take only a temporary period of high unemployment to ratchet down the inflation rate to a new and lower level. So if people really dislike inflation, they should welcome a downturn in the economy. In short, a recession can be viewed as an investment in a more inflation-free future.

Paul Volcker, with the support of the Reagan administration, made a big investment in reducing inflation in the early 1980s. The 1990–1991 recession can be viewed as a mechanism for preserving the gains. Everyone seems to want as mild a recession as possible, but people ought to be aware that a mild recession is not consistent with the goal of reducing the inflation rate to zero.

The next goal on my list is lowering unemployment. In the mid-1980s I told the Joint Economic Committee and the House Committee on Banking that it would be possible to reduce the unemployment rate to about 5-1/2 percent in the late 1980s without its being inflationary. At the time most other economists were arguing that the inflation-safe rate of unemployment was considerably higher. I think history proves that I was right. I also think that at an unemployment rate of about 5 percent we reach the limits of what macroeconomic policy alone can achieve.

If we wanted to push the unemployment rate any lower, we would have to rely on job placement, training, and possibly direct job-creation measures targeted on the so-called structurally unemployed. Current efforts in this area are paltry. The Employment Service is widely regarded as outmoded and ineffective. The nation's major training program, the Job Training Partnership Act of 1982, is inadequately funded. There is no targeted job creation program. I do not know whether the high rates of joblessness in inner-city areas are the result of a lack of opportunities or a lack of interest on the part of the residents of these communities. But I do know a good way to find out—by mounting a few small-scale demonstrations that would offer minimum-wage jobs in either the public or the private sector to people without the skills and contacts to find them on their own. If no one showed up to take the jobs, we could conclude that the problem is on the supply side of the labor market. If the response was large, we could conclude the opposite.

The third goal on my list is promoting economic growth. By economic growth I do not mean the increase in output and employment that naturally occurs as part of a business cycle recovery when factories with idle capacity and jobless people can be put back to work. Rather, I mean the ability of the economy to expand after all its resources are fully employed. This expansion requires creating new capacity, using new technology, and improving the quality of the work force or increasing its size. Because the economy operated below its capacity during the 1980s and is once again in a recession, growth has been only a theoretical issue. But if and when we achieve an unemployment rate near 5 percent and a capacity utilization rate in the neighborhood of 85 percent, the U.S. economy will not be able to grow any faster without an expansion of supply.

So far I see no evidence that lower tax rates and the other supply-side measures introduced in the early 1980s have had much effect on U.S. productivity growth. The result is that growth in the capacity to produce goods and services is stuck between 2.0 and 2.5 percent a year. Most economists would argue that it is extremely difficult to influence this particular policy target. Changing the long-term rate of economic growth by even a couple of tenths of a percentage point is very difficult to do. Nevertheless, most economists think we should try, and most agree that the best way to produce a healthier rate of growth is to reduce the budget deficit, possibly even to run a surplus in the hopes that more public saving will reduce interest rates and encourage private investment.

I believe that more public investment is also needed in the form of adequate attention to the health and education of children, the condition of the nation's infrastructure, and the vitality of its basic research. Here, I would reemphasize Lawrence Summers's point about the need to invest in what is distinctively American. But the only way to obtain major new investments in infrastructure and in the quality of the education system is by paying more attention to the quantity and quality of the public investments in those areas. From a budgetary perspective, there may be merit in distinguishing between federal outlays that represent investment rather than consumption.

The problem with promoting economic growth is that, like achieving the other economic objectives I have discussed, there is a price to pay. In this case the price is decreasing consumption or lowering our standard of living in the short run. Yet because no one seems to want to level with the public about these costs, there is no real mandate for growth. Until policymakers are willing to declare that growth will require tax increases or cuts in middle-class entitlements such as Social Security, they ought to admit that they have chosen a policy of laissez-faire or benign neglect with respect to the nation's economic future. Hand wringing aside, this is a legitimate choice. It is the equivalent of parents telling their children that they are not going to inherit any money because the parents have decided to spend it on themselves. We do not necessarily owe them anything, and, as my Urban Institute colleague Rudolph Penner likes to say, what have our children done for us lately anyway? Needless to say, one does not say that to them; one simply spends the inheritance while mouthing soothing words about the importance of their future.

I want to conclude with a few comments about what Democrats usually call fairness and Republicans usually call opportunity, realizing that these terms are not precisely the same thing. The Reagan administration did not consider the redistribution of income an appropriate object of economic policy. The Bush administration, with its language about a "kinder and gentler America," at first appeared to be signaling a different intent, but its position on capital gains taxation clashed with its rhetoric on this issue. In any case, for various reasons, the distribution of income is more unequal now than it has been at any time in the postwar period, and the incidence of poverty is higher than it was at any time in the 1970s. We could do something about this. The U.S. tax system is less progressive than it once was, mainly because of the increase in payroll taxes, which now take a bigger bite of the average middle-class family's income than do income taxes. The safety net is thinner than it used to be. Although the 1990 budget bill gave the working poor important assistance and provided for a fairer distribution of the tax system, it did not return us to the pre-Reagan status quo. Again, I make a plea for honesty. The nation must either make a serious commitment to reducing poverty and other inequities or admit that it has eliminated this objective from its economic agenda.

I offer these remarks with the intention of provoking policymakers and the public into thinking about their own goals in each of these areas. What are people willing to give up to achieve their goals, and what does that imply in terms of an overall economic strategy? More debate of these issues would help to clarify where the nation is going and whether it can be fairly said that the United States has an economic policy or whether it is simply muddling through.

NOTE

1. *Report of the National Economic Commission* (Washington, D.C.: U.S. Government Printing Office, March 1, 1989).

Comment

William A. Niskanen

Lawrence Summers portrays an image in which the world economy is rapidly becoming integrated. I think this image is somewhat overstated for a number of reasons. First, the world economy is clearly much less integrated than it was about a hundred years ago. This is best illustrated by the fact that for about fifty years before World War I the British maintained a current account surplus of about 4 percent of their GNP. (The current account surplus is a measure of the net value of foreign investment by a nation.) The relative amount of net foreign investment has never been higher than during this period. World capital markets were much more integrated in the period from the late nineteenth century until World War I than they are now.

It is important to distinguish between the integration of financial markets and the integration of capital markets. Financial transactions can be made almost instantaneously these days. To integrate the capital market, however, you must have a real flow of goods and services across national borders, secure property rights, some means of enforcing contracts and property rights and of collecting bad debts, and so forth.

It is also important to distinguish between what has happened to technology and what has happened to the institutions of foreign trade and investment. The technology of the world economy has increased, although I think not as rapidly in this century as it did in the previous century. For example, the difference between satellite communication and submarine cable communication is not great compared to the difference between a submarine cable and a mail pouch on a steam packet. Technology is probably not improving as rapidly now as it was then.

More important, the institutions that integrated the world economy, particularly the world capital market, in many cases have eroded. Many countries have formal restraints on the repatriation of earnings, and the security of property rights across international borders is not nearly as high as it was in the nineteenth century. Sovereign governments now regularly default on their loans. Not long ago that was a dangerous thing for governments to do, because Britain and other Western nations, including the

United States, would send in marines to take over the customs house if sovereign governments did not perform on their foreign debts. The world economy is probably becoming more integrated in recent years and, if there is a genuine rapprochement with the Soviet Union and an opening to the East, it will probably become more integrated than ever. The fundamental institutions that led to the substantially great integration in the late nineteenth century, however, would have to be revived in some form to achieve much more substantial integration.

Second, Summers endorses increased coordination among the exchequers of the world and among the regulators of the world. That may serve the interest of governments, but it would be disastrous for the rest of us. In effect, he is promoting a cartel among the exchequers of the world so that they would not compete with one another on tax rates. This would be similar to allowing the American governors to agree that none of them is going to compete with the others on tax rates among the American states. The governors could use this restriction on competition to raise more revenue, but it is not clear that such an agreement is in the interest of the rest of us. Free trade with interjurisdictional competition in taxes and regulation has the effect of leveling down taxes and regulation, in most cases, to conditions that best serve the interest of consumers and taxpayers. The kind of cartel among exchequers or among regulators that Summers seems to be promoting would level *up* such taxes and regulation.

The key to the effect of the European Community 1992 project is exactly that. If the EC project leads the participants to a single market, and that is all the participants do, the spontaneous competition among jurisdictions would level down tax rates and regulation within Europe. But if the Eurocrats in Brussels have their way, and formally coordinate tax rates across the European countries and implement European-wide regulations, that is very likely to level up both tax rates and regulations, more than overwhelming the favorable consequences of the breakdown of trade barriers.

My view is that we are much better served by the combination of free trade and interjurisdictional fiscal competition and regulatory competition than by any kind of coordination among exchequers and regulators that Summers seems to promote.

Third, Summers encourages increased investments in education and infrastructure. I am a little suspicious when a university professor promotes investments in education because there may be a conflict of interest. (I also believe that he overstates the mobility of capital relative to labor.) New flows of capital are quite mobile across countries, but the existing stock is in place and is subject to considerable exploitation. Labor, and particularly skilled labor, can be very mobile across a country. Ireland, Israel, and India each made a big investment in education and in recent years have seen a substantial part of their skilled labor force leave their home countries. In many cases these skilled workers come to the United States; find employment at a university as assistant professors, trying to get their green card; and then find a way to stay. It is not clear that labor is less mobile than capital, and it is not clear that increased investments in schooling have a very high payoff. I want to distinguish between schooling and education. The United States invests more in schooling than any nation. I wholly agree with Summers that increased investments in education can have a high payoff. The question is whether schooling has much to do with education. Real spending per student in U.S. public schools has doubled about every twenty years since World War II. Real spending per student is now about four times the amount it was when I graduated from public high school. During most of that period the principal measures of the quality of schooling have declined. SAT scores declined from 1963 through 1979, and they have since increased only slightly. About a quarter of college freshmen now are enrolled in one or more remedial courses. It is not clear that increased investment in schooling has a very high rate of return. It is not at all clear that our school systems, including our college and university systems, have that much of a marginal product in terms of education.

We just do not know enough to say that the federal government or other governments ought to channel public monies, whether they are in the form of spending or tax preferences, to particular kinds of investments. In general, I agree with Summers that it probably does not pay for Massachusetts or any American state to invest in basic research and development, because the benefits of R&D flow like water around the world. This may be a problem even for national governments. Some good studies have suggested that the proportion of the benefits that can be captured by the nation that generates the R&D has declined in recent years, thus reducing the payoff to an individual nation of investing in R&D. There are reasons to believe that the United States may underinvest in R&D and in physical infrastructure, but we do not know enough to channel investments into particular factors of production on the premise that our labor force and not our capital is what is characteristically American or is most likely to stay here.

Fourth, Summers makes a strong pitch for free trade except under conditions in which other countries do not have free trade. In other words, he insists on what he calls symmetrically free trade. That may sound like a desirable goal, but the implications are, for example, that if foreign countries take an action that harms their own consumers to benefit some of their producers, we should do something similar ourselves: we should harm our own consumers to help some of our producers. The unfortunate, real world effects of most experience with what is now called strategic trade policy is that all that is left in place are the retaliatory measures.

A good example is the so-called chicken war of the 1960s, when the Europeans put tight restraints on the import of American chickens. We responded to that by placing a 25 percent tariff on light trucks. The Europeans still have tight restraints on the purchase of American chickens, and we still have a 25 percent tariff on light trucks. We have not had one single success in opening the European market by such measures.

We have had a few successes with respect to Japan and some of the other Pacific Rim countries, but most benefits from those measures will not actually accrue to the United States. The United States has pressured Japan, for example, to substitute very high tariffs for their quotas on beef and citrus product imports, but at least with respect to beef, most of the benefits will accrue to Australia and not to the United States. We have, by considerable pressure, broken the Japanese tobacco monopolies so that the decline in cigarette sales in the United States can be matched by an increase in the sale of American cigarettes in Japan. Probably our biggest success is that after months of negotiations we persuaded the Japanese government to change the rules of a Japanese softball league so that the Japanese might have the right to buy American aluminum softball bats. Such is the way that a great power, or at least a once-great power, is using its leverage over its good friends.

Finally, Summers makes the point that, at least until the world economy is perfectly integrated, macropolicy is still important. I want to make a stronger point: macropolicy is important even with a fully integrated world economy. If we have a completely integrated world capital market, macropolicy cannot affect the level of domestic investment, but it can still affect the level of domestic saving. In an integrated capital market, investment will flow to where the returns are highest—at least corrected for the security of property rights, taxes, and so forth—regardless of the level of savings in a given country. That is happening more and more in the United States and in the world as the levels of domestic investment are increasingly diverging from levels of domestic savings. By and large that is a good thing. But even in a perfectly integrated world capital market, the level of domestic saving is a function of macropolicy. In that particular area, and maybe only in that area, I think Summers understates his case.

8. The Debate over Social Policy: The Larger Issues

Nathan Glazer

The United States has been distinguished among the great nations of the world by a basic optimism. America is not afflicted, as some nations are, by a heritage of oppressive class oppression and class warfare; it has not been subject to foreign occupation and domination; it has the greatest wealth of natural resources in the world; and it is a society of immigrants, who by definition come with the hope that life can be better than in the old country. All this may be changing, and, if it is, one reason is that America's optimism over its ability to deal with social problems has been shaken again and again in the past twenty-five years, either by absolute failure, by some measures, or at least by no very substantial progress.

These reflections are inspired by Richard Nathan's book, *Social Science in Government,* which tries to sum up America's experience in using knowledge to guide government in its dealings with social problems. He contrasts the days of the Kennedy and Johnson administrations with today. An "optimistic, almost euphoric, belief on the part of social scientists and many politicians that social science scholarship can be useful in the governmental process" has been replaced by a fading optimism. "In recent years political leaders have been less willing to apply social scientific knowledge in a systematic way in government." [1] It is not hard to think of reasons why this might be true. Social science once promised much, in the design of social programs and in their testing and evaluation. Insofar as our testing and evaluation have improved—and I believe they have—they have demonstrated that our designs for policy were not very good.

The Expectations of the 1960s: Knowledge Guiding Power

The story of this growing sobriety among political leaders, social scientists, and policymakers, begins twenty-five years ago or more, when a high optimism about what could be done by the federal government coincided with an equally high optimism about what could be proposed by social scientists. It was a time when the first unified, comprehensive attacks on inner-city problems—then much more modest than today—were being launched under the auspices of the Ford Foundation. Robert Kennedy and his advisers saw in those models programs that could be applied everywhere to attack not only juvenile delinquency and crime (his mandate as attorney general) but the whole complex of problems associated with poverty. And so political appointees who were temporarily in government, consultants from foundations and universities, permanent civil servants, and intellectuals and journalists met to develop federal government programs of a scope and comprehensiveness never before seen. The general opinion was that if we attacked our problems of poverty and crime and family breakup and inadequate education with energy and originality, dismissing or going around local and state bureaucracies, breaking with rule-bound bureaucratic behavior, and with the backing of an activist federal administration, a rapid improvement would follow in the condition of the poor and problem-ridden.

To explain the presence of the rather odd assortment of people then engaged in creating the poverty program, one must recall that the issue of poverty in American life had been brought to the attention of the president by a long article in the *New Yorker* by Dwight Macdonald, which summarized and commented on Michael Harrington's book, *The Other America*.[2] Energetic Kennedyites in those days, along with their intellectual and academic friends, took a rather contemptuous attitude toward those who labored permanently in the government agencies on these problems: they felt they could do better, out of simple energy and commitment or through greater intelligence and ingenuity or by using the tools of social science, of which they (and social scientists) then had a rather exaggerated opinion.

Charles R. Morris, in an interesting book that deals in part with the origins of the poverty program, gives an accurate picture of what it was like in that dawn, in Washington, to be alive and working on the great problems of society:

When the decision was taken to eliminate poverty [I assume some irony is intended], Johnson's top advisors—mostly holdover Kennedy technocrats, including a number of recruits from [Robert] McNamara's Pentagon—set about the task with the brisk, no-nonsense, sleeves rolled up, let's get it over with, grim good humor that fit the cherished legend of their fallen hero.

The programs were supposed to produce results quickly. [Sargent] Shriver's main criterion for including proposals in the final package was that they had to promise visible progress before the 1966 midterm congressional elections. He courted conservative congressmen assiduously with detailed estimates of the cash savings that would accrue to the nation from reduced welfare, reduced crime, increased tax payments. . . .

Such a massive conspiracy of self-delusion is altogether astonishing. . . . The slightest scraps of data and the broadest sociological associations—as that between education and crime, for instance—were used to underpin huge, wobbly towers of interventionist hypothesis.[3]

Remarkable hubris, one might think. But the bright policy analysts from the Pentagon and the Rand Corporation (who were then moving into domestic research) believed they had accomplished great things by applying advanced statistical and mathematical techniques to determining what weapons systems or deployment strategy gave the greatest benefit. They were joined by social scientists and economists who were equally in a stage of surprisingly limited self-doubt. "Cost-benefit" analyses—as in Sargent Shriver's approach to members of Congress—were all the rage. Shortly thereafter came PPBS, the Planning-Programing-Budgeting System, with the same Pentagon-Rand origins. We would be surprised these days to find such mixed sources for a determined attack on social problems, but the Kennedy ethos combined a high and militant posture abroad with an equally high-posture attack on social problems at home. The two orientations have in subsequent years become somewhat divorced.

Knowledge guiding power was the main theme, and the main hope. The knowledge was to be comprehensive, since it was clear that all the problems of the poor were linked. If analysts were concerned with crime, they had to deal with education; if education, with teen-age pregnancy and limited horizons; if teen-age pregnancy and limited horizons, with the supply of jobs; if the supply of jobs, with job training; and so on. It was easy to make the links and to determine that all agencies should work together, along with outside institutions, from community block organizations to foundations. And America went through the sequence of the poverty program, the Model Cities program, and a variety of others, a history that has been well recorded. Unfortunately, the record rarely brought up clear successes. Richard Nathan quotes a student in one of his seminars who says, "Liberal advocates of social progress shoot themselves in the foot by emphasizing studies that often show the limits and pitfalls of social programs and rarely show their successes." [4] There is an obvious reason why they do that. There are not many successes to show.

At the Housing and Home Finance Agency, where I worked, then under the guidance of the able economist Robert Weaver, who was to become the first black cabinet official when his agency became Housing and Urban Development, it seemed clear that if all the resources of government were concentrated on one problem housing project we could improve matters. We at the HHFA had the problem housing project, Pruitt-Igoe in St. Louis, recently built, but already 25 percent vacant, at a time when most housing projects were full. The Department of Health, Education, and Welfare, then under Abraham Ribicoff, had the social programs. We met around a huge table to see how we could concentrate welfare, social services, education, and many other programs of HEW on the troubled project. It was a revelation to me to discover how many social programs were already in existence, even in those early days before the poverty program. An equal revelation was how hard it was to get them to work together, despite the best will in the world on the part of all the participants. We were able to do some things. We set up welfare and other social services in the project itself. We commissioned a major research study of the project. But only a few years later these great buildings, now almost completely deserted by the poor, who refused to live in them, were dynamited, and the picture made the cover pages in journals of city planning and architecture around the world.

One argument to explain our failures was that not enough money was spent. But indeed the increase in expenditures for social programs was substantial and did not slow down until well into the 1970s. And had the expenditure been doubled, does anyone with knowledge of these programs believe it would have made much difference?

It was often pointed out then that it would take only $11 billion or some such figure to bring all those below the poverty line up to the poverty line. That calculation was possibly accurate, but it turned out it was simply not relevant—not because Congress would not appropriate the money but because there was no way to demonstrate how one could eliminate that gap with the $11 billion that would in theory do so. "Eliminating the income gap" was not as simple as filling a container to the point at which the liquid meets a measure. People were not passive receivers of income.

They changed their behavior in response to the income and kind of income they received. Some stopped working or worked less; some wives left their husbands; and some husbands left their wives. When social scientists undertook the massive social experiments that were designed to guide us in determining how an income-maintenance program to eliminate poverty would work, the results were disappointing. There would apparently be more of such program-defeating behavior than expected. No one ever figured out how to fill the gap.

One problem then with knowledge leading power was the state of knowledge. Social scientists believed they knew more than it turned out they did. When members of Congress asked skeptical questions about various kinds of income-maintenance programs, it may not have been because they distrusted the projections of the social scientists but because they were worried about how much it would cost. Or they wondered how their working constituents would respond to a program that gave money and services to nonworking people in the hope that it would encourage them to work. Or perhaps they distrusted the income-maintenance approach from a simple and old-fashioned conservative Calvinism. There are always influences on power other than knowledge, even assuming the knowledge is sound. The social scientists in policy studies knew that. Politicians must respond to constituents, contributors, party leaders, and so on. But as time went on it turned out that the assurances legislators were given by the policy analysts—assurances based on the best information the analysts could muster—were probably wrong.

Knowledge about such matters as income maintenance has increased—it would have had to. There is far more sophistication and knowledge about social programs today than there was twenty-five years ago. But the main lesson learned is how hard it is to come to any conclusions that social scientists can with assurance provide politicians. Indeed, the policy analysis enterprise has learned how complicated government is; how hard it is to guarantee that when money is provided for some purpose it will be used for that purpose; how hard it is to change the practices of the myriad employees of government who after all must run the programs; how easy it is for them to slip back to traditional approaches after the "experimental" or "demonstration" money is gone; how hard it is for federal hopes and intentions to work their way on state and local government to affect the recipients of aid; and so on.

Even taking into account all the problems of doing anything new in government, the result of the enterprise overall has been disappointment. It was easier to use social science to evaluate programs than to create them, although even the evaluation effort had its pitfalls. The evaluations showed little or no change. According to Peter Rossi, "the expected value of any net impact assessment of any large scale program is zero," and the better designed the assessment, the more likely the estimate of net impact will be zero. The better social scientists become in their processes of assessment and evaluation, the worse the programs look. Rossi's conclusion—and few experts in policy analysis would diverge much—is that over the past two decades "the American establishment of policy makers, agency officials, professionals and social scientists did not know how to design and implement social programs that were minimally effective, let alone spectacularly so." [5]

Even the best of the programs is not that successful. For example, one program that had a good reputation is the Job Corps. This intensive program for unemployed youths operates in a residential setting, to take them away from an "unhealthy" environment. Such intensive programs are expensive, no cheaper generally than the same time spent in college or in jail. Because these programs are expensive, government properly asks what is gotten for the money, and policy analysts try to determine a "cost-benefit" ratio—what is spent on the program and what society gets back. I hope members of Congress ask searching questions when they are told about cost-benefit ratios. In the case of the Job Corps program,

researchers found a cost-benefit ratio for the society of 1:1.46. It needs to be noted, however, that 40% of the benefits came from reductions in criminal behavior, despite the obvious difficulty in measuring the costs to the society of crimes not committed. In the Job Corps case, the values assigned to injury and loss of life due to reduced criminal behavior had a very large effect on cost-benefit findings. ... A murder was estimated to cost society $125,305. The cost-benefit ratio of the Job Corps would have been negative ... if crime reduction had not been considered and if increased production had been the only benefit considered.[6]

Questioning Policy Proposals

Richard Nathan tells us, "Politicians are bound to ask, 'Does it work?' " I believe one can get a great deal of insight into the policy enterprise by analyzing closely that three-word question and the real difficulties in answering it. When a politician asks that question, the "it" he or she has in mind may be a proposal to spend another $100,000,000 on some new social initiative—welfare, education, health, whatever. But despite the specificity of the expenditure, the "it" is going to be undefined. The program inevitably will involve different states and different cities, people to implement it who are different from those who proposed it, clients who have come into the system for different reasons, from different racial and ethnic groups with different values and experiences and expectations. Whatever "it" will be—advice on how to get jobs, requirements to search for jobs, baby-sitting arrangements so that mothers can seek jobs, an allowance for clothes so that they can go to interviews—it is going to be somewhat different in each place it is conducted, indeed, in each interaction between a welfare worker and a client or between an administrator and a welfare worker. What policy analysts will come up with in their evaluation of the "it," to determine whether it is a good idea, are findings about something that is related to the original pristine idea, the Platonic idea, if you will, in a vague and general way.

This was the problem, for example, with all the debates on whether desegregation works. "It"—desegregation—was radically different from place to place: a public-minded university town doing what it thought was right was very different from a resistant community clubbed into a desegregation plan by a federal judge. How could analysts make a judgment that "it" works or does not work?

This is only the beginning of the consideration of why the question "Does it work?" will reduce sophisticated policy analysts to despair. This is not to say they will not undertake the research to find out, making the best stab at what "it" is or will turn out to be. Why not? It will keep their graduate students and staff employed, they will learn more about policy research, and in the end they can write another paper or book on the difficulties of policy research. Indeed, this genre of work is probably at this point the most reliable and authoritative product of policy research.

But then there is that other little word in the politician's question "Does it work?" That is, "work." One can mean many things when one asks whether it works. One representative means, will it reduce costs? Another, does the program provide my district or state with more benefits than some alternative? A third, is it the kind of program that can actually be implemented? A fourth, does it improve the lives of the people who will be affected by this program? Some of these meanings of "work" can be dismissed as not proper questions to address to a policy proposal, important as they are and must be to the individual member of Congress.

Determining Society's Larger Goals

In questioning whether policy proposals work, let us consider only the meanings of "work" that everyone would agree are proper to address to the proposal. Does this proposal make things better for the people it is expected to help? Or does it make things better for society?

We have learned a great deal about this matter from that maverick social policy analyst, Charles Murray. In his book *Losing Ground* and in his even more intriguing book *In Pursuit of Happiness and Good Government*, he has asked the question, what is society really after when it creates welfare or health or housing or education programs?[7] One problem with that $11 billion people once talked about to close the poverty gap and one reason there would have been dissatisfaction even if there was a way for that $11 billion to close the poverty gap is that when people talk about poverty they are not really talking about—or not really talking only about—insufficient money by some standard.

A good number of people living below the poverty line at any moment are not a concern at all. They are working, raising a family, not making trouble. It would be an egregious act of government to seek them out to give them more, although they would undoubtedly appreciate it.

Perhaps society should be happy just to give the money to those who have less than most. But the objective of an antipoverty program is more than simply reducing the number in poverty. The public has an image of crumbling urban neighborhoods and housing projects, ridden with drugs and crime, and wonders properly what the effects of increasing the money flow into the area are on those issues, not only on income. A good deal, some claim, already goes into drugs. Will the proposed program simply increase the amount available?

Similarly, when people in general think about inadequate housing they are not thinking of housing per se. Indeed, public housing projects are generally built to excellent structural standards and should last for decades. More than one housing project has been dynamited long before the end of its intended structural life because, for social reasons, people refused to live in it. Twice, presidential candidates have been pictured in the wasteland of the South Bronx saying something would be done. After Jimmy Carter was elected, a major housing proposal was indeed designed for the South Bronx. I recall that Sen. Daniel Patrick Moynihan, no mean policy analyst, said something like, "Why are we building more housing there when people are burning down the housing they have?" It was an excellent question, and it demonstrated exactly that the problem with poor housing was not simply housing.

Much of the same can be said for public health problems. Roger Starr describes a situation in New York City in which a specialized ward is devoted to the treatment of patients with subacute bacterial endocarditis who have contracted the disease by using infected needles to inject drugs:

> The process of curing these people from their once always fatal disease is long and expensive. It requires bed care, sophisticated antibiotic drugs and a course of treatment lasting six weeks or more. In addition ... the patients suffer from ... unpleasant withdrawal symptoms. They are graceless, even insulting, impatient, destructive, dirty, doomed people, snatched from addiction unwillingly and usually prepared to return to it upon their release from the hospital.[8]

If a program to increase our resources to treat this disease in drug addicts is proposed, and legislators ask, will it work, do they mean, will it cure people, or do they mean, will it do anything about the awful conditions of which this disease is only a symptom and for lives in which it serves as an episode?

The doctors concerned with this problem and other advocates of the program will insist it is unfair to broaden the question: it is enough to cure the sick. But how can one restrict oneself to that? It would be as hard as to restrict oneself, in considering a huge program to build new housing in the South Bronx, to the structural soundness of the proposed buildings when one knew that perfectly good housing was being destroyed by arson in the very neighborhoods in which the new housing was to be built.

The point is that in the programs under discussion, however narrowly directed, the public is really after larger goals, which is why even achieving the purported goals of some program is often unsatisfying. In the late 1980s a television program was aired on what is considered one of our best social programs, WIC—which provides women, infants, and children with nutritional supplements and advice. The program showed two women who received WIC benefits. One had nine children and no husband. If we consider its legislative purpose, WIC is a success. But Congress had in mind, did it not, other things, when it passed that legislation. What it was after in WIC was undoubtedly to ensure that pregnant women and young mothers and their children had a good diet. The fact is, however, that was not the *only* thing Congress was after, even if no other objectives were written into the legislation and the program guidelines. It was hoping for a good life for more people. That is what Charles Murray was reminding all of us sharply, and that point is so important that all the technical criticisms of his criticism of social policy ultimately lose their force.

Roger Starr spells out the nature of the discontent the public might properly feel at the triumph of medicine and public policy he has described:

The treatment of the patients in this ward is paid for by government or given free by the hospital, in keeping with medical ethics and the principles of the society. The patients are, in effect, treated no differently than they might be if they had incurred an infection trying to save someone else's life rather than in the process of trying, in a long and tortuous passage, to end their own. It is altogether proper that they should be saved. No one can conscientiously advocate saving money by letting them die, as they inevitably would were their disease to be left untreated. Yet, somehow, to say that they should be saved is not quite enough. What seems missing is the passing of judgment on the matter.[9]

Charles Murray argued, in his first book, that America's social policies expanded along with the social problems they were meant to address. That's a large, crude statement, and he would agree that not all social programs expanded and not all social problems increased. More controversially, he said that the presence of those social programs contributed to the increase of social problems. They offered alternatives to the norms of ordinary life, based on commonly accepted values. The criticism he received, from people such as David Ellwood, Lawrence Summers, Mary Jo Bane, Sheldon Danziger, and Peter Gottschalk, was technically excellent. He could not show, for example, that illegitimacy and family abandonment increased with the size of the welfare benefit that went to provide for it.

And yet something had happened that made him largely correct. "What seems missing is the passing of judgment on the matter," Roger Starr wrote about the treatment of the infected drug addicts. Society had changed, Summer and Ellwood argued, and it was that, not the social programs, that explained more illegitimacy, child abandonment, family breakup, youth unemployment, and so on. Quite so, society had changed; and it could be argued that social policy was simply accommodating itself as best it could to the casualties of that change. Its expansion, if in pace with the rise in social problems, had contributed nothing to that—there were other causes. When Murray answered his critics, he said the changes were all of a piece; each was implicated in the other. Social changes did make for social problems, but social policy made for further social change. And by implication he said that when his critics faulted him on the relationship between one social program and one social problem, they were ignoring what the end of that social program after all was—a better life for people, a better society, not the reduction of one sharply targeted number which policymakers used to measure the problem. So Murray's critics were right when they said he had not proved his case, program by program, problem by problem. But I think Murray was right to point to changes in society in which social policy was implicated: It offered, in the large, alternatives to a long established norm of steady work and stable family life.

The liberal, reform, social democratic vision of society has much that is attractive in it: We soberly attack one problem after another, create one safety net after another. If new problems arise we devise new programs. The American contribution is that we scientifically test the success of these programs so that we can vary them, correct them, improve them. But what seems to be at fault with it at bottom is that it excludes—or at least considerably reduces—the element of judgment, of the discouragement of the worse and the encouragement of the better. Beyond all the technical arguments between the critics of expanded social policy and those who want to expand it further, there lies disagreement on the weight to be laid on traditional values and judgment of their violation.

NOTES

1. Richard P. Nathan, *Social Science in Government: Uses and Misuses* (New York: Basic Books, 1988), 1.
2. Michael Harrington, *The Other America* (New York: Macmillan, 1962).
3. Charles R. Morris, *A Time of Passion: America, 1960–1980* (New York: Harper and Row, 1984), 90–92.
4. Nathan, *Social Science in Government,* 18.
5. Peter Rossi, "The Iron Law of Evaluation and Other Metallic Rules," in *Research in Social Problems and Public Policy,* vol. 4, ed. Joanne Miller and Michael Lewis (Greenwich, Conn.: JAI Press, 1987), quoted in Charles A. Murray, *In Pursuit of Happiness and Good Government* (New York: Simon and Schuster, 1988), 207–208.
6. Nathan, *Social Science in Government,* 92–93.
7. Charles A. Murray, *Losing Ground: American Social Policy, 1950–1980* (New York: Basic Books, 1984); Murray, *In Pursuit of Happiness.*
8. Roger Starr, *The Rise and Fall of New York City* (New York: Basic Books, 1985), 164.
9. Ibid., 165.

Comment

Laurence E. Lynn, Jr.

Nathan Glazer's paper is challenging, but I think he has it wrong. Since he acknowledges that his thinking was influenced by his participation in the events on which he comments, I want to make a similar acknowledgment and draw on my own experience in formulating my reactions.

I began my professional life in the mid-1960s as the kind of optimistic policy analyst he writes about. I was part of the Systems Analysis Office in Robert S. McNamara's Department of Defense, helping to rethink and reshape America's national security. Using sophisticated modeling techniques, I calculated the precise economic value of U.S. ownership of military base rights on Okinawa, a significant intellectual breakthrough as theretofore all foreign base rights had been regarded as priceless.

Later I moved to the domestic side of government with my Pentagon-ingrained analytic habits and worked as the assistant secretary for planning and evaluation at the Department of Health, Education, and Welfare. While there, I built some models, collected and analyzed data, and conducted economic analysis. Affected with the optimism of the times, I did something that Glazer ought to cite because it confirms his case about the hubris of social policy analysts with grand designs. Under the leadership of Secretary Elliot Richardson, my colleagues and I were the authors of what we were pleased to call "the megaproposal"—let the naïve audacity of that concept sink in! We applied the best available analytic talent to the task of rethinking the shape of social welfare in America and the role of the Department of Health, Education, and Welfare in implementing that grand design.

In hindsight, I am still pleased that we made that effort. My colleagues and I produced ideas that were useful then and, in many respects, are useful now. Admittedly, what we were doing could be construed, as Glazer quotes Charles R. Morris, as building "huge, wobbly towers of interventionist hypothesis" (although, since this was a Republican administration, we included some noninterventionist hypothesis as well). But I think there is a better light in which to view that and similar intellectual efforts, which, in Glazer's retrospective view, represent a dangerously feckless naïveté.

Recently, I reread a letter I wrote in the late 1960s to someone I was trying to recruit into the Pentagon, an idealistic young man from the Harvard Business School. (Lest that seem an oxymoron, let me remind you that in the 1960s idealists were everywhere.) In trying to explain why I thought that he, with his ideals and his talent, should come to work for the Defense Department, I included a couple of quotations that I thought made a persuasive point.

The first was from the Gospel according to St. Luke. Jesus said, "For which of you, intending to build a tower, sitteth not down first and counteth the cost, whether ye have sufficient to finish it. . . . Or what king, going to make war against another king sitteth not down first, and consulteth whether he be able with ten thousand to meet him that cometh against him with twenty thousand." [1] I did cost-effectiveness analysis, in other words, not only because it was intellectually the right thing to do but because my Lord commanded me to do it.

But I had another, secular, view with a contemporary ring to it. In his history of World War II, Winston Churchill described his experience in taking over the Admiralty during the early stages of that war:

One of the first steps I took in taking charge . . . was to form a statistical department of my own. I now installed [my friend and confidant of many years] with half a dozen statisticians and economists whom we could trust to pay no attention to anything but realities. This group of capable men, with access to all official information, was able . . . to present me continually with tables and diagrams. . . . They examined and analyzed with relentless pertinacity . . . and also pursued all the inquiries which I wanted to make myself.

At this time . . . each department presented its tale on its own figures and data. . . . [Some departments,] though meaning the same thing, talked different dialects. I had, however, from the beginning my own sure, steady source of information, every part of which was integrally related to all the rest. . . . It was most helpful to me in forming a just and comprehensible view of the immeasurable facts and figures which flowed out upon us. [2]

I believe those quotations capture the spirit of the 1960s. At least, it was the spirit that animated me and, I think, many of us during those years. There are other testaments to that spirit. If there is a book from that time that continues to stand up as a fine, public-spirited work, it is *The Economics of Defense in the Nuclear Age* by Charles Hitch and Roland McKean. [3] If there are perceptive chronicles of the thinking of those years, they are the books by Alice Rivlin and Charles Schultze.[4] These two scholar-participants stressed that the essential tasks of the "purveyors of grand designs" could be expressed in terms such as practicing "systematic thinking," assembling "relevant facts," linking cause and effect, and evaluating "opportunity cost"—providing a counterweight to parochialism and to narrow, unjust views.

None of us analysts believed that we were, or ought to be, the predominant influence on decision making. Alain Enthoven, then assistant secretary of defense for systems analysis and a seminal figure of the period, and others emphasized that analysis is an aid to judgment, not a substitute. We regarded ourselves, nonetheless, as part of an important movement that had as its goal the achievement of highly skilled statecraft in the Churchillian sense.

What should we conclude about those people and their deeds? Was the period an aberration that we should be relieved to put behind us, as Glazer appears to counsel and as we are evidently doing? I am not a historian, but I think a historical perspective puts an interesting light on those years of efforts by scientists, intellectuals, academics, and elite reformers to produce grand designs out of a passion for social improvement, to try to serve as sources of knowledge in guiding the exercise of power. These social engineers continued an important tradition in American public life:

- The American Philosophical Society and Thomas Jefferson launched the Lewis and Clark expedition to replace a mass of confusing rumors and conjectures with a body of compact, reliable, and believable information on the western half of the continent.
- The asylum movement in the decades before the Civil War, which led to the creation of a new set of social institutions, was an important effort motivated by perfectionist reformers, physicians, and other intellectuals who were determined to improve the lot of the dependent needy.
- The Freedmen's Bureau, created after the Civil War to assist in settling freed slaves, was an unprecedented intervention in behalf of a visionary social goal.
- Efforts begun in the latter part of the nineteenth century to promote mental hygiene, and the emergence of a mental health movement based on developments in psychological science, culminated in the adoption of psychological screening and testing and, eventually, in the creation of community-based mental health facilities and deinstitutionalization of the mentally ill.

- A movement to reform public administration beginning in the late nineteenth century and extending through the progressive era, motivated in part by Woodrow Wilson and an academic school of thought, suggested that government could be rescued from reckless partisanship and made more professional and efficient.

- New Deal social legislation is a prime example of social engineering based on grand designs. One of my favorite pieces of policy evaluation was done by Lester Salamon some years ago. He looked at an obscure New Deal program that distributed agricultural land to blacks in the South and was designed to give them economic resources for self-sufficiency. Thirty years or so later he attempted to determine what had happened. He tracked down the people and their families and heirs to see what had changed in their lives. His study produced some wonderful social intelligence on important and beneficial social changes that resulted from a program nobody remembers.[5]

There have been many eras during which grand designers were ascendant. We have seen dedicated efforts on the part of scholars, intellectuals, academics, and other elites to create grand designs and advocate their adoption. But these designs and their designers usually suffered a similar fate—frustration and disappointment, at least to some significant degree. The realities of social and political arrangements always seem to distort or defeat the intentions of would-be social engineers.

One of the most significant vetoes in social policy history, for example, was President Franklin Pierce's veto of congressional legislation that would have distributed federal land to the states for the purpose of creating social institutions such as asylums. Pierce said such legislation was inconsistent with our history, and, at a stroke of his pen, the perfectionist reform movement was broken. The dream of the asylums began going sour almost immediately; after the Civil War they had become a problem, no longer, if they ever were, domains of humane treatment. The Freedmen's Bureau was abolished in 1872, many would say prematurely. The New Deal notion that the adult categories of the Social Security Act would wither away as people became fully engaged in the work force succumbed to reality, and these programs now constitute the corrosive "welfare problem." The controversies over postwar social legislation are well known.

So the story is one of grand designs followed by disappointment. Recent experience is of a piece with historical experience, and we should be neither surprised nor unduly dismayed. Society is never left unchanged by reform efforts, however, and a strong case can be made that the changes that do occur are on balance beneficial to the nation's overall well being and to its inherited wisdom about the practice of democracy.

But that still leaves a question unanswered. How much and what kind of disappointment is justified in this most recent case? Glazer cites Charles Murray's argument in *Losing Ground* as persuasive.[6] I think there are two better books, one on each side of the story.

On the side of the libertarian-conservative critics, Richard Morgan's *Disabling America* presents a richly documented analysis of a string of Supreme Court decisions beginning in the 1960s that dramatically altered the incentives governing the behavior of U.S. institutions, communities, and citizens.[7] Morgan argues that one of the most serious negative consequences of our recent history is that the task of policing the interpretation of the Constitution by judges is no longer the common intellectual responsibility of the country's social, economic, and academic leadership but has largely come under the control of an increasingly closed guild of Supreme Court lawyers, with specialized language and a claim to special expertise, who represent a rights industry that is profoundly disaffected from American culture and society. This shift in responsibility, he contends, has had profound implications for public policymaking. We now have a rights industry armed with an impressive constitutional rhetoric. It operates through courts and administrative agencies to create rules and regulations in the empty policy space between majorities that says in effect to Congress and the country, "Come and get me if you can." This book points the finger at lawyers and not at economists, but its greater virtue is that it states Murray's primary argument more persuasively than Murray does.

A book for the optimists is John Schwartz's *America's Hidden Success*.[8] Schwartz addresses the success of the policies of the 1960s and 1970s, in both environmental protection and the alleviation of poverty. In 1980, he says, one in fifteen Americans faced the desperation of poverty, compared to one in five just a generation earlier. This improvement was accomplished almost entirely by government. Schwartz goes on to say—and this point does not get nearly the attention that it deserves—that this progress occurred despite what he calls the crushing avalanche of American workers entering the labor market during that period. While we were trying to alleviate poverty, we were also experiencing sharp growth in the labor force and the increased participation of women in the labor force. The nearly thirty million workers entering the labor force from 1965 to 1980, he points out, amounted to more than half the entire labor force of Japan and surpassed the total labor force of either France or West Germany. Twelve million new jobs were created and filled in the five years between 1975 and 1980, compared with fewer than seven million during the entire decade of the 1950s. These workers were better educated than earlier generations of workers. Thus an entire cohort of workers was moving into the economic mainstream at the same time that poverty was being reduced and the environment was being cleaned up. This perspective is as deserving of respectful attention as anything that Charles Murray has put forward.

What can one conclude from this review? Glazer says that, in formulating public policies, policymakers should rely on the element of judgment and be skeptical of grand designs and their designers. His view certainly appears to be in the ascendant. The 1988 presidential election was largely innocent of grand designs, and the United States appears to have presidential leadership that is pragmatic and skeptical of ideas. (If you want governance without grand designs, without intellectuals, and without policy analysts, come to Chicago. Governance in Chicago is based almost entirely on the judgment of tribal leaders and very little on anything that one would consider to be a grand design.)

My feeling is that the proper function of policy analysts and intellectuals is to induce a higher order of statecraft in our policy leadership, a greater awareness of the possibilities of both intervention and nonintervention, a greater appreciation of what we know and do not know, a stronger sense of what experience has taught and can teach us. The importance of that function grows with the complexity of the challenges facing the leadership.

I recently had occasion to reflect on my model-building days in the Pentagon, when I was developing linear programming models and allocating resources among ships and aircraft (which, incidentally, we ought to be doing now). The conclusion is inescapable, I thought, that if left to their own devices, the military services would have ignored the transport mission—moving troops, equipment, and supplies from peacetime bases to theaters of war—and its military significance. They simply did not want to think about this operation or devote to it more resources than absolutely necessary. Only the civilian analysts insisted on considering the military value of this mission. It was a civilian analyst who inspired a spirited, focused, precisely formulated debate on an essentially military matter. That example brings me back to Churchill. Who can be relied upon to analyze with relentless pertinacity? Who will decipher and translate the various dialects heard in policy debates? Who will provide "a just and comprehensible view"? Who will offer intellectual assistance to the art of statecraft and to the art of judgment? Who will speak truth to power?[9] However bad we may look in some of our vain self-preoccupations as a community of policy intellectuals, we were conceived in and are essentially still motivated by that larger purpose of forming just and comprehensible views. I think that such a function is essential to the governance of this society.

NOTES

1. Luke 14:28, 31.
2. Winston S. Churchill, *The Gathering Storm,* The Second World War, vol. 1 (Boston: Houghton Mifflin, 1948), 467–468.
3. Charles Johnston Hitch and Roland N. McKean, *The Economics of Defense in the Nuclear Age* (Cambridge: Harvard University Press, 1960).
4. Alice M. Rivlin, *Systematic Thinking for Social Action* (Washington, D.C.: Brookings Institution, 1971); Charles L. Schultze, *The Politics and Economics of Public Spending* (Washington, D.C.: Brookings Institution, 1968).
5. Lester M. Salamon, "The Time Dimension in Policy Evaluation: The Case of the New Deal Land Reform Experiments," *Public Policy* 27 (Spring 1979): 129–183.
6. Charles A. Murray, *Losing Ground: American Social Policy, 1950–1980* (New York: Basic Books, 1984).
7. Richard E. Morgan, *Disabling America: The "Rights Industry" in Our Time* (New York: Basic Books, 1984).
8. John E. Schwartz, *America's Hidden Success: A Reassessment of Public Policy from Kennedy to Reagan* (New York: Norton, 1988).
9. Aaron Wildavsky, *Speaking Truth to Power: The Art and Craft of Policy Analysis* (Boston: Little, Brown, 1979).

Comment

Richard P. Nathan

The main difference between Nathan Glazer's views and mine is that I am not as pessimistic as he is about the role of applied social science research in government. Henry Aaron's thoughtful book on this subject, *Politics and the Professors,* inspired me to write about the role of social science in the policy process.[1] Aaron, like Glazer, is pessimistic. He says that social science has had a "corrosive" effect, that it has hurt the credibility and undermined the promise and prospects of social programs. In a similar vein, but not as sharply, Glazer says that although social science has made progress it cannot provide government policymakers with useful answers and ideas. I respectfully disagree. Social scientists can answer some questions for policymakers, but we must be modest and specific about what the answers are.

There are three kinds of inputs into the policy process to consider. The first one concerns values and beliefs. A policymaker says, "I want to do this, and do it this way, because I believe it is right to do so." This is surely reasonable in light of how little social scientists know with certainty, even taking into account my more optimistic view of the role of applied social science research in the governmental process. The second kind of input into the policy process is political. A policymaker might say, "I want to do this because my constituents need it and care about it." This approach is surely appropriate in a democracy. The third kind of input is based on scientific knowledge and expertise. Knowledge based on applied social science research comes under this heading. Systematic social science knowledge grounded in research cannot, as we thought in the 1960s, be the dominant input into policy, but I believe it can be a stronger input than is implied in much of the literature. This is where Nathan Glazer and I think about our subject differently.

Let me define three kinds of applied social science research. The first kind is concerned with studies of conditions and trends. It is most appropriate and useful when it engages researchers in studies that use primary data. This kind of research attempts to define problems, although I sometimes think social scientists go too far in defining problems. When they do this, they are acting too much like politicians by saying what they would like to see society do.

The second kind of research involves demonstration studies. By demonstration studies, I mean pilot studies of possible new programs designed to learn what works. Policymakers can look at pilot studies to decide whether the government should replicate and generalize a new policy or program. For example, the Manpower Demonstration Research Corporation (MDRC) has conducted important demonstration research in employment and welfare focused on the most disadvantaged groups. These and similar demonstration studies have their roots in the experience of policy analysis for the Defense Department. MDRC studies provided the knowledge base for the Family Support Act of 1988. To a considerable extent this act was the product of a body of demonstration research that randomly assigned people to control and experimental groups and showed positive, consistent, and significant (though not huge) results from interventions to aid women on welfare to enter the labor force. Sen. Daniel Patrick Moynihan and others who fashioned this legislation said they relied on this research. Judith Gueron, the president of MDRC, testified at the hearings on this legislation. Her essential message was, "We have confidence about what we learned from these demonstration studies conducted in eleven states in which 35,000 people participated and on which basis Congress may want to generalize about new work/welfare programs." The Family Support Act, based on social science research, led welfare policy in a direction that I think is sound and encouraging for the 1990s.

The third kind of applied social science research is evaluation research. Evaluation research projects, as I use the term, study programs that have already been adopted. They question the effects of a policy once it is adopted nationally or at the state level. Evaluation research is the frontier of applied social science.

Three questions are important in conducting evaluation research. The first involves implementation: You have a new idea. Was it carried out? The U.S. governmental system does not go far enough beyond new ideas. Policymakers are so busy working on the next new idea that they often fail to examine the implementation of ideas already adopted. Using evaluation research, we need to determine whether a new policy penetrates the bureaucracy. Does it influence the behavior and the services that were supposed to change when Washington or Trenton or Albany passed a new law?

The second question to ask in evaluation research is, If institutional penetration occurred and the bureaucracy responded, was the response sustained? In Massachusetts, when the officials who ran Gov. Michael Dukakis's employment and training program for welfare family heads departed the government, was their strong and effective influence on the bureaucracy sustained?

The third set of questions in evaluation research concerns the effects on individuals. After a new program has been set up and is generalized, we might ask the following questions: Did it make a difference? Did a work/welfare program increase earnings? Did it reduce welfare? Did it increase time worked? How did it affect children, families, and communities? Those are important dependent variables.

Nathan Glazer is an astute observer of contemporary social science, but I believe he is overly pessimistic about the usefulness of social science in government. Although applied social science is not the fount of all wisdom or the way to run technocratic government, it can provide the policy process with a valuable input, particularly if it is multidisciplinary.

NOTE

1. Henry J. Aaron, *Politics and the Professors: The Great Society in Perspective* (Washington, D.C.: Brookings Institution, 1978).

III

Knowledge and Power in Foreign Legislatures

9. Knowledge, Power, and Legislatures: A British Perspective

Denis Healey

I n Britain we once had a chancellor of the exchequer who was not adept at making speeches and had his private secretary write them for him. On one famous occasion when he was addressing the "frozen penguins" in the city of London during his annual speech at the Mansion House, he started off like all chancellors of the exchequer: "My Lord Mayor, your Royal Highness, your Lord Bishops, sheriffs, ladies and gentlemen. The problem we face today is perhaps the most daunting our country has ever known. Unless we can solve it in three short months, I see nothing but catastrophe ahead. There is only one way forward." Then he turned the page and read out, "From now on you are on your own, you bastard!"

There is a basic truth in the saying, "You're on your own," because in Britain few speeches are written other than by the people who deliver them. In the House of Commons it is forbidden for members to read a speech. Members can speak from penciled notes. If they are clearly reading, everybody shouts, "Reading, reading!" and they have to put them away. Then you really are on your own.

Differences Between the British Parliament and the U.S. Congress

Members of Parliament are really very much on their own in collecting the knowledge they need to do their job. In the British tradition they are wealthy amateurs who do politics in their spare time. For 150 years members of Parliament got no payment at all. When I came into the House of Commons in 1952, the MP's salary was a thousand pounds a year, which was then less than three thousand dollars. We had no money for a secretary, none for a researcher. We had to pay for our own postage. Since then the situation has improved, but MPs still get only enough to live on. The salary is now the equivalent of about forty thousand dollars a year, and we get free postage and free travel to our constituencies; however, we get only enough money for one secretary and half a researcher. Few members of Parliament find it possible to employ half a researcher, and so they share a researcher with another member. One researcher working half time, however, cannot provide an MP with much information. Some conservative members get help from firms of which they are directors; some Labour members get help from the trade unions that sponsor them. They still do not have money to employ people to provide them with extensive information.

We are paid less than our American counterparts for several reasons. The first is that we have small constituencies compared with those in the United States. The average constituency in Britain is slightly more than sixty thousand. As I understand it, the average member of the House has as many as half a million constituents. And senators may have forty million constituents. So the burden of work falling on members of the U.S. Congress is enormous compared with that which falls on the average British MP.

British MPs do not necessarily take much interest in their constituents. They tend to get elected because they are the representative of the party that their constituents wanted to put into power. In Roman days Caligula was able to make his horse a consul. Although that does not happen in the Senate these days, in Britain, on the whole, anybody who stands with the Conservatives can be elected in a middle-class seat and anybody taking the Labour interest can win a working-class seat. The personality of the MP is comparatively unimportant.

Furthermore, few people in British politics get financial help from lobbyists. I once read that somebody in the U.S. Congress had received $1,000,000 in two years from defense firms. I also read that in the 1988 Senate election three candidates each got more than $200,000 from twenty-seven pro-Israel political action committees said to have been secretly coordinated by the American-Israel Public Affairs Committee.[1] Help from lobbyists on that scale is unknown in Britain. In any case it is difficult for an individual MP to provide a lobbyist with value for money because our constitution is so different from the U.S. Constitution. British MPs have comparatively little personal influence on the government departments, which decide the issues that concern lobbyists.

This difference is relevant to the relationship between knowledge and power. In the British system the elected government takes all the decisions on policy, on legislation, and on appointments; the opposition can only criticize. The opposition can hardly ever expect to win a vote, except perhaps on the detail of legislation in a committee or sometimes on a matter that is not essentially a party matter. For example, Mrs. Thatcher supported the death penalty, but the majority of the House of Commons opposed it. So the death penalty does not exist in Britain. Similar issues are abortion and corporal punishment.

In Britain, unlike the United States, party discipline, although not absolute, is nearly always effective in determining major issues. I asked former representative John Brademas a few years ago when he was the chief whip in the House of Representatives whether he had much trouble delivering his party's vote. He replied, "Hell, Denis, I can't even deliver my fellow whips." That is not the case in Britain. In Britain the government party can almost always rely on having a majority on any issue, unless the government's overall majority in the House is very small indeed and can be defeated by a handful of its members.

The British system, however, has some advantages. The prime minister and members of the cabinet are nearly always people who, while in opposition, were members of what we call the shadow cabinet. As the opposition, they studied the work they would be doing in office. Moreover, every opposition leader in the shadow cabinet expects to become a minister in the next government. Nothing concentrates a person's mind so powerfully on responsibility as knowing that he or she may be doing the job in a few months' time. In other words, in England the opposition is seen as training for government. The situation in the U.S. Congress is very different.

How does this system affect knowledge and the role of knowledge in Parliament? I believe that active and intelligent members of Parliament can get all the knowledge they need without the enormous amount of assistance available to members of Congress from their staffs and from other sources. On the other hand, wise British MPs learn about the subject they want to concentrate on before they get into Parliament. Some of the most effective politicians in Britain started off as officials of their party organizations—in my party, Peter Shore and me; in the Conservative party,

Ted Heath, Enoch Powell, Reggie Maudling, and Ian Macleod. Each of us did research before taking the job. Members of Parliament can also learn by addressing written questions to the government. Mrs. Thatcher had to admit, for example, that her government was taking thirty-five pounds a month more from the average worker than I did when I was the Labour chancellor of the exchequer.

British MPs can learn from select committees, which are molded on U.S. congressional committees. These are an important source of knowledge for the opposition and for government members. Members of Parliament can read the newspapers. Furthermore, British institutes, such as the Royal Institute of International Affairs (Chatham House) and the International Institute of Strategic Studies, perform the same role that similar institutions, such as the Brookings Institution, do in the United States. And, of course, MPs are lobbied on political issues interminably, whether the cause is saving the whale, stopping the fur trade, or campaigning for nuclear disarmament. These lobbying groups deluge members with information.

In Britain, experience is another source of knowledge for MPs. Each leading member of the major parties probably has spent some years as a minister, to learn how to fight the bull, and that is important. Jack Kennedy used to quote a translation by Robert Graves of a Spanish poet: "Bullfight critics ranked in rows/crowd the enormous plaza full/but the only man who really knows/is the man who fights the bull." [2] Ministers soon acquire the single most important bit of political knowledge: government is choosing. Leaders cannot do everything they want. They must decide their priorities. A bright minister can learn the weight of the different considerations that should determine a decision. This is quite impossible to learn from research staffs.

I was lucky because I was defense secretary for six years after having thought about these problems in opposition with American experts. When I became chancellor of the exchequer, I knew nothing about economics, but I had a five-year course as a mature student in managing the economy when I was at the treasury. I know considerably more about economics now than when I began. One weakness of the American system is that this kind of knowledge does not exist in the U.S. Congress. It is unlikely that a representative or senator who gets a job in the administration will ever return to Congress. I learned a lot by traveling and talking to people, because my major interests, until I became chancellor, were foreign affairs and defense. I got to know George Kennan and Paul Nitze, for example,

in the late 1940s, when they were working for the policy planning staff
at the State Department. George Ball has been my friend since that time.
I got to know Henry Kissinger somewhat later.

Let me tell a story about Henry. I was at a meeting at the Institute of
Strategic Studies in England, just before the election that Nixon won in
1968. We were traveling back from Alistair Buchan's house outside Oxford. Henry said he had been approached by one of Nixon's staff, to see
whether he would be prepared to work for Nixon if Nixon won the
election. Henry said to me, "I'm very doubtful whether I should accept
this invitation, first, because I worked hard for Nelson Rockefeller against
Nixon, but secondly, because I'm not sure I could survive in the Washington environment." That is one of the few cases of bad judgment for
which Henry has ever been responsible.

One of the people I got to know early on when he was still at the State
Department in charge of special projects was Dean Rusk. He made a
remark to me that is relevant to this problem of knowledge and power.
He said the difference between academic life (he had been a professor at
Mills College before going into government) and government service is
the difference between arguing to a conclusion and arguing to a decision.
The best definition I know of a government minister is that he or she is
someone who makes important decisions based on inadequate information. Ministers never know as much as they need to know, even with the
resources of the entire civil service behind them.

It is important to remember that the true worth of knowledge is not
so much having the facts (which, in my experience, are easy to obtain,
even the so-called secret facts, if you work at it) but in understanding the
facts and their relevance. That is a difficult undertaking, because the experts
often do not understand the subjects they study. The three areas of study
in which the disagreements among the experts are greatest are the most
important in politics.

First in importance is economics. People disagree violently about the
theory and practice of economics. We do not even have the facts of
economics. We do not know what is going on now, never mind being able
to forecast the future. An economist, as you know, is a man who, when
you ask him for a telephone number, gives you an estimate. There is
another good definition of an economist: An economist is a man who
knows sixty-five ways of making love but does not know any girls.

Military strategy is just as bad as economics. It was not considered a
subject for academic study until about thirty years ago, when people on

both sides of the Atlantic tried to understand the effect of nuclear weapons on strategy. There are still deep divisions on that issue. The United States tore itself to shreds about whether the other side would try to take out a fraction of its total strategic capacity in a surprise attack; the MX tragicomedy was based on that fear.

Nor do we understand foreign policy, a complex area indeed. For example, we do not yet comprehend how nuclear weapons have influenced foreign policy, although Henry Kissinger wrote a long book on this subject in the mid-1950s.[3] What strikes me now is that scientists try to understand what is happening in the world in terms of cause and effect—what medical people call etiology—but it is usually easier to understand what is going on in terms of process—what medical people call pathogenesis. Understanding a process requires knowledge and experience of the past as well as about the present. Ernest May and Dick Neustadt wrote a book called *Thinking in Time* that contains good sense for decision makers.[4] Although it is imperative that decision makers try to understand the historical and human background of problems, this is one of the most difficult things to learn from academia. Historians can be helpful in that area.

A British View of the U.S. Government

Now I move into a rather difficult area, looking at the U.S. system of government from the British perspective. Let me begin by quoting the words of one of the supreme thinkers about politics, though an ineffective politician, an Italian called Niccolò Machiavelli. On his deathbed Machiavelli was asked by the priest to renounce Satan and all his arts. He replied, "This is no time to be making enemies." So I am going to be cautious in what I say.

First, comparing the U.S. Congress with the British Parliament, I am struck by the enormous burden that American representatives and senators carry. House members, with constituencies much larger than their British counterparts, must fight an election every two years. The dedication of such legislators staggers me. For example, Lee Hamilton, D-Ind., has committed himself to understanding such topics as foreign policy and intelligence, when his constituents have no interest in these problems. Members of Congress are also subject to local lobbying on local issues, an inevitability when there are such huge constituencies.

Second, it strikes me that American political parties are held together

more by the pork barrel than by principle or platform. There is less difference between the average Democrat and Republican in Boston or Vermont than between a New England Democrat and one from Texas or
Florida. An American friend of mine once told me that a platform is
something you stand on to get in—it is not something that takes you
anywhere. This still tends to be true, although sometimes newly elected
presidents may ask you to watch their lips.

Third, American legislators have enormous staffs. I was told a few years
ago that thirty thousand people were working on Capitol Hill; the number
could well be more now. Although these young men and women are able
and dedicated, their objective—indeed, their duty—is to help the representatives they serve. As a rule, they are less sensitive to the interests of
the United States as a whole, either at home or abroad, than to the interests
of their representatives. Indeed, it may cost legislators votes to take a
national interest seriously if their constituency is miles from the center.

Finally, the level of political participation in the United States is low,
lower than that of any other democratic country I know. George Bush
was elected president by less than one-fifth of the people who had the
right to vote. One-third of American adults do not bother even to register;
of those who register only about half vote. These figures are indeed worrisome because they cast doubt upon the whole theory of a popular mandate. I can never understand why there is not more pressure, particularly
from the Democratic party, to register the people who do not register.

Now, turning to the U.S. Constitution, I wonder if it is adequate for
the problems facing the United States as it moves into the twenty-first
century. The conflict between Congress and the administration seems less
constructive than that in Britain between the government and the opposition. The fault is not just on the side of Congress. It is difficult for a
foreigner to comprehend that the people who form a new administration,
from the president down, may have no experience in national government.
In fact, Carter and Reagan did not. That is equally true of many of their
cabinet appointees. Moreover, the continuity that we get in Europe with
a nonpolitical civil service is greatly reduced in the United States since,
when the government changes, the three thousand top civil servants in the
federal departments may be replaced by political appointees. I am not sure
that the American system is adequate for the problems confronting it.

Now a word about Congress. When I was a young man, visiting Washington once or twice a year after 1949, the congressional system worked

well with the administration because so many members of Congress were either stupid or corrupt. A boss in either party could control a large vote and deliver the vote when the administration wanted it. That assurance began to disappear when Dick Bolling abolished the seniority rule. Now, unfortunately, there are many intelligent and honest members of Congress, and the Constitution has become almost impossible to work. It is important to think about why this has happened.

Now that Congress has well-briefed, intelligent, and honest members, it is bound to have more power and to use that power. Power without responsibility, as some Englishman said, has been the prerogative of the harlot throughout the ages. The real question, then, is can Congress learn the responsibility for national and international affairs that should accompany the power it is now capable of yielding? Carlo Benedetti, the head of Olivetti, once said that the American Constitution was the last great political invention of the English. It could also be said that the Japanese constitution was the last great political invention of the Americans. Changing one's own constitution, as we discovered on several occasions when we tried to do it in Britain, is the most dangerous and difficult thing on which a government can embark.

Knowledge and Power in the Future

Let me finish with a personal appeal. Paul Kennedy and others have written about the decline and fall of the United States.[5] These accounts are mainly based on an illusion—that there was a period when the United States was omnipotent. Many people believed that, of course. The great debate in my early years in politics was about who lost China, as if China was America's to lose. There is no doubt that America's relative power is less than it used to be, but it is still the greatest nation in the world. Millions of people on every continent regard it as a beacon of opportunity and freedom. People pour into the United States the way they do not pour into any other country. Although U.S. military and economic strength is relatively smaller than it was, the United States still is likely to remain the greatest military power. The United States still is the greatest economic power, although it will not remain so unless it reduces its military spending. Our world presents us with bewildering challenges. Jim Wright made a relevant point here. The old men leading the Western democracies have learned a good deal through their half-century in politics, but the world they learned about is vastly different from the one into which we are moving.

My generation was brought up when we were mobilizing opinion against Hitler. My adult life was preempted by the Cold War and attempts to control that situation. Technology has now changed the world in ways we have not yet come to grips with. Nuclear weapons preclude total war as an instrument of policy between big countries. The difficulty of containing a limited war makes even that option between big powers too dangerous for the big countries to contemplate. Little countries can still slaughter one another with impunity.

Information technology has transformed the international financial markets. The combination of globalization, deregulation, and innovation, such as the leveraged buy out, has produced a fragile Western banking system that is vulnerable to shock, whether it comes from sovereign debt in Latin America or from the savings and loans industries in the United States.

Finally, the chemists have put their oar in, and chemicals are poisoning our air and our water and even the food we eat. We had a terrible scare in Britain a few years ago about salmonella in eggs, listeria from cheese. An American comedian said that Britain was the only country in the world where the sex was safer than the food.

All these problems created by technology are essentially world problems. They are not national problems. They are not Western problems. They are not communist problems. The only world leader who has had the wit to notice this is Mikhail Gorbachev, who has been making speeches on this issue since Chernobyl. I think the United States and the Soviet Union will attempt to control these new technologies; however, the rest of the world is not going to replace domination by its senior partners with a Soviet-American hegemony. So we must find new ways to get all countries to work together, to return to the kind of world on which the United Nations charter was based.

These new challenges require new kinds of knowledge, new approaches to understanding. The American Congress has an obligation to acquire the knowledge that will enable it to use its new powers responsibly, not only its powers as the legislative branch vis-à-vis the administration, but its powers as an instrumental body in the American polity that will help to guide American policy in the world to come.

Perhaps the most important idea that I can impart is that thought is more important than information. The mass of facts available is just too bewildering. One should not be deluded by academics who think they are providing knowledge when they arrange these facts into a pretty pattern. To understand how the world economy and the American economy are working, how nuclear weapons have changed foreign policy, how the sciences are changing the world environment requires thinking and understanding. It is still true that the most important space in the space age is the space between the ears. I hope you all make good use of it.

NOTES

1. John J. Fialka, "Pro-Israel Lobbying Group Is Accused of Breaking U.S. Campaign-Funds Law," *Wall Street Journal*, January 13, 1989, A14.
2. This quotation, in a slightly different translation, was attributed to President Kennedy by Rep. F. Edward H. Hebert in a letter Hebert sent to the *Washington Post*. The letter said, "President Kennedy was fond of quoting some lines from the Spanish poet García Lorca." The lines, however, are from Domingo Ortega. See Suzy Platt, ed., *Respectfully Quoted: A Dictionary of Quotations Requested from the Congressional Research Service* (Washington, D.C.: Library of Congress, 1989), 5.
3. Henry A. Kissinger, *Nuclear Weapons and Foreign Policy* (New York: Harper and Row, 1957).
4. Richard E. Neustadt and Ernest R. May, *Thinking in Time* (New York: Free Press, 1986).
5. Paul Kennedy, *The Rise and Fall of the Great Powers: Economic Change and Military Conflict from 1500 to 2000* (New York: Random House, 1987).

10. Lessons from History: Knowledge and Power in National Legislatures

Gordon A. Craig

The history of European legislatures in the nineteenth and early twentieth centuries, seen from the perspective of knowledge and power, shows that such bodies were not invariably characterized by a high degree of knowledge in any true sense, nor did they always have the power to do what they knew they should do or what they wanted to do, although sometimes their preoccupation with power led them to do things that they should have known were unwise. Even in the mother of parliaments members tended to be less men of knowledge than knowledgeable men. In the first part of the nineteenth century, when Henry Peter Brougham, after many years in the House of Commons, was made lord chancellor, the highest judicial officer in the land, one of his colleagues was heard to murmur, "Now if he only knew a little about the law, he would know a little about everything."

This was not, of course, necessarily a disability. Judged by his legislative record, Brougham was a much more effective parliamentarian than such deeply learned persons as John Stuart Mill in the House of Commons or, to take a German example, Theodor Mommsen in the Reichstag. A legislature composed of generalists of diverse talents and skills, such as Brougham, was usually effective in dealing with the ordinary business of the nation and could always, when necessary, mobilize the special knowledge and find the experts to help with more complicated matters. As a result of the increase of European population in the first half of the nineteenth century, the rapid expansion of industrialization, and the coming of what was called the social question, such recourse became increasingly urgent as the century advanced, and—although legislatures were not equipped with extensive research and information-gathering agencies—they were pretty good at improvising, when they wanted to do so and when they were allowed to do so.

Unfortunately, this was not always the case. Legislatures were often inhibited or prevented from acting on the basis of available knowledge by considerations of power, by the fact, perhaps, that the national constitution or the nature of the existing regime denied them the authority to take the initiative in the decision-making process, or, when that was not true, because their ability to do what reason and knowledge recommended was made impossible by party or ideological division or their will lamed by calculations of private interest or fear.

Achievements in European Legislatures Before World War I

It is easy enough to find historical examples of effective mobilization of knowledge by legislatures. Between the years 1830 and 1869 the national legislature of Zurich transformed that hitherto aristocratic backwater into the most liberal and progressive canton in Switzerland, as well as into the industrial and intellectual center of the new Bundestaat that emerged, not least of all because of its own efforts, from the cantonal strife and national war of the 1840s. To accomplish this, the legislature set about performing a number of highly technical tasks: it overhauled the administrative structure of the canton, supplying the reorganized districts with effective agencies and courts and establishing rules for popular participation in community government; it reformed the judicial system and wrote a new code of criminal justice; it abolished the feudal remnants and passed the canton's first comprehensive tax law; it ended guild restrictions on employment and wrote a law on the freedom of occupation *(Werbefreiheit)*; it initiated an extensive program of urban renewal to stimulate communication and trade; it enacted new company laws to encourage railroad building and the establishment of the kind of banks that could promote economic growth; and, finally, it reformed and expanded the educational system. All this required a degree of expert knowledge that exceeded the collective intellectual resources and energy of a legislature required to perform the day-by-day tasks of running the country. The Zurich legislature therefore delegated the task of gathering, collating, and analyzing data and, on that basis and in accordance with assigned guidelines, drafting the necessary legislation to a number of cantonal councils and commissions. These worked with an energy and speed that, by modern standards, seems incredible. The Educational Council, for example, completed a revolutionary reform of both higher education and elementary and secondary schooling in less than eighteen months, and the system that emerged was far in advance of anything that existed in England or France at the time. It established a high degree of literacy and was declared by Matthew Arnold, when he inspected it at the behest of the British Parliament in 1867, to possess the best elementary and secondary schools in Europe.

At the same time that these reforms were being carried through, the British Parliament was confronting for the first time the ills of uncontrolled industrialization. Or perhaps confronting is not the word, for there was no fund of exact knowledge concerning conditions in the factories and workshops of England, and there existed in Parliament a profound reluctance to interfere with the working of the economic system. The prevailing attitudes in that body were either theoretical or philosophical, like the view of Lord Brougham, who held that capitalism was so logical in its working that working people should learn to take an aesthetic pleasure in its beautiful regularity, no matter how it affected them personally, and the conviction of Sir James Graham, who believed, in the words of Sidney and Beatrice Webb, that "a melancholy economic necessity ruled the will and intelligence of man in all his social relationships" and that "the fate of the mass of the nation was irreparable." But no one really knew the facts, and it was only when royal commissions headed by Michael Sadler and Lord Ashley revealed the deplorable conditions in factory towns, many of which had neither sewage systems nor adequate water supply nor housing for the workers except of the most primitive sort; the shameful situation in the mines, where women and children were found working like animals; and the hardly less wretched conditions in the textile mills that the conscience of Parliament was stirred and the basis provided for the Mining Act and the Ten Hours Act and other landmark legislation that sensibly lowered social tension in the country and, incidentally, helped England escape the convulsions of 1848.

Legislative Failures

Examples of failure to act upon knowledge, although the probable consequences of this failure were palpable, also leap to mind. In 1908, when Emperor William II, by reckless remarks about foreign policy to an English newspaperman, had caused a major international crisis and revealed how dangerously irresponsible and adventurist national policy had become, the German Reichstag had an excellent opportunity to demand a diminution of royal prerogative, a greater degree of responsibility of the chancellor to the Reichstag, and the granting to that body of the right of interpellation in policy matters. Despite overwhelming evidence of a strong public desire for such action, the Reichstag did not make such demands, largely, one supposes, because German parliamentarians as a group had never acquired the self-confidence and sense of collegial solidarity that members of Parliament in England or members of Congress in the United States enjoyed. Moreover, they had always, since Bismarck's days, been unenthusiastic about the prospect of challenging the political establishment—that is, the Crown and its agencies—in matters of political importance, and perhaps because they had read too much Hegel in the university, they were uncertain about the legitimacy of doing so. So they ignored their subconscious knowledge that failure to act would confirm the government in its dangerous ways and did nothing.

Twenty-two years later, after a ruinous war had been fought in part because of that early failure, the German Reichstag—followed four years later by the French Assembly—provided posterity with another fateful example of the inadequacy of knowledge and common sense to prevail in circumstances in which the very existence of parliamentary government was at stake. The problem in both cases was how to alleviate the crisis caused by the world depression. The precise issue was whether the social partners represented by the parliamentary coalitions seeking to deal with this problem were willing to make equal sacrifices (in matters such as contributions to unemployment insurance funds, for example) to effect this result. In both cases, plans drawn up by competent and objective economists were available that might have succeeded in checking the mounting crisis. Yet both the Reichstag and the French Assembly sacrificed reason to party or private interest and to ideological zeal, the coalition governments dissolved and were replaced by emergency governments with no clear electoral legitimacy (Brüning in Germany, Laval and Pétain in France), and Germany went down the slope to Hitler and France to the muddle and defeatism of 1938–1940.

Now that Hitler has been mentioned, it is not an inappropriate time to think of the question that Cassius, in Shakespeare's play about another dictator, asked his friend Brutus

Upon what meat doth this our Caesar feed
That he is grown so great?

and to ask ourselves why Hitler's career, unlike Caesar's, was not cut short at its inception and prevented from running its fearful course. Who supplied the provender that so nurtured his ambitions and self-confidence that his dreadful designs could be frustrated only by a ruinous war that cost the lives of seventeen million military personnel and eighteen million noncombatants and created the problematical world in which we live?

To give an adequate answer to that question would require more time than this paper allows, but I can note at least that prominent among those who lavished the heady nutrient of power upon Hitler were Western parliamentarians who closed their minds to palpable evidence of his aggressive intentions and, by adopting a doctrinaire antimilitarism, failed to provide the means of putting an end to them at an early stage. The debates in the House of Commons on the military budget between 1933 and 1938, as recorded in *Hansard,* show a sorry record of legislative failure to act vigorously upon the basis of known facts to repair inadequate power in the nation's interest.

As for the national legislature of the United States, there are surely few episodes in the history of Congress's participation in the making of American foreign policy as discreditable as the story of the Neutrality Act. First passed in 1935 and made permanent two years later, this unrealistic and illogical piece of legislation was designed to prevent the United States from being drawn into foreign quarrels. It sought to achieve this by enjoining the president from extending aid or assistance to any of the belligerents involved in a state of war, even if some of them might be the victims of naked aggression. This encouraged the international gangsters and hurt their victims, as was shown in the case of the Abyssinian War in 1935 and the Spanish Civil War in 1936, yet Congress steadfastly refused to reconsider its action. In August 1939, in a dramatic meeting with congressional leaders, President Franklin Roosevelt pleaded with them to repeal the law, which he said would prevent the United States from helping its friends in a war that his intelligence sources told him was inevitable and imminent. Sen. William Borah of Idaho, a leading isolationist, recorded that his sources told him that the rumors of war were vastly exaggerated, at which John Nance Garner, Roosevelt's vice president, turned to him with a shrug and said, "Cap'n, we just ain't got the votes!"

These depressing stories of legislative failure were relieved by no examples of great, even if unsuccessful, leadership. In 1930 in Germany and in 1934 in France there were, to be sure, a few members of parliament who raised hesitant objections to the actions of the majority, but none who sought to describe the issues in terms of history and principle and to portray the inevitable consequence of failing to deal with them. This was unfortunate and probably means that those legislatures deserved the fate that shortly befell them. The history of legislative bodies is not free of the names of parliamentary leaders whose record of success has inspired later generations—one thinks of William Ewart Gladstone and his influence upon Woodrow Wilson and through him on Franklin Roosevelt—but it has perhaps been the noble failures, the persons who stood up for conscience and honor when all the odds were against them and the personal risk was far from negligible, who have had the greatest power to move us to reflection.

The story of the decline and fall of the Senate of Rome would mean little to us if it were not for our recollection of the valiant efforts of Marcus Tullius Cicero to prevent it, the mighty *quo usque* (once known to every American schoolboy) that he hurled at the head of the conspirator Catiline, his unavailing efforts to invoke and reinvigorate the idea of the *res publica* and to persuade the Senate to hold to its ancient ideals, and his isolation and death as his colleagues scuttled for cover during the cutthroat politics of the period of the Second Triumvirate. And the lamentable story of the governmental ineptitude and parliamentary mismanagement of American affairs that led to Britain's loss of her colonies and to the independence of this country is relieved to some extent by the memory of Edmund Burke's attempts to prevent it by calling for a policy of conciliation. Burke, like Cicero, was a man of great knowledge. William Hazlitt said of him that "his stock of ideas did not consist of a few meager facts, meagerly stated, of half a dozen common-places tortured in a thousand different ways; but his mine of wealth was a profound understanding, inexhaustible as the human heart and various as the sources of nature." But Burke was too learned for most of his merely knowledgeable parliamentary colleagues, who fidgeted or dozed, as Cicero's senatorial colleagues must have fidgeted and dozed, during the ebb and flow of his eloquence and were deaf to his warnings, even when he was reminding them, in the American debates, that to deny to their dependencies the rights that were enjoyed by the home country could not but be fatal, or later—in the famous attack on Warren Hastings—when he predicted that corruption and exploitation once condoned even in the farthest reaches of the empire would soon proliferate at home. Perhaps because legislative bodies have a tendency to respect power more than knowledge, Burke's colleagues remained unmoved by his exposition of the abuses of power; but what we remember of these ancient quarrels is that he was right and they were wrong.

A last example, who deserves to stand with Cicero and Burke as one whose greatest parliamentary performances were as ineffective as the laments of Cassandra, was Alexis de Tocqueville. Tocqueville had the misfortune of being a member of the French legislature in the 1840s, when the Guizot system was at its height and the deputies, convinced of the wisdom of their chief's dictum that the key to the solution of social ills was to encourage all citizens to get rich *(Enrichissez-vous!)*, were oblivious to the real needs of the country. He wrote later,

France grew unconsciously accustomed to look upon the debates in the Chamber as exercises of the intellect rather than as serious discussions and upon all the differences between the various parliamentary parties . . . as domestic quarrels between the children of one family trying to trick one another. A few glaring instances of corruption, discovered by accident, led the country to presuppose a great number of hidden cases and convinced it that the whole of the governing class was corrupt.

Tocqueville tried to convince his colleagues that this perception, coupled with their own indifference to prevalent social misery, was ruinous. "I believe," he said in a speech in January 1848, "we are at this moment sleeping on a volcano. . . . In God's name change the spirit of the government, for . . . that spirit will lead you to the abyss." How right he was became clear when revolution swept away the Guizot system a month later.

Tocqueville and the Question of Civic Virtue

Tocqueville commends himself especially to our attention because he was fascinated by American politics. He was convinced that the endurance of the democratic experiment would depend not upon its ability to wield power effectively or to use knowledge wisely but upon the extent to which it inspired civic virtue among its citizens. It is difficult to find a very precise definition of this term in *Democracy in America*, but Tocqueville explains what he means in Chapter 5 of the first book when he writes, "Americans rightly think that patriotism is a sort of religion strengthened by practical service." This, in his view, was the foundation of liberty and the source of its sustenance, and he believed that it was to be found in its strongest form in the New England township. "In the restricted sphere within his scope," Tocqueville wrote, "[the New Englander] learns to rule society; he gets to know those formalities without which freedom can advance only through revolutions, and becoming imbued with their spirit, develops a taste for order, understands the harmony of powers, and in the end accumulates clear, practical ideas about the nature of his duties and the extent of his rights."

The question that troubled Tocqueville was whether this ideal of civic virtue could survive outside the local framework and whether it could animate larger legislative bodies than the New England town meetings. For in the wider American world, values tended to change and coarsen, and the quest for wealth that was so highly approved by the American ethos was basically inimical to civic virtue. Would it not be true—he raised the question tentatively, even diffidently—that in the higher reaches of politics, and in the national legislature itself, those essential passions that he described as "the desire for esteem, the pursuit of substantial interests, and the taste for power and self-advertisement" would always tend to defeat the claims of virtue and wisdom. It was the same question that Cicero and Burke had raised in somewhat different forms. It was the same question that was raised in the winter of 1989 during the dispute over the congressional pay raise, when an attempt to solve a difficult and perennial problem by mobilizing knowledge by means of a special commission was defeated by a welling up of public protest that was Tocquevillian both in its energy and in its rhetoric. It is not an irrelevant question, nor will it become one as long as so much is said in the nation's capital about ethics, also an intractable problem and certainly one that is not susceptible to solution by either knowledge or power.

Contributors

Jodie T. Allen is editor of the *Washington Post*'s Outlook section. Her editorials and signed columns have covered the federal budget, taxation, federal-state relations, health, welfare, labor, population, and toxic hazards. In the 1960s and 1970s she served in the departments of Defense, Labor, and Health, Education, and Welfare.

David Brady, professor of political science at Stanford University, is the Bowen H. and Jane Arthur McCoy Professor in the Graduate School of Business. His most recent book is *Critical Elections and Congressional Policy Making* (1988).

Joseph Cooper is the provost at Johns Hopkins University and professor of political science. He was staff director of the House Commission on Administrative Review (Obey commission) from 1976 to 1978. His main interests are congressional history, organization, and leadership and presidential-congressional relations. He has written numerous books and articles on Congress.

Gordon A. Craig, author and historian, is the J. E. Wallace Sterling Professor of Humanities Emeritus at Stanford University. His writings include *The Triumph of Liberalism: Zurich in the Golden Age* (1989), *The End of Prussia* (1984), *The Germans* (1982), *Germany, 1866–1945* (1978), and *The Politics of the Prussian Army, 1640–1945* (1955).

Thomas S. Foley is Speaker of the House of Representatives. He was majority leader of the 101st Congress and served on the Permanent Select Intelligence and Budget committees. Before his election to Congress in 1964 to represent the Fifth District of Washington State, he was in private practice of law and government service.

Frank Freidel is the Charles Warren Professor of American History Emeritus at Harvard University and Bullitt Professor of American History Emeritus at the University of Washington. He has written four volumes on Franklin D. Roosevelt's early career and a biography, *Franklin D. Roosevelt: A Rendezvous with Destiny* (1990). He is the coeditor of the *Harvard Guide to American History* (1974) and author of *Our Country's Presidents* (1966) and *America in the Twentieth Century* (1960).

Newt Gingrich, first elected to the House in 1978 to represent Georgia's Sixth District, is minority whip. He serves on the House Administration Committee and the Joint Committee on Printing. He is the author of *Window of Opportunity: A Blueprint for the Future* (1986) and has written numerous articles on public policy issues.

Nathan Glazer is professor of education and social structure at Harvard University. An eminent sociologist, he is the author of *The Limits of Social Policy* (1988), *Ethnic Dilemmas* (1983), and *Affirmative Discrimination* (1975); he is the coauthor of *Beyond the Melting Pot* (1963) and *The Lonely Crowd* (1950).

Denis Healey is a member of the British House of Commons and has been deputy leader of the British Labour party. He has served as secretary of state for defense, chancellor of the exchequer, and opposition spokesman for foreign affairs. Among his publications are *When Shrimps Learn to Whistle* (1990), *The Time of My Life* (1989), and *The Curtain Falls* (1952).

Theodore J. Lowi is the John L. Senior Professor of American Institutions at Cornell University. His writings include *The Personal President* (1985) and *The End of Liberalism* (2d ed., 1979).

Laurence E. Lynn, Jr., is professor and former dean at the University of Chicago's School of Social Service Administration and professor in the Harris School of Public Policy Studies. During the 1970s he served as assistant secretary in the Department of Health, Education, and Welfare and the Department of the Interior. He is the author of *Managing Public Policy* (1987), *Managing the Public's Business* (1981), *Designing Public Policy* (1980), and *The State and Human Services* (1980).

Ernest R. May is the Charles Warren Professor of History at Harvard University. His current research concerns the effects of weaponry on international relations and the history of intelligence agencies. His recent publications include *Thinking in Time: The Uses of History for Decision-Makers,* with Richard E. Neustadt (1987), and *Knowing One's Enemies: Assessment Before the Two World Wars* (1986).

Richard P. Nathan is provost of the Rockefeller College of Public Affairs and Policy at the State University of New York at Albany and director of the Rockefeller Institute of Government. His main interests are U.S. domestic policy, federalism, and urban affairs. *Social Science in Government: Uses and Misuses* (1988) is his most recent book.

William A. Niskanen, economist, is chairman of the Cato Institute. He has served as assistant director of the Office of Management and Budget and was a member of the Council of Economic Advisers. He has written on international trade, the federal budget, taxation, and bureaucracy. Among his publications are *Reaganomics* (1988) and *Bureaucracy and Representative Government* (1971).

Mancur Olson is chair and principal investigator of the Project on Institutional Reform and the Informal Sector, funded by the U.S. Agency for International Development, and professor of economics at the University of Maryland at College Park. He is the author of *The Rise and Decline of Nations* (1982) and *The Logic of Collective Action* (1965).

Nelson W. Polsby is director of the Institute of Governmental Studies and professor of political science at the University of California at Berkeley. His books include *Presidential Elections,* with Aaron Wildavsky (8th ed., 1991), *Congress and the Presidency* (4th ed., 1986), *Political Innovation in America* (1984), *Consequences of Party Reform* (1983), and *Community Power and Political Theory* (2d ed., 1980).

David E. Price, who represents North Carolina's Fourth District in the House of Representatives, was first elected to serve in the 100th Congress. He sits on the Appropriations Committee. Previously, he was professor of political science and public policy at Duke University. Among his writings are *Bringing Back the Parties* (1984), *The Commerce Committees* (1975), and *Who Makes the Laws?* (1972).

William H. Robinson has been deputy director of the Congressional Research Service since 1986. His current research interests include legislative policy analysis and comparative legislative development. Recent publications include a chapter in *Organizations for Policy Analysis,* edited by Carol H. Weiss (1991), and book reviews in the journal *Governance.*

Isabel Sawhill, economist and senior fellow at the Urban Institute, has served as director of the National Commission on Employment Policy. She was an author or editor of *Challenge to Leadership* (1988), *Perspective on the Reagan Years* (1986), *The Reagan Record* (1984), and *Economic Policy in the Reagan Years* (1984).

Allen Schick, director of the Bureau of Governmental Research at the University of Maryland, is an expert in the federal budget process. Among his writings are *The Capacity to Budget* (1990), *Crisis in the Budget Process* (1985), *Making Economic Policy in Congress* (1982), and *Congress and Money* (1980).

Stephen J. Solarz was first elected to the House of Representatives in 1974 to represent New York's Thirteenth District. He is chairman of the Asian and Pacific Affairs Subcommittee and serves on the Joint Economic Committee, the Merchant Marine and Fisheries Committee, and the Select Committee on Intelligence. He has published numerous articles on foreign affairs.

Lawrence H. Summers, vice president and chief economist at the World Bank, is professor of economics at Harvard University, specializing in labor economics. He has written extensively on topics of labor force transitions, labor force participation, and the dynamics of unemployment. His most recent book is *Understanding Unemployment* (1990).

Carol H. Weiss, professor in Harvard University's Graduate School of Education, is a sociologist specializing in the link between knowledge and policy. Among her writings are *Organizations for Policy Analysis: Helping Government Think* (1991), *Social Sciences and Modern States* (1991), *Reporting of Social Science in the National Media* (1988), and *Social Science Research and Decision-Making* (1980).

Clay H. Wellborn is a policy research manager with the Government Division of Congressional Research Service. Before coming to the Library of Congress, he was vice president for research at *National Journal*. He is on the faculty of Boston University and is active in providing technical assistance to Latin American legislatures that are building information and policy analysis support agencies.

Gordon S. Wood is University Professor and professor of history at Brown University. He is the author of *The Radicalism of the American Revolution* (forthcoming), *The Rising Glory of America: 1760–1820* (2d ed., 1990), and *The Creation of the American Republic: 1776–1787* (1969) and is coauthor of *The Great Republic* (4th ed., forthcoming).

James C. Wright, Jr., who represented the Twelfth District of Texas from 1955 until 1989, served as Speaker of the House in the 100th Congress. His writings include *Reflections of a Public Man* (1984), *Of*

Swords and Plowshares (1968), *The Coming Water Famine* (1966), and *You and Your Congressman* (1965).

James Sterling Young, professor of government at the University of Virginia, directs the presidency research program at the Miller Center of Public Affairs. Among his writings are *The Washington Community, 1800–1828*, which won the 1967 Bancroft Prize. He is now completing *The Puzzle of the Presidency: Nation Leading in America.*

Index

Knowledge, Power, and the Congress

"The creation of the Library of Congress under Thomas Jefferson provided a unique place of intersection between knowledge and power in our fledgling republic in its early days. We honor Congress in our own time by exploring areas of potential improvement and by comparing our experiences with those of the growing number of other legislative republics. It is with a view toward the future that we undertook this inventory of past and present experience."
—From the Foreword by *James H. Billington, Librarian of Congress*

William H. Robinson has served as deputy director of the Congressional Research Service of the Library of Congress since 1986. His current research interests include legislative policy analysis and comparative legislative development. *Clay H. Wellborn* is a policy research manager with the Government Division of the Congressional Research Service. Before coming to the Library of Congress, he was vice president for research at *National Journal.*

 Congressional Quarterly Inc.

ISBN 0-87187-631-0

DATE DUE

MAY 9 1995			
MAR 2 1 1996			
GAYLORD			PRINTED IN U.S.A.